Working From Home

for dummies®

A Wiley Brand

Working From Home

by Tara Powers, MS, et al.

A Wiley Brand

Working From Home For Dummies®

Published by: **John Wiley & Sons, Inc.,** 111 River Street, Hoboken, NJ 07030-5774, www.wiley.com

Copyright © 2020 by John Wiley & Sons, Inc., Hoboken, New Jersey

Published simultaneously in Canada

For general information on our other products and services, please contact our Customer Care Department within the U.S. at 877-762-2974, outside the U.S. at 317-572-3993, or fax 317-572-4002. For technical support, please visit https://hub.wiley.com/community/support/dummies.

Wiley publishes in a variety of print and electronic formats and by print-on-demand. Some material included with standard print versions of this book may not be included in e-books or in print-on-demand. If this book refers to media such as a CD or DVD that is not included in the version you purchased, you may download this material at http://booksupport.wiley.com. For more information about Wiley products, visit www.wiley.com.

Library of Congress Control Number: 2020941268

ISBN 978-1-119-74849-6 (pbk); ISBN 978-1-119-74835-9 (ebk); ISBN 978-1-119-74837-3 (ebk)

Manufactured in the United States of America

SKY10021563_093020

Contents at a Glance

Table of Contents

Introduction

In today's modern global economy, working from home is no longer a novelty. Organizations around the world are embracing the advantages of letting employees work outside the office, and the results are eye-opening: Managers save money and resources and have access to talent outside their zip codes, while employees enjoy greater job opportunities, productivity, independence, and satisfaction. Remote work really can be sustainable for professionals who want flexibility.

Whether you're new to having a home office or you've been working outside an office for years, *Working From Home For Dummies* can help you prepare for working virtually — and thriving.

About This Book

Working From Home For Dummies helps you acquire and cultivate some of the most important attributes needed for remote work. Here, you get pointers on setting up a home workspace; strengthening important skills like managing your time, establishing routines, and setting boundaries; and using your manners in virtual team meetings. You find help with three popular work-at-home technology programs: Slack, Zoom, and Microsoft Teams. You also get tips for managing a virtual team and balancing your time between your work and your personal life, even when both take place at home.

In this book, sidebars (shaded boxes of text) provide an in-depth look at particular topics. You may find them interesting and illuminating, but they aren't crucial to understanding the rest of this book. Feel free to read them or skip them.

You can also pass over the text marked with the Technical Stuff icon (see the later section, "Icons Used in This Book"). The text accompanied by this icon gives some technical, informative details about working from home, but you can still get the most important information you need without reading it.

Whenever we quote prices in this book, they're listed in U.S. dollars. When in doubt about a price, check the company's website for the latest information.

One last note: Within this book, you may note that some web addresses break across two lines of text. If you're reading this book in print and you want to visit one of these web pages, simply key in the web address exactly as it's noted in the text, pretending as though the line break doesn't exist. If you're reading this as an e-book, you've got it easy — just click the web address to be taken directly to the web page.

Foolish Assumptions

You may have picked up this book for one or more of the following reasons:

» You're new to working from home, and you need guidance on setting up a workspace, developing skills for success, and figuring out new technology.

» You've been working at home for months or years, but you still want some new tips to boost your productivity, computer skills, and work–life balance.

» You're managing employees who work from home, and you need help transitioning from an old-school setup to a virtual team.

Icons Used in This Book

Handy icons appear in this book's margins. Here's what they mean.

When you see text highlighted by this icon, stash it in your brain, whether you're new to working from home or a pro.

The text marked with this icon may not be crucial to your success in working from home, but you may still find it enlightening.

This icon denotes a piece of advice that may make working from home easier.

Pay attention to this icon. The guidance can prevent work-at-home headaches.

Beyond the Book

In addition to the material in the print or digital book you're reading right now, *Working From Home For Dummies* comes with other great content available online. To get the Cheat Sheet, simply go to www.dummies.com and type **Working From Home For Dummies Cheat Sheet** in the Search box.

Where to Go from Here

You may not need to read every chapter of this book to build your confidence as you start (or continue) working from home, so feel free to jump around. If you're looking for a particular topic — such as how to work with different technology platforms or how to manage employees virtually — check out the table of contents or the index to guide you in the right direction. But if you're a work-at-home newbie, start with Part 1, which details how to set up your workspace, the most important skills and behaviors you need for remote work, and useful virtual team meeting etiquette. Good luck, and welcome to the world of working from home!

1

Getting Started with Working From Home

Set up your workspace in the right spot and with the right gear.

Develop skills and behaviors to ensure success, such as establishing goals and priorities, managing your time effectively, and boosting your productivity and motivation.

Follow virtual meeting etiquette, from checking your background to minimizing noise and more.

» **Equipping your home office**

» **Imposing order on the chaos of working from home**

» **Personalizing your workspace**

Chapter **1**

Setting Up Your Workspace

Working from home brings both benefits and challenges. Initially, it may seem like the ability to work from home is the most important option for any job you're considering. Given that you can save hours of time not commuting, walk your dog whenever you want, and stay in sweatpants all day if you feel like it, working from home can feel like a dream come true.

However, many professionals quickly find that working from home is frustrating, distracting, and uncomfortable if they don't have a designated workspace and proper setup that allows them to be productive, available, and efficient in their home environment.

The bottom line is that productive work can happen in a variety of home workspaces. You don't need to build an addition to your house for the perfect executive-level home office suite. Instead, some tried-and-true best practices can yield a functional and comfortable workspace. *Hint:* It's not your bed or the living room sofa.

This chapter walks you through all the factors to consider when setting up your home office, including picking the best location for your office, ensuring you have all the right equipment, and keeping your workspace organized, ergonomically friendly, and pleasant.

Choosing the Right Spot in Your Home

The first order of business when working from home is setting up a workspace that's as functional and comfortable as possible, even if you have limited space. If you work from home, whether you're an entrepreneur, a freelancer, or a remote team member, you need to have a dedicated space to get work done.

Home offices are as individual and varied as the people who work in them. They come in all sizes, shapes, colors, degrees of privacy, and ability to control noise and interruptions. What works for some can be completely nonfunctional for others.

If you're fortunate enough to have a dedicated office space in your home, good for you! But if your home office is in your basement without natural light and with terrible Wi-Fi reception, you may need to rethink where to work each day. In the following sections, I walk you through the top factors to consider when choosing the perfect spot for your home office.

Picking the best room

When you're finding a place for your home office, you'll want to consider factors such as location, lighting, the amount of space, and the level of privacy.

REMEMBER

A separate room in your home is not required to get work done. So, as you read through the following sections, consider all your options to find the spot in your home that meets your needs, whether that's a spare bedroom or a corner of your living room.

When you're choosing a place for your home office, consider the following factors:

>> **Location:** Consider the type of work you do and the equipment you need. If you're a graphic designer, you may require a design table, along with a desk for your computer. If you're a consultant, you'll most likely need space for filing cabinets, shelves for books, and possibly a seating area to meet with clients.

TIP

Try to find a space in your home that provides some quiet and privacy (for example, when you're having an important meeting). Ideally, your home office will have a door so you can block out distractions and noise, have phone and video calls, and effectively separate your work space from your home space. If you don't have a separate room to dedicate to your home office, try to find a place that's removed enough from the main living space that you can get some quiet when you need it (maybe by asking your housemates to go in another room for short periods of time).

Whether you have a door or not, choosing a dedicated location to get work done will set a boundary for housemates, letting them know that when you're there, you're working and you may not be available.

>> **Light:** There are many reasons to consider lighting in the early stages of your workspace planning. Having enough light is necessary to reduce eye strain, headaches, drowsiness, fatigue, and depression.

Whenever possible, try to get light from natural light sources (sunlight streaming through a window) as opposed to artificial ones (a lamp). The benefits of natural light include alertness and an overall sense of well-being. And where there's natural light, there is likely to be a view of the outdoors. Turning away from your computer every few minutes and looking outside can create a moment of mindfulness and peace. This simple strategy can affect your overall productivity and motivation. It doesn't take much natural light to fill a small space and elevate your mood.

Even if your workspace gets plenty of natural light during the day, you'll need to add a light source to have enough light for winter months and evenings. Be sure to keep supplemental lighting indirect, and avoid working under the direct glare of overhead lights. Use lampshades to soften and diffuse the light.

Floor lamps can provide a lot of light but also take up coveted space in small areas and can make it feel cramped. Consider hanging pendant lights to keep the light source off the ground and free up valuable space.

>> **Wi-Fi:** Having access to a strong, reliable Internet connection is essential for home-based workers. Before you settle on your workspace, make sure you can get online and stay online consistently throughout your workday.

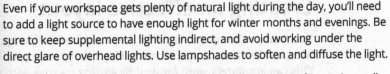

Choosing a space that's close to your router can help provide a stronger Wi-Fi connection.

>> **Electrical outlets:** You need power outlets near your workspace to plug in a computer, printer, lighting, phone charger, and potentially a router or a wireless booster. Consider whether you'll be doing a lot of video calls and test out a mock call in potential workspace areas of your house to see how it looks. A plain wall that isn't too distracting is a good backdrop, and proper lighting will make the video quality better, too.

Don't worry if your workspace isn't ideal. You don't need a soundproof home office. Ask yourself the following questions before randomly choosing your work-space. You don't want to set up shop in one area of the home only to have to move to another spot if it's not working for you.

>> What is the regular work that you'll be doing and how much space do you need to spread out?

>> Where is your router? If you can't set up your workspace near your router, can you get a booster if your router isn't close by?

>> Will you need some type of room divider to separate your workspace from your personal space?

>> Where is the natural light best in your home?

>> Are there enough electrical outlets for all your gadgets and a surge protector?

>> Is the workspace quiet or can it be if necessary?

>> Is there enough room for necessary equipment like a computer, printer, storage, shelves, chair, desk, monitor, and/or paper shredder?

>> Is the background acceptable for video calls and meetings with clients?

Creating an effective layout

Your home office may need to fit into a small or unique space or even share space with another room in your house, like a living room, dining room, or bedroom. This can absolutely work for you! By getting creative with space, form, and function, you can create an optimal home office space that is effective and allows you to be productive during the workday.

Using the space you have

When space is limited, you'll have to get creative when figuring out where your designated workspace will be. If you're using your living room or bedroom for this dual purpose, consider putting your desk behind your couch and adding a throw rug under the desk to create an area that's at least visually separate from the rest of the room. If you're using your bedroom, a room divider can help to keep your personal space, well, personal.

TIP

Try using an entire wall in a room for your workspace. That strategy can create a clear, organized area for work without distracting from the rest of the room. Consider adding shelving on both sides of the wall for your office equipment and storage.

Don't overlook those nooks and odd corners in your house that are currently being used as decorative space. If you follow the flow of the room, you can keep it pleasing to the eye and easily fit your workspace there.

TIP

If you like to visualize how you can move around your furniture to make a space in your home for an office, several online design tools can help you get creative and determine what will work best:

>> **Planner5D:** www.planner5d.com

>> **RoomSketcher:** www.roomsketcher.com

>> **Roomstyler 3D Home Planner:** www.roomstyler.com/3dplanner

Applying the principles of feng shui

The Chinese philosophy of feng shui is a practice of arranging your living space and working environment to achieve harmony and balance with the natural world. The Chinese words *feng* and *shui* translate to mean "wind" and "water," respectively. Feng shui offers smart guidelines to consider when setting up your workspace at home:

>> Try to create as much division as possible between your workspace and your bedroom.

>> Eliminate all unnecessary clutter.

>> Incorporate natural elements like wood and plants, or even a small desktop water fountain if you have the space.

>> Position your desk in a strong position (not up against a wall, preferably looking out a window or door).

>> Focus on function. Do you need space for taking notes, spreading out, and to see monitors clearly?

>> Make sure you have fresh air circulating.

>> Position your desk near a window so that you have natural light.

>> Decorate in ways that motivate you and remind you of your goals.

Getting All the Equipment You Need

After you've picked the perfect spot for your workspace, it's time to set up your new home office with all the furniture, equipment, and supplies you need to be productive. Start by thinking about the kind of work you'll be doing. Do you need space to spread out materials or papers? Do you need a desk that's big enough for multiple monitors? Do you need a printer and scanner? How many hours a day will you be in your home office? What type of technology will you be using to connect with clients or team members?

Answering these questions will help you determine the basic equipment you'll need to get started working from home.

Desk and chair

Whatever type of work you'll be doing, start by picking out your most important items first: a desk and chair. As with most office supplies, the options are endless. So, keep in mind two things: form and function.

Deciding on a desk

Here are several options to choose from when finding a desk for your home office:

>> **Writing desk:** If all you need is a place to write, you can opt for something straightforward and simple, maybe even a simple table. No bells or whistles, just a flat horizonal surface that can be a blank canvas for what you need it to be.

>> **Floating desk:** A floating desk is built into the wall, so it doesn't take up unnecessary space with bulky legs or other pieces that can overwhelm a room. Floating desks can be great for small offices and can even be installed to fold down when not in use. They're great for saving space and keeping your floor space open and clutter-free.

>> **Computer desk:** A computer desk has all the space for technological devices like computer towers, monitors, and all the cables and hookups so your devices work as efficiently as possible. Most computer desks are built with computer keyboard trays or laptop trays that slide away when in not in use.

>> **Corner desk:** Corner desks use less foot space and keep the main part of the room open for other uses.

>> **Executive desk:** An executive desk is often a large piece of furniture, with plenty of desktop space, lots of drawers, and shelf space for books, a printer, files, and decor.

>> **Standing desk:** If your line of work doesn't require a lot of time sitting at a computer, or you just prefer to stand to do your work, a standing desk can be a great choice. Some standing desks are convertible and can easily switch between a standing position and a desktop sitting position.

Chair

A good office chair will greatly increase your productivity and define your office as a professional workspace. Take the time to get a chair that is both comfortable and stylish, something you'll want to spend hours in. If you don't love your office chair, you'll never sit at your desk.

TIP

PAYING ATTENTION TO ERGONOMICS

You want your home office to be a safe and healthy place to work. Following a few simple ergonomic rules is your best bet for reducing your chance of injury and increasing your comfort, all of which helps you stay productive and focused:

- Choose a chair with an adjustable backrest that follows the shape of the spine and the curve in the lower back.

- You should be able to rest your feet flat on the floor comfortably. If you can't, adjust the chair height or add a footrest.

- Make sure the arm rests are close to the body and allow the shoulder to relax. The arm height should be adjustable and match the height of the desk to prevent shoulder strain.

- The back of the chair should come to the middle of the shoulder blades in order to provide adequate support; above the shoulders is even better.

- The seat of the chair should be long enough to put two or three finger lengths between it and the knee.

- The top of your computer screen should be at eye level or a little below.

- Position your keyboard so your forearms are parallel to the floor.

TIP

Be sure to choose a chair that's adjustable. Think about it: What's the first thing you do when you get in the driver's seat of a new car? You adjust the mirrors, the seat, maybe even the steering wheel. Your office chair should be no different. You need to be able to customize it to your body, your desk, and your computer screen so that it's ergonomically correct for your body (see the nearby sidebar for more on ergonomics).

To protect your back and neck, choose a chair with full back support — no bar stools allowed. Make sure your chair swivels so you can move easily between one part of your desk and another. Choose a chair with the correct wheels and strong casters so you can move on carpet or hard surfaces.

Computer and monitor

If you're a remote worker, your employer will probably supply your computer. If you're an entrepreneur or freelancer, you'll need to supply your own.

Depending on the work you do, you may need a second monitor so you can always have more than one window open at a time or so you can easily toggle back and forth from a project design to a video conference on two separate screens. Having an additional monitor can increase productivity by up to 50 percent.

TIP

If you're using a standing desk, you'll probably want a wireless keyboard in addition to the keyboard on your computer so that you can have the keyboard at the correct height. What's most important is that you have the right computer specifications for the work you'll be doing.

Here are some questions to help you define your specs before getting your home office computer:

>> **Does it matter whether you're on a Mac or a PC?** These days, you can do most things on any computer, but you may require software that runs only on a Mac or only on a PC, so make sure the computer you buy meets the needs of your line of work.

>> **Will you do all your work at home or will you be mobile?** If you plan to be away from your desk at least some of the time, opt for a laptop instead of a desktop.

TIP

You can connect your laptop to an external monitor, keyboard, and mouse when you're at your desk, effectively making your laptop look and feel like a desktop computer.

>> **How fast do you need your computer to be?** If you're working with photos or videos, you probably feel the need for speed. If you're working mainly with Microsoft Word documents, speed may not matter as much.

>> **How much storage do you need?** Again, if you're working with large files, like photos and videos, you'll need a big hard drive (and maybe some external hard drives, too).

Get clarity on your requirements before you spend thousands of dollars on a top-end computer setup that you don't really need.

Printer and scanner

You'll probably need a printer when working from home. You may also need a scanner to scan important documents to send to your company, clients, manager, or teammates. Depending on how often you'll be scanning documents, investing in a printer/scanner combo can be a good idea. They aren't expensive, and if you don't need to print in color you can buy a black-and-white version, which will reduce the cost even more.

If you don't require high-quality scans and you don't have many pages to scan at once, you may be able to get by with one of the many smartphone apps available for scanning documents. For example, Scanner Pro (https://readdle.com/scannerpro) is an app that allows you to use your iPhone to take a picture of a document and save it as a PDF or JPG. It works great for scanning short documents like contracts.

Internet access

Reliable, high-speed Internet is one of the most important things you need to work from home. You may need to upgrade your Internet service to make sure you have the fastest and most reliable speed available in your area. If you frequently engage in videoconferencing, you may need a hard-wired Internet connection (where you connect directly to your modem using an Ethernet cable, instead of relying on Wi-Fi), so you don't lose your video connection.

The quality of your Internet service is especially important if others in the home are going to be online at the same time. Be sure to check what Internet speed is offered in your area and shop around to get the best Internet service available.

Phone service

Some employers require remote workers to have a phone line that's strictly for work. If you're self-employed, you may decide just to use your personal cell phone for work, too.

You don't always have to get a separate landline for your office. You may be able to get a phone number on Skype (www.skype.com) or Google Voice (https://voice.google.com) that is redirected to your cell phone.

The kind of work you do may require that you have a landline that doesn't go down if the Internet goes down. You can purchase telephones inexpensively online, and your Internet service provider can help you add a landline.

Noise-cancelling headset and camera

When working from home, you may be making and receiving calls, engaging in and leading videoconferences, and possibly recording audio or video for your clients or team members. Chances are, there will be days when you need to block out noise, record clear audio and video, or listen intently without being interrupted. All good reasons why investing in a noise-cancelling headset and camera is essential, especially if the webcam on your computer is poor quality.

Storage

Filing cabinets aren't the most exciting purchase you'll make for your home office, but you do need a place to store papers, or you'll find that they quickly pile up around you. Consider getting fireproof storage for important documents that you aren't storing in the cloud.

TIP

If you're the sort of person who needs a visual reminder of files, try wall storage or a magazine rack. If you need bookshelves, make sure they're large enough for different sizes of books, files, and pieces of decor. Bookshelves can also look great as a backdrop on video calls.

Organizing Your Work Life (And Keeping It That Way)

Organization is often overlooked when designing a home office, but it can have a significant impact on your productivity. A clear space provides a clear mind, so think about your workflow, how work comes in, where it lives while you're working on it, and where it goes when it's complete.

Surround yourself with things that inspire you and keep you motivated to show up and get your work done. You'll be spending a lot of time in this space, so it's important that it be as functional and comfortable as possible.

Time

Start each day by identifying your goals to help you focus your energy and decide what to have in front of you at your desk. Only your top priorities for the day should be on your desk. This will keep you productive and efficient and won't confuse the subconscious brain.

Use time blocking on your daily and weekly calendar to block off time to complete the most important priorities of the day. This concept works because it creates deadlines and time limits for tasks, helping you organize your daily time more effectively. It also helps you say "no" to interruptions, calls, and meetings that aren't necessary.

Workspace

While sitting in your workspace, your subconscious mind is processing everything you can see — regardless of whether it's important in that moment. This inevitably causes your brain to get distracted and overwhelmed and increases inefficiencies. Your brain will end up focusing on the low-priority tasks that are in front of you rather than what's most important.

Having a clear workspace that is free of clutter, piles, and gadgets, and holds only what you're currently working on or items you use regularly, is a key technique for staying focused and getting work completed. This is only possible when you have a simple and effective filing system for your paperwork and other materials.

TIP

Keep items you use multiple times a day within reach at your desk. These items may include pens, pencils, a calculator, a stapler, your phone, a notebook, a headset, your computer, and your printer. Keeping these items near your desk or in a desk drawer will maximize productivity and make organization easier.

REMEMBER

Your electronic inbox is also its own workspace. Organize it the same way you would organize your paperwork with files and folders so everything is searchable and can be located online in a minute or less.

Paperwork

You need a filing system for your home office. The last thing you want to do is lose important information and spend hours searching for client paperwork and valuable notes because you don't have a system in place.

TIP

Use the "touch it once" rule when managing your paperwork. When you touch something, it either gets done, passed on, put in a reading pile, queued up in your action folders, recycled, or filed. Don't keep shuffling it around on your desk — touch it once and be done with it.

There are two things to consider when organizing your paperwork: when to process it and how. Depending on the amount of paperwork you have, you may need to process paperwork more than once a day or weekly. Consider processing all incoming items on the following timeline:

>> First thing in the morning each day or on Monday morning

>> Before or after lunch or midweek

>> Before you stop working at the end of the day or at the end of your workweek

When you process your paperwork regularly, you calm the subconscious mind from worrying about what you may be missing. Your subconscious knows you have unprocessed paperwork on your desk, which creates a mild sense of anxiety regarding the unknown. You'll find yourself looking at the same paperwork over again and again if it's sitting on your desk.

TIP

Queue up your work in terms of priority and timeline to create a filing system that works. Sort your to-do paperwork into color-coded folders labeled as shown in Table 1-1. Color-coding and labeling your to-do folders is important when it comes to retrieval. It allows you to quickly determine importance and time frames so you don't have to remember it later. This provides a feeling of security, calm, and productivity. Remember to update your folders weekly to ensure priorities are queued up appropriately.

TABLE 1-1   **Color-Coding Your File Folders**

Color	Label	Used For
Red	Today/top priority	Projects that need to be addressed in the next 48 hours
Yellow	This week	Projects to complete this week
Orange	This month	Projects to complete this month
Green	Follow up	Calls to be made to clients, business development opportunities to be followed up on
Purple	Wish list	When you have time
Blue	Pending	Waiting for someone to get back to you

REMEMBER

Find a filing system that works for you and the work that you do. If you work with clients, you may make different files for each project or client. If you provide services, you may have files for the various services you provide for each client receiving that service. Or you may file based on activity — for example, active clients or projects are in an active file alphabetically or by service topic, inactive clients or projects are filed separately, and archived files represent files that you rarely look at or need and most likely will recycle after one year.

Computers and other devices

Having an electronic filing system is just as important as having a paper system. Queueing up tasks by priority and deadline using your calendar or task list on email is an easy way to create action items that you reference daily.

TIP

Use the same "touch it once" rule when managing electronic information as you use for paperwork. Designate a few times during the day for checking email, texts, and Slack; handle requests during those times. Determine what to do with that information or request in the moment. For example, does it need your immediate attention or should you convert it to a task for later in the week? Can you file it in a client folder or topic folder? Can it be organized in a subject folder for reading at a later time?

Set up rules that help you to automatically organize your email and purge your electronic communication consistently, or it will quickly get out of hand and you'll feel anxious every time you open your inbox, wondering if you missed something.

Books and other reference materials

Create an in basket in your workspace where you keep books, reading material, magazine articles, reports, and other reference materials that you'd like to go through. Put the most important materials on top of the pile. Then block time in your calendar each week to sort through these items and decide what to keep, what to read, and what to recycle.

Use your bookshelf to organize your books and reference materials by topic or genre so you can find what you need quickly when doing research.

Adding Some Personal Touches

Many remote workers are former office workers and have had some experience with generic, impersonal office spaces. One of the best things about working from home is that you can create a workspace that is tailored for *you* and represents your interests and values. You're in charge of how your home office looks and feels!

TIP

Think about what inspires you. Think about your "why," the thing that motivates you and keeps you going on tough days. It can be a favorite affirmation, family photos, or a photograph of the place where you're happiest. Think about what makes you smile and provides a sense of calm.

Consider including plants in your home office. Being surrounded by plants is like bringing the outside in. Plus, plants have clear mental health benefits.

Because you're at home, you can even add an aromatherapy diffuser to your desk and a set of speakers to play your favorite music. No one in the next cube will complain!

The goal is to only allow things on your desk that have high value to *you*.

Another approach for decorating your office is to think about your style. Maybe you're more productive in minimalist surroundings. Maybe your style is more colorful and chaotic. What might seem chaotic and noisy to one person may be another person's motivation.

The key is to take the time to make your home office space your own. These personal touches will go a long way toward boosting your productivity and focus. Your home workspace, no matter where you put it, should motivate you to come to work every day.

Chapter **2**

Ensuring Success with Important Work-at-Home Skills and Behaviors

Working from home requires a different set of skills and behaviors than working in an office — everything from setting up your home office (see Chapter 1) to troubleshooting technology to making your schedule and creating personal and professional boundaries to protect your home life and your work life.

If you've always worked in an office surrounded by other people, working from home is a major shift in terms of staying productive and engaged and getting things done. Whether you realize it or not, those people who may have distracted you with their long-winded stories at the water cooler also provided you with many things — like companionship, support, communication, collaboration, camaraderie, motivation, and accountability — that contributed to your success and happiness at work. Working from home has plenty of its own advantages, but acknowledging the things you may miss when you're not in an office, and how to accommodate for their absence, is important.

This chapter covers the self-directed skills and behavioral best practices to plan for and develop if you want to succeed working from home.

Setting Goals and Priorities

Setting your goals and priorities is an essential skill for both personal and professional success. If you aren't setting goals or prioritizing your work, chances are, you're likely not making any progress or you're continually being overrun by other people's priorities.

REMEMBER

When working from home, staying engaged and excited about your work can be a challenge. Getting to know your personal strengths and aspirations will help you set goals and priorities that matter and are motivating to you. Take time to journal and reflect about what's important in your life and career.

Here are some questions to get you started:

>> What do you want to learn, do, or accomplish?

>> How do you want to make a difference and have an impact?

>> What would you like to become an expert at or be known for?

>> Where do you see yourself five years from now in your career?

>> When was the last time you lost track of time in your work and you were in the flow?

The answers to these questions will help you discover your strengths and identify personal goals that are important to you. If you can align your personal goals and aspirations with your work goals, you'll be more engaged and determined to accomplish them.

This section explores how to establish SMART goals, ask the right questions to understand the resources needed for success, and use a virtual scoreboard to keep updated on priorities and progress.

Starting with goals

One of the most important behavioral characteristics to build and hone when working from home is self-direction. It's up to you to determine what's most important, organize your time, plan your goals and tasks, and meet deadlines. The ability to control your workflow can be empowering, but without anyone holding you accountable or checking in on your progress, you must consistently set goals and priorities on your own.

Entire books have been written about how to set effective goals, but the thing to keep in mind is to create your goals and priorities through the filter of working from home and what matters to you. A good place to start is applying the principle of SMART goals because it helps to make your goals clear and measurable.

REMEMBER

The best way to build SMART goals is to focus on making your goals:

>> **Specific and synergistic:** Include details on how to achieve goals and align with your personal aspirations.

>> **Measurable and motivating:** Define what the end result should look like and why it's exciting for you to accomplish.

>> **Achievable and agreed on:** Confirm that the goal is possible given your knowledge and resources, and agree that it's important. The bigger the goal, the more resources are usually needed and the more time it will take.

>> **Relevant and rewarding:** Relate your goals to the work you do and understand the impact achieving your goals will have on others.

>> **Time-bound and thoughtful:** Have a start date and deadline and a well-thought-out plan to achieve your goals. If working with a team, determine important milestones for each goal and estimate the amount of time needed to achieve each goal by the deadline. Crosscheck these milestones against the amount of focused work time you have available to get it done.

TIP

Motivating goals are important to keep visible by displaying them prominently in your workspace and reviewing them weekly to gauge your progress. You may not have coworkers to keep you accountable, but seeing your goals every day will keep you focused.

Flexibility is key. Even the best-laid plans often require modifications. Don't beat yourself up if you need to do some tweaking to the timeline on your goals or ask your team or client for an extension. Make the necessary adjustments and keep moving forward.

Deciding on priorities

Every goal is achieved through incremental progress. On a weekly basis, create a priority action plan with the top tasks and due dates outlined that will move you down the path toward achieving your goal and check in on your progress using a scoreboard.

To establish your true priorities, ask yourself the following questions:

» If there was one thing you needed to accomplish today, what would that be?

» Do you own the task?

» What would be the consequences if you didn't do it?

» Is it important or urgent?

The answers to these questions will help you establish what absolutely must get done today or this week, what should get done but isn't as time sensitive, and what isn't necessary but would be nice to do.

Using a scoreboard that is visible and that you share with others will help you stay motivated and build momentum to keep going. It can be as simple as creating a document with your top and medium priorities identified and due dates listed, along with a progress key, where you indicate which goals you're making progress on, which have stalled, which are in trouble, and which you should scrap because they don't matter anymore.

TIP

You can use your scoreboard to decide where to refocus your time and attention on a weekly or monthly basis. Post your scoreboard on Microsoft Teams (see Part 4) or Slack (see Part 2) so that it's readily available to your team members, helping them stay focused on the collective results you're working toward. Use your scoreboard to help you decide where you need to say no, delegate tasks to others, or delay tasks so you can focus on what matters.

Managing Your Time Well

Working from home has its share of advantages and challenges when it comes to managing your time. The advantages include fewer distractions normally found at the office, including phone calls, meetings, and interruptions from colleagues. But it also has significant challenges, including the never-ending pile of laundry waiting to be done, pets begging to be fed, the escape of social media at your fingertips, and more. You also don't have coworkers or your manager to keep you accountable for getting things done.

Effective time-management skills are often seen as the biggest factor to success when working from home. These sections identify several best practices that you can use to quickly upgrade your self-management skills when it comes to time.

Creating and sticking to a schedule

Effective time management is essential if you want to hit your deadlines when you're working from home, so use your calendar as a success tool and use it wisely. Instead of leaving your calendar as a blank open slate for others to populate, block time to support a healthy body and mind and to do focused work when you're most productive and alert.

TIP

Aim to go to sleep and wake up at the same time each day so that your schedule is consistent. Allowing yourself two weekly schedules to choose from for different types of work (for example, project work versus networking/relationship building) can address boredom, sustain your attention, and reduce the chance of multitasking, which can eat up 80 percent of your productive time.

Time chunking

The best way to get things done when no one's watching is to organize your time as efficiently as possible. People used to think that multitasking was an efficient way to accomplish many tasks as quickly as possible. That's true for some simple tasks. But as soon as you attempt two simultaneous tasks that require critical thinking, they'll both suffer. Multitasking fractures your attention and frequently ends in frustration.

The alternative to multitasking is *time chunking*, which is the concept of breaking up your day into larger chunks of time for important work, instead of reacting to constant interruptions. It's the answer to "working smarter, not harder." The more chunks of time you can devote to specific tasks, the less start-up and restart time you'll have and the more efficient you'll be. And because you set aside a specific amount of time to accomplish a specific task, you'll be more focused and do it better.

REMEMBER

Here are the simple rules of time chunking:

>> **Block your time by breaking your work hours into chunks of hours for specific purposes.** For example, you may chunk time for project work, administrative work, follow-up calls, sales calls, team meetings, personal time, planning, downtime, and exercise.

>> **Block time for harder tasks for when you know you'll be in the right headspace for them.** Maybe you're best during the first few hours of the day,

or maybe you're most focused right after lunch. Use slower points of the day to knock out less demanding tasks on your plate (for example, answering email). Block time on your calendar to align with those energy windows. Discuss how to coordinate those energy windows with the energy windows of the others on your team.

>> **Do one task at a time and avoid interruptions of any kind during these times.**

>> **Stick to your plan.**

TIP

When you're starting out, it's a good idea to keep tabs on how much time you spend on each task by setting up an activity log. If you're an independent contractor, this is helpful for billing purposes. If you're an employee, it's a good way to document for your team how you're spending your time and where. Ultimately, seeing when you're most productive during the day will allow you to carry out complex tasks during that time.

REMEMBER

A good time manager creates an at-home work schedule that pairs periods of sustained focus with periods of rest and exercise in a way that works with her natural energy and brain.

Taking breaks

Sitting at your desk all day, eating lunch in front of your laptop, and staring at a computer screen for hours on end is a recipe for disaster. Without taking adequate breaks from work, your productivity, mental well-being, happiness, and overall performance will suffer.

Remote workers already feel like they need to be available and online at all hours of the workday, so they're at a higher risk of working long hours without breaks and sitting for long periods of time.

Take advantage of one of the top perks of working from home, which is having a flexible schedule. Schedule breaks throughout your day. Be sure to include short breaks every hour just to step away from your desk, stretch and breathe for five minutes, and grab a snack, as well as longer breaks in which you can exercise, walk your dog, work in your garden, or call a friend. Being outside is ideal, but anything you can do to recharge your batteries midday is valuable to your energy and focus and ultimately your work.

The research is clear on the benefits of taking regular breaks. Here are a few examples:

>> **Increased productivity:** Taking breaks may sound counterintuitive to boosting productivity, but the gains in focus and energy after stepping away

from your desk are real. Taking an actual lunch break, where you step away from your workspace, can help prevent a midafternoon slump.

>> **Improved mental well-being:** Everyone should set aside time throughout the day to recharge. Reducing stress and improving mental health can be as easy as taking a quick walk outside or cooking a healthy breakfast.

>> **A boost in creativity:** Taking a break, clearing your head, and getting oxygen to your brain can give you a fresh perspective on a challenging project.

>> **More time for healthy habits:** Regular breaks give you time to get fresh air, exercise, meditate, or engage in any other self-care activity.

Building in quiet time

Scheduling quiet time is often the only way to get things done when working from home. This is a time you decide to shut off phones, shut down email and instant messaging, not allow interruptions from housemates, and allow yourself to fully immerse for a certain amount of time in a project or just to think and ponder next steps.

REMEMBER

Nobody crushes every minute of the workday. Your motivation and energy naturally ebb and flow throughout the day. When you're working from home, it's even more important to understand your energy peaks and valleys and plan your schedule around it.

Making to-do lists

TIP

Organize your time with weekly priorities and daily tasks in the form of a to-do list. You can do this on a notepad or an online organizer. Having a to-do list will add an extra layer of structure to your workweek, reduce worry and stress that you're forgetting things, and provide a feeling of accomplishment when tasks get completed. You can make your own to-do lists — purchase paper organizers like those available at Planner Pad (www.plannerpads.com) or go online with tools that are mobile.

Here are a few online options to consider building lists and calendars for yourself and that you can use with a team:

>> **Any.do:** www.any.do

>> **Asana:** www.asana.com

>> **monday.com:** www.monday.com

>> **Todoist:** www.todoist.com

» **Trello:** www.trello.com

» **Wunderlist:** www.wunderlist.com

Start with a master list every week where you brain-dump all your to-do's, including both personal and work tasks. Do this at the beginning of each week and continue adding to the master list as additional ideas, tasks, and requests come up throughout the week. Don't worry if your list seems too long — you'll evaluate it every day and eventually transfer outstanding tasks to a new master list, usually every two weeks.

Every night or first thing every morning, review your master list, identify the tasks that must get done that day, and transfer them to your daily to-do list. Use time chunking to block time on your calendar to get your to-do's done (see "Time chunking," earlier in this chapter). Be sure that your daily to-do list takes into account standing appointments on your calendar and your red and yellow action folders that need your immediate attention (see Chapter 1 for more on folders).

REMEMBER

You also need time for exercise, personal time, and family time, so be realistic about what tasks you can actually accomplish in any given day. Your daily to-do list will help you build your daily plan.

By getting in the habit of using this simple system, you'll find that you accomplish more each week and keep track of everything that's important for your work life and your personal life.

Conquering procrastination

If you're a "wait until the last minute" or "do it later" type of person, this is a habit you'll want to break when working from home. Procrastinating impacts your ability to be an effective time manager and can have dismal consequences for your personal life, dreams, and goals. Procrastination makes everything take longer and often thwarts your ability to experience a sense of accomplishment and joy.

The first step to managing procrastination is to admit that you do it. This admission can be even more powerful if you track and analyze your time during the workweek using a spreadsheet. Break down your day into half-hour increments, and note the following:

» What you were doing during that block of time

» The priority of the activity (high, medium, or low)

>> Whether the activity got you closer to your goals

>> How the activity made you feel

With a simple daily tracker that you have right on your desk, you can track the number of interruptions that get in the way of real work, and the number of low-priority or just plain unimportant tasks you engage in. At the end of the week, analyze your time and make new choices if appropriate for the following week. Use the tips in this chapter — including goal setting, prioritizing, and time blocking — to accomplish the things that matter to you, incentivize and reward yourself for getting them done, and then celebrate with others.

REMEMBER

When you're working from home, the most important commitment you need to make is to yourself, your dreams, and your goals.

Establishing Routines

The benefits of following a routine are clear. Routines helps people cope with change, reduce stress, create healthy habits, and get things done efficiently. And when you work at home without colleagues to support you, a routine provides much-needed structure.

A daily routine doesn't have to be rigid. In fact, working from home gives you a chance to be more flexible with your work hours, a major upside for remote workers. A daily routine is simply there to help make sure you're dedicating time to the things that matter most. Humans are creatures of habit and routines help us do the right thing even when we're tempted to lie in bed watching movies all day.

Establish a routine for working at home by following these suggestions:

>> **Go to sleep and set your alarm for the same time every day.**

>> **Exercise, meditate, or do light stretching in the morning.** These activities will put you in a positive mindset and warm up your body for the day.

WARNING

Refrain from checking the news, Slack, or social media when you first get up. This is almost never helpful for your mindset.

>> **Shower and get dressed for work.** Everyone knows how tempting it is to wear pajamas all day. But resist the urge — it really blurs the lines between working and relaxing. Yes, you can dress comfortably, but getting dressed for work signals an important mental shift.

>> **Have a healthy breakfast and drink water.**

>> **Prepare for your day by building your to-do list, setting goals, and planning connection time with team members or friends.**

>> **Start work at the same time every day.**

>> **Establish a daily routine for taking quick breaks, stretch breaks (see Chapter 21 for pointers), lunch, exercise, and fresh air every day.**

>> **At the end of every day, spend 15 minutes preparing for the next day and reviewing your appointments and high-priority items.** This will help create a sense of clarity and calm for the mind so you can truly "shut off" from work at the end of the day.

>> **Quit work at about the same time every day.** That means closing your laptop, silencing your phone, and walking away from your workspace. Creating this boundary is essential for your emotional well-being. Find out more about setting boundaries later in this chapter.

Being Your Own IT Department

Technology is the driving force behind the growth of remote work. Thanks to the power of the Internet, the wide reach of high-speed Wi-Fi, and the explosion of collaborative business-ready apps (like those in Parts 2, 3, and 4), more people are now able to work wherever and whenever they want. Having a basic understanding of technology will help you be immeasurably more successful when working from home.

You've probably been using a computer for all your professional life, but that doesn't mean you know how to keep your tech running smoothly. As a home-based worker, whether you're an independent contractor or a telecommuter for a larger company, you're largely on your own. For example, even if you work for an organization with a robust IT department who can support your tech needs and offer phone or web support, someone from IT will most likely not be coming to your home office to solve your tech issues.

So, first things first, you need to understand the technology and equipment you're using, including how it works and basic troubleshooting to keep you up and running. You also need a plan for what to do if you need more advanced support.

When it comes to your office equipment including phone, computer, software, Wi-Fi network, camera, microphone, printer, or scanner, be sure to read through product manuals, attend online training if offered, and consider purchasing a support package to call for additional assistance anytime you need it. If you're serious about working from home long-term, make sure you're familiar with everything in your home office.

At a minimum, you need to know how to handle basic technical skills yourself, such as how to

>> Reboot your Wi-Fi

>> Save files to the cloud and/or back up files

>> Run antivirus software

>> Keep your operating system up to date

>> Troubleshoot your printer

>> Use all your software, apps, and programs

REMEMBER

Some technical issues will need more than a simple reboot to solve. You should be prepared to fix most computer problems yourself, but some solutions will definitely be outside of your abilities to fix. Make sure you have tech-support vendors on call. If your computer or any other essential technology goes down or is out of commission for more than a day, it's time to rely on the experts.

Increasing Your Healthy Productivity

Your productivity is driven by more than just the speed of your laptop. In fact, studies have proven that when companies make health and well-being a priority and provide wellness education and programs, companies see significant improvements with both health and productivity.

For remote workers, the priority of health is no less important. Many companies offer employees access to wellness portals where employees can access nutrition information, meditation sessions, and exercise programs virtually (see Chapter 19 for more information). If you're an independent worker, there are several ways to boost your productivity by focusing on your health all on your own. Here are some healthy productivity habits for anyone to follow, especially remote workers:

>> **Get enough sleep.** Don't fall into bad sleeping habits. Turn off electronics an hour before bed and wait to check your email or social media until an hour after waking up. Go to bed and wake up at the same time every day. Aim for seven or eight hours of sleep per night — that's hours of *sleep,* not hours spent lying in bed looking at your phone.

- **Eat well.** If you have junk food around, it's hard to avoid it when working from home. Plan ahead to have healthy snacks and lunch on hand. Think of eating healthy lunches as another form of self-care, because it gives you the nourishment you need to have consistent energy throughout the day.

- **Stay hydrated.** Start the day with a full bottle of water at your desk and refill it at lunchtime. Make it a goal to drink several bottles of water (at least 64 ounces) every day. Many times, when you feel hungry, your body is actually thirsty. Using a bottle to monitor your water intake can help ensure you're getting enough water and curb that hungry feeling.

- **Get moving.** Schedule time for exercise every day. Getting your body moving provides many benefits, including increased immune function, and it helps you approach work with a fresh perspective.

- **Stretch.** Put a clock on your desk to avoid sitting for too long. Schedule five-minute stretching breaks every hour (see Chapter 21 for tips).

- **Get outdoors.** Get outside and breathe in fresh air and sunshine, even in the winter. Just ten minutes of fresh air and direct sunlight, which is the body's main source of vitamin D, can fight off disease and depression.

- **Practice mindfulness.** Mindfulness is about paying attention to everything that is happening in the present moment — sounds, smells, feelings, and touch — and accepting it in a nonjudgmental way. It's a powerful tool to sharpen your focus, decrease mistakes, enhance creativity, and reduce stress. (See Chapter 20 for details.)

- **Set daily intentions.** Setting a daily intention activates your receptivity. Intentions also provide you with reminders of how you want to live your life. They're often related to internal things like motivation and inspiration.

REMEMBER

Self-care and healthy habits aren't selfish; for an at-home worker, they're essential to productivity and engagement. When you work from home, away from the bustle and activity of an office, finding healthy ways to take care of yourself is not just helpful — it's one of the most important ways to stay on top of your game, with energy and focus that can last all day. (Part 6 has more information.)

Watching Out for Distractions

Fighting distractions while in an office environment has always been an issue, but when you work from home, those distractions are different and possibly multiplied. Things like household chores, kids, pets, spouse, noise, social media, and easy access to a TV can prevent at-home workers from accomplishing as much as they need to. Keeping your focus on work and not on doing laundry or watching TV can be achieved through awareness and discipline.

First, you need to be aware what your personal distractions or avoidance behaviors are. For some people, checking social media is a major avoidance behavior when they don't want to start a difficult project or handle a challenging situation. Other people feel that they can't focus on work with a sink full of dirty dishes or an unmade bed. Additionally, having the TV on all day keeps some at-home workers company but doesn't distract, whereas others get sucked into whatever program is on.

Start by defining your own distractions, and then make a plan for setting them aside. For example, if social media is your distraction, set your phone aside and close all the social media feeds on your computer. Allow yourself to check your social accounts only at scheduled times of the day, for a set amount of time. If dirty dishes are causing your lack of focus, make sure the kitchen is clean before you start work in the morning.

REMEMBER

Distractions vary from one person to the next. The key is to discover *your* avoidance behaviors and how they're hindering your work, and then come up with a plan for avoiding them during the day and maintaining focus on work. Building self-awareness of your distractions is an important activity, especially for remote workers who must be self-directed and disciplined in order to be productive at home.

Overcoming Isolation

The dependence on technology at work and in our personal lives has led to a heavy reliance on the Internet for our social lives. Being social no longer requires a car — all you need is an Internet connection. Working from home means you accept a certain amount of isolation. Yes, you can connect with your clients and your team via video calls, but much of your communication and connection is through screens.

TECHNICAL STUFF

Despite the ease of human connection using technology, people are feeling lonelier and more isolated than ever. The Australian Coalition to End Loneliness states that "loneliness occurs when the quality of our relationships are felt to be inadequate. It can occur even if we are surrounded by people." According to a 2018 survey from *The Economist* and the Kaiser Family Foundation, more than two in ten adults in the United States (22 percent) and the United Kingdom (23 percent) say they always or often feel lonely, lack companionship, or feel left out or isolated. In a survey of 20,000 Americans, nearly half reported always or sometimes feeling lonely or left out, and the survey found that young adults ages 18 to 22 are the loneliest generation of all.

REMEMBER

Working from home doesn't need to lead to loneliness or isolation, but it does require intention, thoughtfulness, and planning. Interacting with others — whether team members, clients, or friends — should be on your schedule every workday. When your workday is solitary, it's a good idea to make sure you connect with and see another face during the day.

Here are some of the ways to actively combat isolation when working from home:

>> **Schedule one-on-one meetings.** Put on your calendar several one-on-one meetings with team members or your boss. If you're a freelancer, set up quick coffee meetings online or in person to serve several goals, including creating opportunities for connection, a commitment to networking, and getting out of your home office.

>> **Use a buddy system.** Find a buddy — either professional or personal — who you can connect with regularly during your workday. It may be a colleague or neighbor whom you walk with in person or virtually every morning or a team member you connect with each week via videoconference for a personal check-in.

>> **Attend a virtual social hour.** If you're part of a team, take advantage of any virtual social events hosted by your leader, even if you don't feel like it. These connections serve as trust builders and culture shapers and require your participation to feel more connected to your team. Don't bail on the virtual happy hour or lunch-and-learn.

>> **Engage in instant messages (IMs) and chats.** Use the informal communication vehicles of IMs and chats to connect regularly with colleagues throughout your day. Set up a fun Slack channel to share jokes, memes, or funny experiences happening at home with your kids. Just make sure they're work appropriate. (Turn to Part 2 for more about Slack.)

>> **Join employee resource groups (ERGs).** Find a shared interest or hobby — like music, sports, reading, or cooking — with others on your team. Form a group that you commit to connecting with regularly and sharing insights, thoughts, or recipes.

Staying Positive and Motivated

For many people, the energy and buzz of an office full of people is a great source of positive energy and motivation. Working from home can generate its own form of positive energy and motivation, including having a flexible schedule and a comfortable, quiet workspace, surrounded by things that make you happy and peaceful. But if solitary workdays start to feel uninspired or your work is feeling lackluster, you can take some steps to get your energy and motivation back.

Putting positivity into practice

Staying positive is important no matter where you work. You can inject more positivity into your day by making just small shifts in the way you connect with others and respond to your situations by focusing on your "why" and building your resiliency muscles.

By checking in with yourself regularly and staying present, you can increase your ability to quickly tap into your positive and negative emotions as they're happening and then lean on tools and best practices for staying positive.

Focusing on your "why"

Keeping your "why" front and center is a very strong motivator. Your "why" provides focus and direction in the chaos of your workday. It pushes you to keep going through tough challenges. Of course, getting paid well for the work you do is a reward, but it's your "why" that fuels your behaviors and attitudes about your work.

Your "why" should be something fundamental, something core to who you are. To find your "why," reflect and journal on these four questions:

>> What gets you excited and makes you want to get out of bed every day?

>> What do you want people to say about you when you're not around?

>> What do you want to be remembered for? What difference do you want to make?

>> What are your goals? Why are they important and why do they matter to you?

REMEMBER

The surest path to achieving lasting happiness in life and with your work becomes much clearer when you make your life and work about something bigger. Clarity on your "why" brings meaning and purpose to your everyday actions and becomes the ultimate source of personal strength, conviction, and perseverance. The prescription for extraordinary results is knowing what matters to you and taking daily steps that align with what matters.

Boosting your resilience

Some people seem to have a knack for managing the stressors of everyday life with grace and ease. The secret to maintaining a sense of stability rather than quickly falling apart when stressful events occur is having emotional resilience.

It's no surprise we're hearing more and more about resiliency. Being hyper-connected and responsive to work anytime, anywhere is extremely stressful and cognitively exhausting. The result is a frenetic way of working that can quickly lead to burnout. Many companies are now including resiliency as an important behavioral characteristic to look for when hiring new team members. Assessing a potential new hire who can roll with the punches and adapt to adversity quickly is required for the future of work.

The good news is that resiliency is not a quality that you either have or don't have — it can be learned. Think of resiliency like a muscle that you can build with regular and consistent practice. Anyone can develop these skills to help in the face of chronic stress and increasing demands.

Here are common traits of highly resilient people — that experts agree can be learned through practice to help you build your resilience:

>> **Mindfulness:** Mindfulness is a state of active, open attention in the present. When you're mindful, you observe your thoughts and feelings from a distance, without judging them as good or bad. We all react differently to stress and trauma. Being in the presence of the moment without judgment or avoidance takes practice, but it's one of the best forms of healing and resilience-building. See Chapter 20 for more about mindfulness.

>> **Empathy:** Empathy helps build our own self-worth when we see ourselves and everyone around us as having value. Another bonus of practicing empathy is the "happy" effect of oxytocin, the hormone that is released when we care for others. Empathy and business effectiveness are not mutually exclusive. Instead, individual, team, and organizational success rely on a compassionate work culture.

>> **Acceptance:** When a problem arises, own what's happening to you. Resilient people understand that experiencing stress and pain is a part of living that ebbs and flows. As hard as it is in the moment, it's better to come to terms with it rather than ignore it, repress it, or deny it. Ask the necessary questions to be able to solve the problem. Use critical thinking, reasoning, and problem-solving techniques. Resist the urge to blame others or external forces. Acceptance helps you learn from your mistakes and find meaning in life's challenges instead of seeing yourself as a victim.

>> **Internal control:** Resilient people believe that they, rather than outside forces, are in control of their own lives. They have a realistic view of the world and can be more proactive in dealing with stressors in their lives, more solution-oriented, and feel a greater sense of control, which brings less stress.

>> **Optimism:** Resilient people see the positives in most situations and believe in their own strength. This can shift how they handle problems from a victim mentality to an empowered one.

>> **Support:** Resilient people tend to be strong, but they know the value of social support and surround themselves with supportive friends and family. Supportive people give you the space to work through your emotions. They know how to listen and when to offer just enough encouragement, without trying to solve all your problems with their advice.

>> **Sense of humor:** People with emotional resilience are able to laugh at life's difficulties. This trait is a huge asset because it provides a greater perspective and the ability to perceive issues as a challenge, rather than a threat. And, of course, laughter reduces the level of stress hormones and increases the level of health-enhancing hormones, like endorphins.

>> **Self-care:** This idea of taking care of yourself takes into account many things. For some people, it's rest, reading, journaling, or meditating. For others, it's working out, listening to music, taking a bath, or relaxing with friends. Self-care is any activity that inspires you, nourishes your soul, helps you recharge your batteries, and fills your cup. Resilient people know what works for them, and they make it a priority in their lives.

REMEMBER

Building your resiliency muscles will serve you well in an increasingly stressful world and position you as a strong team member or business partner that can be counted on to make it through difficult situations.

Understanding personal motivation

Motivation is personal, it comes from within, and it's up to you to find your own natural motivation in order to flourish when working from home. Self-determination theory proposes that human beings have an innate drive to be autonomous, competent, and connected to one another, and that when that drive is liberated, people achieve more and live richer lives. This is great news for the work-from-home crowd because you have a great deal of influence over these things in your work environment:

>> **Autonomy:** Autonomy is enhanced by being able to make your own choices about when and how you'll work, explaining your rationale behind a decision, and sharing and acknowledging your feelings.

>> **Competence:** Competence is enhanced by engaging in work that is challenging and stretches you to learn something new. It's also promoted by receiving positive feedback on a job well done.

>> **Connection:** Connection is enhanced by a feeling of being included, respected, and valued, as well as a sense of security in the relationships that you have.

Being a team player and knowing you matter

Nothing is as motivating or satisfying as being on a winning team. It's true for football teams, chess teams, and virtual teams alike.

Due to the increased focus on communication, collaboration, trust, and accountability on virtual teams, oftentimes their effectiveness and connection far exceeds teams who work in the same office.

REMEMBER

This level of production and comradery doesn't happen by chance. It happens when the team has a leader in place who sets clear expectations and communicates effectively, and when team members collaborate well, leverage technology, and hold each other accountable. This is what a highly functional and motivated remote team looks like:

>> You talk, chat, or connect daily.

>> Trust is firmly established.

>> You love to share the spotlight and see each other succeed.

>> You and your colleagues behave the same way and say the same things in team meetings as you do in one-on-one conversations or chats.

>> If a line is ever crossed, that behavior is immediately addressed, discussed, and reframed.

>> You don't hesitate to pitch in to help out a colleague.

>> Everyone is deeply respectful of the cultural differences of teammates.

>> You effortlessly connect on a personal level with teammates.

>> When issues arise, you deal with them and move on without grudges, simmering resentment, or sidebar conversations.

>> There is lively give and take, listening, and understanding during team meetings.

>> People are relaxed, and laughter is a normal occurrence. You have fun together.

Making Sure You Still Have a Personal Life

Creating guidelines and boundaries when working from home is an important aspect of finding balance and avoiding burnout. Being clear on what you're working to accomplish during the week and what support you need from your team and your family will help enlist the support, care and empathy of the people who can help you achieve success. (Part 5 has more information on adding balance and peace to your work-at-home life.)

Establishing expectations

When you have a routine for working from home, you can communicate expectations to others about any work or personal obligations you have, such as caring for an aging parent or being available for your children at different times of the day.

Setting expectations at home may include letting your family or housemates know when you need them to be quiet or free up bandwidth when you're attending an important meeting. If you're working on a global project that requires availability outside of regular work hours, set expectations with your team and manager for how this can work for you. For example, maybe you can respond via email or text after 5 p.m., but virtual meetings or conference calls will need to be scheduled before then.

REMEMBER

Be sure to discuss expectations with the intention of creating a win-win agreement for all involved and plan to revisit expectations anytime they aren't being met or need to change.

Setting boundaries

When you work from home, boundaries and balance are important topics to keep in mind because that division can get blurred very easily. It takes real discipline to be a highly productive worker *and* protect your personal life.

TIP

In the early days of working from home, it can be difficult to resist the urge to overcompensate for not being in the office by working longer than you normally would or not taking breaks. On the flip side, you can't get sidetracked by household chores or other distractions at home and fail to get your work done. To keep your worlds separate, try these tips:

>> **Create physical boundaries.** Set up a workspace that's separate from your home space (see Chapter 1). This should make it easier to shut out the everyday distractions of home life and to stop working at the end of every day.

» **When you're working, act like it.** According to the Colorado Department of Labor, getting dressed for work can help you transition to a work mindset by creating a "mental boundary between relaxation and work time." Also, avoid going into certain areas of the home, or sitting in certain chairs, for example, so that you know when you're in "work mode," and when you're not.

» **Have "no-go" zones for technology.** Laptops and cell phones can be useful for staying in touch with coworkers, but they can also leave you feeling as though you're always "on." This can lead to stress and burnout. Set up "no-go" zones where work devices are banned, like your bedroom, bathroom, or entertainment room. It may be obvious that you've blurred the lines if you're checking your voicemails at all hours and answering emails at midnight.

» **Set break reminders.** Regular short breaks can help to keep you energized and focused. Try setting a countdown timer while you do an hour of work. When the alarm goes off, reward yourself with a five or ten-minute break to grab a coffee, do some stretching, or get fresh air. Getting out of your chair during the day is vital.

» **Set up reliable childcare and pet care.** Have childcare and pet care, in place if necessary, and encourage your children not to disturb you when you're working. You can do this by having them help you create colorful signs that you hang up around your workspace that signal it's okay to interrupt or they need to wait. However, don't be too rigid. One of the great joys of working from home is being available to give your kids a hug when they get home from school.

» **Commute to and from your home office.** Consider taking a short walk before starting your workday. Even a ten-minute stroll can energize you and help to create a break between home tasks and work tasks. When you're finished working for the day, change out of your work clothes to symbolize that work is over.

» **Shut it down.** When you call it quits for the day, you need to mean it. That means closing the laptop, silencing the phone, and walking away from your workspace. Creating this boundary is essential for your emotional well-being. Give yourself, your family, or your housemates your undivided attention during nonwork hours. Your mental health is important, so do what you can to recharge your batteries.

IN THIS CHAPTER

» Checking the background and looking ready

» Watching the noise level

» Speaking clearly and using good eye contact

» Understanding crucial do's and don'ts

» Being patient

Chapter 3

Following Virtual Team Meeting Etiquette

Anyone who works from home will quickly realize that virtual meetings are an absolutely critical component of how work gets done. And you'll quickly become very familiar with video conference calls. They're an important way to create a connection with colleagues and a vital way to bridge the connection gap with global clients when travel isn't possible.

Taking part in a virtual meeting from your home office requires the same level of professionalism as attending a meeting in a conference room. There's no substitute for good manners. The age-old guidelines that comprise good meeting etiquette still apply to virtual meetings, with a few new ones for the digital age. Following these rules of etiquette can go a long way toward fostering a productive business environment.

This chapter shows you what great virtual meeting etiquette looks and sounds like so your clients and team members see you as a professional, capable, and respectful member of the team. (Parts 3 and 4 discuss Zoom and Microsoft Teams, respectively, two popular tools for virtual meetings.)

Checking Your Background

When you're participating in a virtual conference call with clients or team members, concentrating on the conversation or presentation at hand can be a struggle. In fact, a recent survey found that during a regular conference call, 34 percent of the time was wasted by participants "decor peeping" into their coworkers' homes rather than being fully present in a meeting. Additionally, an article published in *The New York Times* stated that "peeping at the flaws and flourishes in others' living spaces is one of the sustaining pleasures of 21st-century self-isolation."

These distractions are a problem, especially when your presentation, interview, sales call, training session, pitch to a new client, or client support is valuable and important, which it probably is.

Your coworkers, clients, and vendors won't take you seriously if you have a pile of dirty clothes or an unmade bed in the corner behind you. So, be sure to consider how to minimize disruptions around you and choose or create a background that helps to maintain focus.

Chapter 1 discusses the importance of adding personal touches to your home office. Be sure that these personal touches don't become background noise when on virtual conference calls. Make sure your background is professional, distraction-free, and work appropriate, and that the lighting is good, keeping in mind that natural lighting is best. Declutter the area that will be visible to others. Neutral-colored walls with a simple picture, plant, and lamp are always a good choice.

TIP

If your background is not ideal or distraction-free, most video conference tools have free digital backgrounds you can use. A quick Internet search will provide hundreds of background images that can seemingly transport you to a tropical paradise, the Eiffel Tower, a professional conference room, or even outer space.

In addition to showcasing a bit of your personality and keeping people focused on your message, using backgrounds can make people feel more comfortable attending a virtual meeting. In a recent poll, close to half of the workers surveyed said that their background setting is the main reason they don't want to turn on their camera, and 75 percent said they would still prefer audio over video. If you agree with these statistics, it's time to use these tips to upgrade your background and embrace virtual conference calls as the most valuable tool to connect, build trust, and foster engagement.

Looking Camera Ready

Just because you work from home doesn't mean you can slack on professionalism. It's easy to fall into a too-casual trap when your commute is a short walk from your kitchen to your home office. Certainly, one of the best perks about working from home is the freedom to wear anything you want to work. However, when you're in a virtual meeting, your professionalism may be judged if you just roll out of bed in sweats and bedhead and hop onto your Monday morning team huddle. When it comes to looking presentable on camera, common sense isn't always common knowledge.

TIP

When heading into your next video call, use these tips to make sure you're "screen-ready":

>> **Get out of your pajamas.** Put on a clean shirt.

>> **Brush your hair.** You don't have to be glamorous, but you should at least look presentable.

>> **Set up your webcam at eye level.** Use books or baskets to raise up your computer screen, if necessary, so people don't feel like they're looking up or down at you. Make sure your camera is on a steady surface to prevent shaking.

>> **Pay attention to the lighting.** Light your face using a lamp or sit near a window where there is natural light so you don't look like you're in the dark.

>> **Consider wearing solid, neutral colors rather than pinstripes or bright neon and big jewelry.** Both can be distracting, and large jewelry can make a distracting noise every time you move.

>> **Find a quiet place and get comfortable.** Joining a video call while your kids are screaming, the dog is barking, or loud music or chatter is happening in the background may not be avoidable, but do your best to find a spot where you can hear and be heard.

>> **Test your video before your call.** This way, you won't be fixing your hair or clothing when the call starts, and you'll prevent yourself from being distracted or embarrassed.

Minimizing Noise and Using the Mute Button

Nothing is more frustrating than hearing that alien echo noise or high-pitch screech from conflicting microphones. If you're working in a noisy cafe, an airport, or anywhere that has a lot of background noise, always keep your microphone muted when you're not speaking. It gives everyone else the ability to chime in without distraction. In large meetings, it's a good idea to keep your mic muted until you need to speak, even if your office is quiet.

Video meetings have enough background noise, so don't add to it. Make sure you're in a quiet room; close the windows, turn off music, cell phones, and TVs; relocate pets; and make sure your roommates, spouse, and kids know you aren't to be disturbed. Minimize the use of your keyboard because the sound is distracting and it also highlights that you may not be fully engaged. Also, mute any alert tones on your computer.

TIP

Depending on the noise level in your home, you may want to consider getting noise-canceling headphones to truly tune out the distractions of traffic and sounds within your home. Here are some factors to consider:

>> **Decide if you want ear buds, earpads, or full-size headphones that fit around your entire ear.** Full-size headphones can do a great job canceling out noise, but you may feel self-conscious on camera with them on.

>> **Think about how you'll use your headphones most often.** Wired headphones can save you some money, but wireless headphones will allow you to be hands-free, which comes in handy.

>> **Check the battery life.** A good set of headphones usually lasts 25 hours on one charge.

>> **Try on the headphones in the store if possible, to check for fit and sound.** Have someone talk to you or play music to see how well they drown out the noise.

>> **Consider how much you're willing to spend.** You'll use them every time you're on a call and they'll impact noise levels and distractions significantly. Invest in headphones that work for you and present you in the best way possible.

>> **Don't expect headphones to be perfect at canceling out noise.** They can't block out everything, but they can get close.

Speaking Clearly and Making Eye Contact

Videoconferencing technology has improved greatly, but it's still a good idea to speak slowly, articulate your words clearly, and don't interrupt. When there are nonnative speakers on the call, slowing down and speaking clearly is even more important. Keep in mind that if you have a decent microphone, you don't need to yell — your normal speaking volume should be fine.

TIP

Great presenters know that making direct eye contact when speaking or presenting is the most powerful way to engage others and reinforce your point. When it's your turn to speak, be sure to look into your camera, not at the smiling faces of your clients or colleagues on the screen. It takes a while to get used to looking into a little black dot and it can be challenging to focus on consistently during a meeting, but when you look at the camera, you look more natural. Plus, looking into the camera helps you connect with others much more effectively and increases your impact.

Most videoconferencing tools provide opportunities to participate in the meeting without interrupting the speaker. Things like using a chat window to comment on what's being said, sharing an emoji to react to a presentation, or "raising your hand" to ask a question are all ways you can engage in the meeting. These tools are even more important if the meeting brings together people meeting in-person and people dialing in.

TIP

Another great option is to record the meeting. It's a great way to minimize the need to take notes, so everyone can participate fully and you know you can share the recording later or have it transcribed for the group. Plus, you can share the recording with team members who couldn't attend.

Many new computers and laptops come with cameras and mics already installed. But not all tech tools are created equal. If you're not confident that your current webcam and mic are up to the task of daily video calls, investing in new technology is probably a good idea. Purchasing an aftermarket webcam or microphone can give your video and audio a significant boost in quality.

Consider the following when shopping for a webcam:

>> **Resolution:** The lower the resolution, the grainer you'll look onscreen.

>> **Frame rate:** Webcams without high frame rates produce images that periodically freeze on the screen. If you're planning to stream video, look for a minimum of 15 frames per second (fps).

>> **Autofocus:** This feature can help refocus you on the screen if you tend to move around a lot when presenting or speaking.

>> **Compatibility:** Be sure that the webcam you're considering runs on your operating system.

Microphone considerations include the following:

>> **Price:** Depending on what you plan to do for work, a simple USB microphone that plugs right into your laptop will most likely do the trick. However, if you'll be recording regular videos, podcasts, and interviews, investing in a high-quality microphone such as the Blue Yeti (www.bluedesigns.com/products/yeti) may be your best choice.

>> **Plug-and-play option:** Most likely, you want a microphone that is simple and that you can use right out of the box by just plugging it into your computer. Then all you have to do is select the microphone as the audio option when you're participating in a call or videoconference.

>> **Size:** If you don't want your microphone to appear in your conference calls, choose a small and portable mic that plugs into your computer. This also makes it easily portable for travel.

Remembering a Few Important Do's and Don'ts

In every team meeting, you have an opportunity to build trust and connection with your clients and coworkers and to increase engagement. Don't squander that opportunity by being unprepared or leaving everything to chance.

Engaging in virtual meeting best practices

Follow these best practices to help you practice rock-star virtual meeting etiquette and ensure participation and engagement in the virtual meetings you attend:

TIP

>> **Do a tech check.** Before joining a meeting, check your settings to ensure that your microphone and camera are turned on. That way, you can participate when asked and others can see and hear you.

If your Internet is running slow from home, check out the following:

- Are others in the house eating up bandwidth by streaming Netflix or being online? Can you ask them to wait until your meeting is finished?

- Do you have 50 other files open on your laptop? Close down all unnecessary programs while attending a virtual meeting.

- Can you plug directly into your modem? This will speed things up considerably.

» **Be ready to join.** Try to join a virtual meeting via your computer. The quality of a video call on a smartphone isn't nearly as reliable or clear. Use a headset or earplugs to improve sound quality and keep the noise down for your housemates, family, or pets.

» **Insist on video when important.** Body language is crucial for interpreting whether your audience is engaged. Video makes people feel more engaged because it allows team members to see each other's emotions and reactions, which immediately humanizes the room. They're no longer just voices on a phone line; they're the faces of your coworkers.

TIP

Turn the video camera on early before the meeting starts so people can chat casually prior to the meeting. If the meeting doesn't require everyone to be on camera, plan to turn it on quickly before the meeting starts, just to say hello. It's a great morale booster and can set up positive energy for the meeting.

» **Don't underestimate the icebreaker.** *Icebreakers* are discussion questions or activities to help participants relax and ease them into a group meeting. Icebreakers can create a positive group atmosphere, break down social barriers, and help people become more familiar and trust each other. Have some fun with virtual icebreakers, such as sharing a meme that you like or a picture of your workspace or the view outside your window. Keep icebreakers quick and positive, not too personal.

» **Request or send an agenda in advance.** If you've been asked to attend a meeting, be sure to request an agenda so that you can think about the content, formulate ideas, and prepare to be engaged. If you're leading the meeting, incorporate collaborative discussions in your agenda so that your meetings are engaging and people want to contribute. Use your tech tools such as breakout rooms, whiteboards, polling, and chat to get everyone involved.

» **Ask for opinions.** Go out of your way to address individuals by name and ask specific questions if you haven't heard from them. Don't let one or two people dominate the discussion. Pay attention to the attendees that you haven't heard from and call on them for their opinions. By verbally engaging your meeting participants, you can ensure that everyone feels included, and they aren't multitasking by messing around on Facebook or doing other work.

» **Follow up.** You know that informal gathering that occurs immediately after an in-person meeting has ended, when attendees have side conversations and process what was said in the meeting? Plan to reach out and follow up with other attendees to have open, transparent, and less guarded conversations about what they really care about or are worried about. This quick follow-up shows that you care and is a great way to build trust.

Steering clear of common mistakes

WARNING

Be sure to observe the following don'ts in virtual meetings:

» **Don't be late.** When you're late, attendees notice, especially if it's a small meeting. Being late can give the impression that you don't care or that the meeting isn't important to you. A better option is to try not to schedule meetings back to back so that you have some time to dial in early. Make sure your audio and video are working and on. Introduce yourself before speaking so that everyone knows who's talking.

» **Don't move around excessively.** It's distracting and can come off as though you're anxious. Keep your body movements minimal or stand if it helps you to stay focused and keeps you from fidgeting. If you like to talk with your hands, make sure they don't distract from your message or get in the way of reading your facial expressions on camera. If you have to move from one room to another because of sound issues or quality, turn off your camera and mute yourself for a minute until you get settled.

» **Don't be too far away.** Some people don't like the way they look up close on the camera, so they sit far away. But proximity plays a big role in how you're perceived as a communicator and can impact your levels of engagement. Be sure that your head, face, neck, and upper torso are visible so that people can see your body language and facial expressions.

» **Don't eat.** Even if the meeting falls during your normal mealtime, don't eat during your video call. Just because people can't smell it doesn't mean they can't hear or see you chewing. No one wants to see you stuff your face while discussing important business matters, unless it's a virtual happy hour or virtual dinner — then go for it!

» **Don't speak too softly.** When meeting virtually, speak *slightly* louder than usual. In addition to making sure others can hear you, it conveys belief and confidence in your message. Think about what volume you would use if you were in a large conference room, and use that voice on your virtual calls as well.

» **Don't interrupt.** A well-run meeting allows everyone a chance to speak and is usually done round-robin or via a virtual conference table that you set up ahead of time. If that practice isn't set up for your meeting, wait until other attendees are done talking before you share your insights. If you have talkative team members who take up too much time, consider giving everyone a time limit when they speak to address this issue.

>> **Don't multitask.** According to a study by InterCall, 65 percent of people do unrelated work, 60 percent read or send emails, and 43 percent admit to checking social media during virtual meetings. All of these behaviors are no-no's. Give the virtual meeting your full attention. It's more productive and more respectful.

>> **Don't carry on side conversations.** You wouldn't do it in a face-to-face meeting, so you shouldn't do it in a virtual one. That includes talking, texting, or chatting with anyone not in the current meeting.

>> **Don't leave the meeting without notice.** Be sure to say "goodbye" when you're leaving the video call, either by speaking up or using the chat window. That may seem unimportant, because people will likely see your image leave the screen when you hang up, but practicing this simple but thoughtful gesture is good meeting etiquette and is never a bad idea.

>> **Don't be silent.** You're in the meeting for a reason and your voice matters. Be mindful of how long it's been since you provided input. Use the rule of three when attending a meeting: Provide three solutions, ask three questions, or give three insights. This shows that you're an engaged and valued member of the team.

Practicing Patience

Technology brings with it new challenges, and not everyone will be equally adept at participating in virtual meetings. Try to be patient as people get the hang of it. During a meeting, if someone doesn't respond immediately, give him a few seconds. The slow response may be an audio delay or he may be desperately trying to unmute himself.

Don't forget to relax and have fun! You're allowed to be yourself, so break the ice with a joke. The more fun you interject, the more people will stay focused and engaged in the meeting.

Video calls and meetings take a little getting used to, but as a home-based worker, talking to your camera will become a natural and frequent part of your workday. Give yourself time and stick with it, because using these tech tools is a vital part of keeping you connected to your team, your clients, your vendors, and other partners.

TIP

Deep breathing can calm the mind, focus the brain, and be grounding for the nervous system. When you find that you're becoming frustrated or impatient during a virtual meeting, take five deep breaths through your nose and out your mouth while filling up your lungs and belly; this practice will quickly ease any anxious feelings you're experiencing. Another option is to request a walking meeting while discussing something that is emotional or difficult. This can help you keep a clear head and stay engaged while minimizing distractions. (See Chapter 20 for more about mindfulness.)

The key is to recognize your impatience as a red flag that you need to slow down and center yourself. Have a handful of strategies to help you, including asking more questions when you feel your impatience building. Asking questions immediately connects you to other virtual attendees and can lead to more authentic communication, which in the end, makes everyone happier — and that's a high-value commodity when working in a virtual environment.

2

Staying in Touch with Slack

Chapter **4**

Getting Started with Slack

S lack significantly improves how people collaborate with each other in many ways. Of course, that won't happen unless you and your colleagues understand how to use it. This chapter discusses the mechanics behind Slack. It provides details on Slack's cost, versions, different user roles, installation, and other key attributes.

REMEMBER

This chapter covers many of Slack's robust features but does not list all of them. There are just too many of them to provide a comprehensive list.

Reviewing Slack's Different Versions

Slack offers a number of different plans to its customers. To state the obvious, the Free plan is the least expensive one.

Free plan

This starter plan allows organizations and their employees to try Slack gratis. The Free plan lets you take advantage of a decent amount of Slack's functionality, but on this plan members can view only a workspace's most recent 10,000 messages. (Workspaces are covered later in this chapter.) Older messages are inaccessible, even in search results. What's more, Slack restricts workspaces to ten third-party apps. If you attempt to add an eleventh, you'll receive the following message:

> Workspaces on free subscriptions can only install 10 apps and your workspace has reached the limit. You can add [app name] if you upgrade your workspace or remove one of your existing apps.

Slack's Free plan doesn't entitle you to use all third-party apps for free in perpetuity; no version does. Apps don't fall under Slack's pricing model. They operate under different plans altogether.

TIP

Slack does not impose a time limit on Free plans; they do not expire.

When it comes to upgrade options, as of this writing these three exist:

>> Standard plan

>> Plus plan

>> Enterprise Grid

Throughout this chapter, these options are collectively referred to as *premium plans*.

Standard plan

Slack markets its least expensive paid option, the Standard plan, to small and midsize businesses. To be fair, though, nothing prevents groups or departments at larger firms from going this route.

Features under this premium plan include guest accounts, single sign-on, multi-workspace channels, and unlimited search. (If there are 257,123 messages in your workspace, you can search them all.) Slack also throws in group calls, screen-sharing, and unlimited apps.

For this plan, Slack charges $6.67 per person per month when billed yearly and $8 per person per month when billed monthly.

Plus plan

Ideal for larger firms or those with advanced administration tools, Slack's Plus plan includes all features of the Standard plan. It also sports a guarantee of at least 99.99 percent uptime, enhanced security, data-export functionality, customized message retention, higher user storage limits, and 24/7 email support. For this plan, Slack charges $12.50 per person per month when billed yearly and $15 per person per month when billed monthly.

TIP

Yes, premium Slack plans lift the ten-app restriction. Don't expect, however, to be able to use all third-party apps for free.

Enterprise Grid

Enterprise Grid represents Slack's newest, most robust, and priciest offering. The industrial-strength, all-you-can-eat plan is ideal for massive organizations that have gone all-in on Slack. Prominent customers include IBM, Target, and *The New York Times*. Enterprise Grid appeals to firms that require more granular security features, unlimited licenses, phone support, an insane 1 terabyte of storage per member, and other powerful features.

Slack doesn't list the price of Enterprise Grid on its website. Still, it's fair to assume two things:

>> The annual fee is considerable.

>> That cost varies based on the number of users in the firm.

In reality, a 20,000-employee firm may ultimately save money by purchasing Enterprise Grid. Think about the total per-user monthly fees that it would incur by paying for the Slack Plus plan.

TIP

People tend not to marry their spouses without having dated them first. Along the same lines, it's typically wise to try one of Slack's other premium plans before signing up for Enterprise Grid.

Note: This book focuses on the features that apply to *all* Slack plans. When necessary, key Enterprise Grid features are mentioned.

Changing Your Slack Plan

Slack allows its customers to easily upgrade and downgrade their plans.

Upgrading

To upgrade from one Slack plan to a more robust one, follow these steps:

1. **Click the main menu.**

2. **From the drop-down menu, select Settings & Administration and then Workspace Settings.**

   A new window or tab opens in your browser.

3. **Click the rocket icon in the upper-right corner of the page.**

   A pop-up menu appears with all options, as well as a link to compare plans.

4. **Select your desired plan and follow the additional instructions.**

Slack walks you through the upgrade process. When you're done, you receive an email from Slack and a Slackbot message confirming your upgrade that resembles the one displayed in Figure 4-1.

FIGURE 4-1:
Slackbot upgrade
confirmation
message.

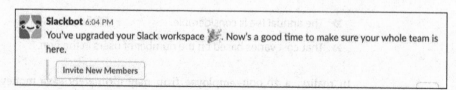

> **Slackbot** 6:04 PM
> You've upgraded your Slack workspace 🚀. Now's a good time to make sure your whole team is here.
>
> Invite New Members

REMEMBER

Upgrading your organization's Slack plan is a *binary*. That is, you can't upgrade yourself to a premium plan while keeping the other members on the free plan. This arrangement makes sense because Slack is a *team* tool, not an individual one.

Downgrading

Your organization can downgrade its Slack plan, too. Depending on your new plan, you may

>> Lose access to certain Slack features

>> Be able to use remaining Slack features to a more limited extent

>> Need to change channel access for existing guests

To downgrade, follow the same instructions in the previous section but select a "lesser" plan.

TIP

For more on the specific consequences of downgrading your Slack plan, go to `https://bit.ly/sl-downgr`.

Beginning Your Slack Journey with the Workspace

What if you go old school for a moment and forget about contemporary technology? Imagine a world without computers, smartphones, apps, and even the Internet.

Think about a massive brick-and-mortar town hall meeting. Everyone can gather around for a group announcement. Most of the real action, however, takes place in an informal, decentralized manner. Attendees break out into different groups based on their interests. They engage in wildly different, meaningful, and focused discussions on the issues that most resonate with them. Everyone shares ideas and opinions. They offer meaningful solutions to problems. They reach agreement on key town issues. To break deadlocks, they vote. Even better, someone in each group takes copious notes and meticulously files them. As a result, anyone can look up who said what when and why. This context is critical.

This town hall meeting is a decidedly low-tech version of Slack's starting point: the *workspace*. Formerly called a *team*, the workspace is a cohesive amalgam of different technologies and communication tools, including

>> Channels (think chat rooms)

>> Individual and group instant messaging

>> Powerful search capability

>> Screensharing (for customers on premium plans)

>> Video calling

What if you put all the ingredients in this list in a large pot and started cooking? You'd wind up with a scrumptious technological bouillabaisse called a workspace.

TIP

Customers on Slack's Enterprise Grid need to know about the *organization*. This entity sits above an individual workspace; it serves as a meta-container. Think of a workspace as one big container of channels. In this vein, an org comprises all the other containers. Of course, if your employer doesn't pay for Enterprise Grid, pretend that the idea of an org doesn't exist because it doesn't.

Creating a new Slack workspace

Depending on what you do and how your organization uses Slack, you may belong to a number of different workspaces. Start with one and add new ones only as needed.

TIP

If employees at your organization already use a Slack workspace and you want to join it, skip the following steps and proceed to the next section.

Follow these steps to create a new workspace:

1. **Go to** www.slack.com/create, **enter your email address, and click Next.**

Slack sends you a six-digit confirmation code. Don't close this browser window or tab. You need that code in the next step.

2. **Retrieve the code from your email and enter it on the page from Step 1.**

3. **Enter the name of your organization or team and press Enter or click Next.**

4. **Enter the name or purpose of your workspace's project and press Enter or click Next.**

Slack creates a workspace with this name as well as the #random and #general channels. (Chapter 5 covers channels in more depth. For now, just think of them as buckets within your workspace in which users discuss specific topics.)

5. **(Optional) Enter the email addresses of people you want to invite to this workspace.**

You can also copy an invite link and email the link to people. Of course, you can skip this step and always add workspace members at a later date, too.

Slack has now created your workspace.

6. **Click the See Your Channel in Slack button.**

Slack launches the workspace in a new browser tab or window. By default, Slack places your cursor in the new channel within the workspace.

7. **Click the Finish Signing Up button.**

8. Enter your full name and a strong password. Then click Next.

9. Name your workspace.

The value in this field defaults from Step 3, but you can rename it here. You can also change the first part of your workspace's URL as long as it's available. Ultimately, your workspace URL will look like this:

```
https://[workspacename].slack.com
```

**TECHNICAL
STUFF**

URL stands for Uniform Resource Locator. Think of it as a web address.

10. Press Enter or click Next.

11. (Optional) Add other people's email addresses or copy a link to share with them via text, email, or any other communication tool or app.

You can also let anyone whose email address shares your domain sign up for the app. If you invite others here, you see a confirmation page.

12. Click the Start the Conversation button.

You see your new Slack workspace. You can start communicating and collaborating with others in Slack.

WARNING

If your organization has purchased Slack's Enterprise Grid, it may follow a different process. Only Workspace Owners and Admins may be allowed to follow the preceding steps.

TIP

If you create several workspaces and decide later that you want to consolidate them, you can.

Signing in to an existing Slack workspace

Slack gives users two options when they want to log into an existing workspace:

» Requesting and receiving an email invitation

» DIY

Contact the person or department responsible and ask for an email invitation. After a Workspace Owner or Admin adds you to the workspace, you'll receive an invitation similar to the one shown in Figure 4-2.

Sign up by clicking the Join Now button in the email.

The Workspace Owner or Admin at your organization may have enabled an open signup process. If so, you don't need a person to invite you to the workspace.

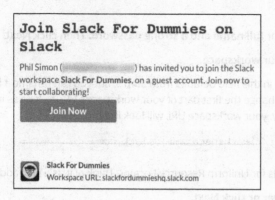

Join Slack For Dummies on Slack

Phil Simon (███████████) has invited you to join the Slack workspace **Slack For Dummies**, on a guest account. Join now to start collaborating!

Join Now

Slack For Dummies
Workspace URL: slackfordummieshq.slack.com

FIGURE 4-2:
Slack workspace
email invitation.

For example, consider the following hypothetical example. Marillion permits anyone with a valid @marillion.com email to sign up. As a result, employees don't need to receive formal workspace invitations. Instead, they can just visit https://marillion.slack.com and sign up.

What if you're a Marillion employee, but you don't know the URL of your company's workspace? Slack's got you covered. Just go to www.slack.com/signin and click the Find Your Workspace link. Slack takes you to the page shown in Figure 4-3.

Start with a workspace

In Slack, everything happens in a workspace. Like a virtual office building, a workspace is where your team can gather in Slack to communicate and get work done.

🔍 **Find your Slack workspace** 〉
Join or sign in to existing workspaces.

➕ **Create a new workspace** 〉
Get your company or organization on Slack.

FIGURE 4-3:
The Start with a
Workspace page.

You choose the first option on Slack and enter your email address. Slack attempts to verify three things:

>> The email address does in fact exist.

>> You can access an existing workspace.

>> The URL of that workspace is `https://marillion.slack.com`. (In fact, you can use the same email address to join multiple workspaces, and Slack identifies them all.)

Slack indicates as much in the browser, as Figure 4-4 shows.

Check your email!

We've emailed a special link to ▮▮▮▮▮▮▮▮. Click the link to confirm your address and get started.

Wrong email? Please re-enter your address.

After Slack has verified all three of these facts, it sends you an email that includes a unique link to the workspace. After you click that link, you can do the following:

>> Create a Slack account.

>> Sign in to the existing Marillion workspace.

>> Start communicating with your colleagues.

To find out how to add others to your workspace, turn to "Expanding your existing workspace," later in this chapter.

TIP

Visit `www.slack.com/get-started#/find` to locate any existing workspaces already associated with your email address.

Accessing your new workspace via a web browser

After you create your new workspace, you can log in to it and use it. Brass tacks: Slack provides a slew of different ways to communicate and collaborate with your colleagues. After you set up a workspace, you can sign into it via

» Any web browser

» Slack's computer app

» A mobile app on your smartphone or tablet

In February 2018, Slack decommissioned its Apple Watch app.

You can't do anything in Slack until you log into a workspace. In this sense, it's a walled garden similar to Facebook. Here's how you access your workspace via a web browser:

1. **Enter your workspace's URL.**

TIP

   If you've forgotten the URL of your workspace, go to www.slack.com/get-started#/find and enter your email address. Slack sends you an email containing all the URLs for all the workspaces associated with that email address.

2. **Enter your email address.**

3. **Enter your password.**

4. **Click the Sign In button.**

TIP

As you'd expect, you can reset your password if you forgot it by clicking the related link.

Using the Slack desktop app

Many if not most current users find it easiest to use the Slack app that corresponds to their computer's operating system. If your desktop or laptop runs macOS, Windows, or even Ubuntu/Linux, Slack has you covered.

TIP

Get started by going to www.slack.com/downloads. Download the Slack app and install it for your computer. In this way, Slack is just like any other contemporary computer program. Of course, the exact process will hinge on your computer's operating system. Keep your workspace name, email address, and password handy, and you shouldn't have any problems. After you log in to your workspace, you can start using Slack in earnest.

TIP

You may love Slack's desktop app, but you'll spend at least a little time using Slack in a web browser. Slack forces users to perform certain functions and configure a few settings exclusively via a browser.

Using the Slack mobile app

Slack wouldn't be a very useful tool today if you could only use it on computers. After all, it's not 1998. Fortunately, you can install the Slack mobile app on just about any device running a contemporary version of iOS and Android. Just follow these steps:

1. **Go to the app store on your smartphone or tablet.**

2. **Install Slack as you would Spotify, Facebook, or any other app.**

3. **Log in with your credentials.**

TIP

Consider installing Slack on your mobile device. If you're worried about your phone blowing up with Slack notifications, don't be. Chapter 7 covers how to customize them and keep your sanity in the process.

TIP

Slack automatically synchronizes data across devices. For example, say that you post a message in the #announcements channel from your Samsung Galaxy Note 10+ phone while at the gym. You immediately see the same message in Slack on your laptop — provided, of course, that you're connected to the Internet.

After you join a workspace, expect to meet Slackbot. Its purpose is to send you automatic tips about how to use the application. Figure 4-5 displays one of these gentle reminders about how to get the most out of Slack.

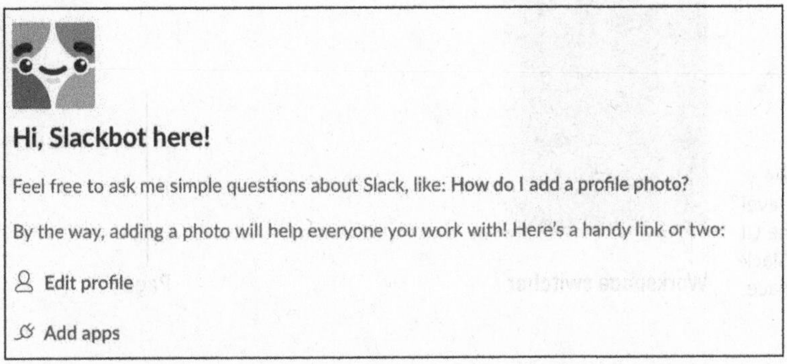

Hi, Slackbot here!

Feel free to ask me simple questions about Slack, like: How do I add a profile photo?

By the way, adding a photo will help everyone you work with! Here's a handy link or two:

ℹ Edit profile

ℹ Add apps

FIGURE 4-5:
Slackbot introductory message with tips.

Introducing the Slack user interface

Slack has created an intuitive and user-friendly application that you'll love using. On a conceptual level, its user interface (UI) contains seven main design elements:

>> **Sidebar:** Easily navigate Slack's views for Threads, Mentions & Reactions, Drafts, Saved, Channels, People, Apps, and Files.

- **>> Main workspace menu:** Allows you to invoke valuable options and settings.

- **>> Workspace switcher:** Easily jump to different workspaces.

- **>> Main navigation bar:** A fixed bar for moving within a workspace, performing searches and viewing history.

- **>> Page header:** A fixed header that always lets you know exactly where you are in Slack.

- **>> Page:** The main "work area" for the selected view.

- **>> Detail view:** Presents more information and options for each view.

Regardless of your employer's plan and how it uses Slack, these elements exist in all workspaces. Figure 4-6 presents a conceptual overview of the Slack UI.

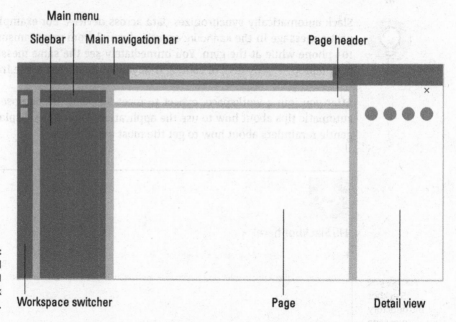

FIGURE 4-6: A high-level diagram of the UI of a Slack workspace.

Figure 4-6 may look great in the abstract, but how does it translate to an actual Slack workspace? To answer that question, here is Figure 4-7.

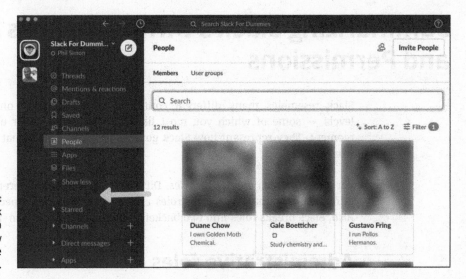

FIGURE 4-7:
A sample Slack
workspace with
People View
selected in the
sidebar.

By way of overview, three useful Slack buttons always appear in the main navigation bar. As such, you can access them in all Slack views. Each of these buttons works like comparable features on your favorite web browser:

>> **Previous button (left arrow):** Takes you to your previous screen.

>> **Next button (right arrow):** If you clicked Previous, click here to go forward.

>> **History (clock):** View your most recent locations.

These buttons help you easily navigate Slack.

Figure 4-7 has a yellow arrow highlighting a narrow bar in the sidebar — one that you won't find in Slack. This book refers to the two halves of the sidebar separated by that horizontal bar. The top half of the sidebar lies above it; the bottom half lies below it.

REMEMBER

The UI is contextual — Slack changes based upon your current view. That is, the view that Slack displays hinges upon what you selected in the sidebar. For example, if you click People, Slack shows you different features and elements than if you click Channels or Apps. Finally, if Slack has bolded one of these views, you should eventually check it out because something new has taken place there.

REMEMBER

Software companies can push updates and new features on a daily basis. No, Slack won't completely revamp its UI every week. By the same token, though, its current UI won't stay the same forever.

Summarizing Slack's Different Roles and Permissions

Slack resembles many different contemporary applications on a number of levels — some of which you most likely use today. Consider user roles for a moment. They represent how Slack governs who gets to do what within a given workspace.

For starters, roles are not binaries. Ditto for permissions. Different users can do different things based on their roles and the organization's specific Slack plan. Also, Slack breaks roles into two buckets: administrative and non-administrative.

Administrative roles

This section describes Slack's three different administrative roles for all plans save for Enterprise Grid. (See the later section "Enterprise Grid roles and permissions" for details.)

Primary Workspace Owner

Slack initially designates the person who creates the workspace as the *Primary Owner*. This special type of Owner technically outranks any other Workspace Owner and sits atop the pecking order. Primary Owners can do everything that Workspace Owners can do, as well as the following:

» Demote Workspace Owners.

» Transfer the role of Primary Owner to someone else.

» Delete workspaces.

Note that Slack bills an organization's Primary Owner, not each of its employees. That is, individual members don't need to provide their credit card information to Slack.

An organization can assign only one Primary Owner per workspace at a time, although an existing Primary Owner can designate someone else. (The idea of designating multiple Primary Owners just doesn't make sense.)

To determine your organization's Primary Owner, follow these steps:

1. **Click the main menu.**

2. **From the drop-down menu, select Settings & Administration and then Workspace Settings.**

    A new window or tab opens in your browser.

3. **On the left side of the page, click About This Workspace.**

4. **Click the Admins & Owners tab.**

Workspace Owners

Slack grants Workspace Owners the next highest workspace privileges. Permissions include managing members, administering channels, setting security controls, exporting data, and handling other essential administrative tasks. Slack allows you to assign multiple individuals to the role of Workspace Owner, but only one person can occupy the role of Primary Owner.

This begs the question: Which people in your organization should occupy the role of Workspace Owner? The answer depends on many factors, but typical examples include

>> Company presidents and founders

>> At large organizations, senior leaders and/or department heads

>> For a semester-long college class, the professor teaching the course

>> For informal groups or families, the person or people who started the workspace

Workspace Admins

Although they aren't exactly slouches, Workspace Admins wield less power than Workspace Owners do. For example, they can't view billing statements, but they can still do quite a bit. Specifically, they can manage members, perform additional actions on channels, and handle other key administrative tasks. Finally, a Workspace Admin may also restrict others' rights to install third-party apps.

TIP

Slack does not limit the number of Owner and Admin accounts that you can assign to a workspace. Make sure that you trust each of them, though. To borrow an oft-used line from *Spiderman*, "With great power comes great responsibility."

Non-administrative roles

Relatively few people in your firm will be Workspace Owners and Admins. The vast majority of Slack users at your employer will occupy the following non-administrative roles.

Members

Members belong to existing workspaces but lack the administrative rights of Workspace Owners and Admins. Their privileges generally include sending messages, as well as joining, creating, and posting in channels. You may allow them to invite guests to your workspace.

Let's say that you've invited Skyler to your workspace but she hasn't accepted your invitation yet. Technically, Slack considers her an *invited* member, but that's not an official role. Slack places a *square* icon to the left of Skyler's name in the bottom half of the sidebar (as opposed to the *circle* icons next to *members'* names).

REMEMBER

Roles are workspace-specific. You may be a member of one workspace but an Admin or Owner of another.

Guests

Let's say you hire Marie, an independent contractor. You want her to hold a single one-day training session at your company. Should you add her as a full Slack member? Should your organization pay Slack's monthly user fee for her to use it? Maybe, but Slack provides some options for this scenario.

Under Slack's premium plans, Workspace Admins, Workspace Owners, and members can create and manage two types of guest accounts:

>> **Multi-channel guests (MCGs):** These folks can join the channels that the inviting workspace member has previously designated. Slack places square icons to the left of MCGs' names in the bottom half of the sidebar.

>> **Single-channel guests (SCGs):** SCGs can't join random channels. They belong to one predetermined channel. Slack places sideways triangle icons to the left of SCGs' names in the bottom half of the sidebar.

REMEMBER

Under the Plus and Standard plans, Slack charges monthly or annual fees for all members. For example, if your workspace consists of an Admin, seven members, and two MCGs, Slack charges you for all ten users. In this scenario, nobody rides for free.

Only customers under premium plans can add SCGs. Slack caps this number at five per paid workspace member. For example, if your organization pays for six user licenses, a maximum of 30 total SCGs can join your workspace.

Managing member roles

Slack realizes that things change over time. As long as your role permits it and someone with greater privileges hasn't disabled the feature, you can elevate or downgrade members' roles in Slack.

WARNING

Tread lightly when promoting members to Owners and Admins. Your role may not permit you to demote them later. As a result, you'd have to involve someone else.

If you want to change someone's current role, follow these steps:

1. **Click the main menu.**

2. **From the drop-down menu, select Settings & Administration.**

3. **From the submenu that appears on the right, select Manage Members.**

   A new window or tab opens in your browser.

4. **Click the ellipsis on the right that corresponds to that member.**

5. **Click Change Account Type.**

6. **Click the radio button to the left of the new role.**

7. **Click the green Save button.**

REMEMBER

Members and guests can't alter their own roles — never mind the roles of others. That is, they can't elevate themselves to Owners or Admins or demote themselves. A workspace member already in an administrative role needs to make this change.

Changing guest access

Slack provides a few different options for handling guests. For example, Workspace Owners and Admins can do the following:

>> Demote members to single- or multi-channel guests.

>> Upgrade guests to members.

For example, say that Steven owns Porcupine Tree Music (PTM), a quirky London-based music store that uses Slack. He frequently hires subcontractors for different reasons. Steven always invites them to the PTM workspace as SCGs. In the workspace, they coordinate details about events, payments, and other details.

One of Steven's subcontractors is Gavin. He holds a few drum clinics at PTM, and they go well. Gavin's got mad chops. Steven decides to hire Gavin as a full-time employee. Gavin gleefully accepts. To quote Homer Simpson, "Done and done."

Slack wouldn't be very flexible if Steven had to create a new account for guests such as Gavin. Fortunately, he doesn't need to do so. Steven can merely upgrade Gavin's account from SCG to member with all the accoutrements associated with his new status.

To upgrade an SCG to a member, simply follow the steps in the earlier section "Managing member roles."

WARNING

Depending on what you're trying to accomplish, you may need to change a member's role twice. For example, maybe you've added Gale Boetticher as an SCG in your workspace, but now you want to make him an Admin. First, you have to make him a member before Slack will let you upgrade Gale's role to an Admin. In other words, in this case, there's no direct path between the two roles.

Deactivating member accounts

Say that a Slack guest just isn't working out. As the Slack Admin, you want to remove the person as a guest and revoke access to your workspace. Follow these steps:

1. **Click the main menu.**

2. **From the drop-down menu, select Settings & Administration and then Workspace Settings.**

3. **From the submenu that appears on the right, select Manage Members.**

   A new window or tab opens in your browser.

4. **Click the ellipsis on the far right that corresponds to the member you want to remove.**

5. **Click Deactivate Account.**

   Slack warns you that this action deactivates the member from the workspace, but active members are still able to view his contributions.

6. **Click the red Deactivate button.**

   The person is no longer an active member.

Note that Slack wisely grays out the names of deactivated members in the People view. You don't see them appear in the sidebar (see Figure 4-8).

Slack disables the ability to send new messages to deactivated members. You can try, but you won't succeed.

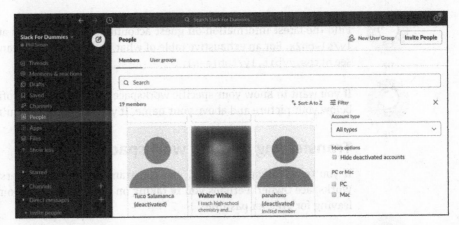

FIGURE 4-8:
Deactivated
accounts in the
People view.

Deleting member accounts

Before deactivation and if their settings permit, individual members can delete direct messages (DMs) and files. However, Slack doesn't let even Workspace Owners and Admins delete entire members' accounts and histories — and it's not hard to understand why. After all, *Slack* stands for Searchable Log of All Conversation and Knowledge. The operative word here is *All*.

What if your firm fired an employee for engaging in inappropriate workplace behavior? For obvious reasons, HR would just as soon purge that employee from all records à la George Orwell's classic book *1984*. For legal reasons, though, Slack doesn't let even Workspace Owners rewrite history. At some point, a court, lawyer, or regulatory body may compel an organization to turn over information. As a company, Slack doesn't want to expose itself to liability.

Reactivating member accounts

Say that you want to reactivate a member's account after deactivating it. Simply go to the same member dashboard and follow these steps:

1. **Click the main menu.**

2. **From the drop-down menu, select Settings & Administration and then Manage Members.**

   A new window or tab opens in your browser.

3. **Click the ellipsis on the far right that corresponds to the member you want to reactivate.**

4. **Click Activate Account.**

TIP

Find the latest information on guest accounts and permissions at `https://bit.ly/sl-ch2x`. For an exhaustive table of what each role can and cannot do in Slack, see `https://bit.ly/table-sl`.

TIP

If you want to know your specific workspace role, go to your profile. Slack lists it below your picture and above your name. If you see nothing, you're a member.

Transferring primary workspace ownership

If you're a Workspace Owner, you can transfer primary ownership to a fellow Workspace Owner. Perhaps you're taking on a new role in the company or you're leaving for greener pastures.

WARNING

This move is immediate, and you can't reverse it by yourself.

Enterprise Grid roles and permissions

Slack's robust Enterprise Grid offering provides for additional administrative roles that transcend individual workspaces. In other words, on Slack's other plans, the Workspace Owner serves as its king or queen. With Enterprise Grid, however, two roles — Org Owner and Org Admins — effectively outrank the Workspace Owner.

Primary Org Owner

This individual retains the highest level of permissions. No one else can transfer ownership of the org. The person in this role can also do everything that Org Owners can do.

Org Owners

Think of Org Owners as seconds in command. As such, they can do the following:

>> Determine an organization's app management policies for all workspaces.

>> Choose which settings individual Workspace Owners can enable and disable. (If you can't perform a "normal" task as a Workspace Owner under the Enterprise Grid plan, it's probably because an Org Owner has disabled that functionality.)

>> Configure single security and access settings such as single sign-on and two-factor authentication.

>> Configure single sign-on (SSO).

Org Admins

Org Admins can do almost everything that Org Owners can do with a few exceptions. For example, they can't override a workspace's app management policy. For a comprehensive table of what Org Admins and Owners can and can't do, see https://bit.ly/eg-slack.

Starting Your New Workspace off on the Right Foot

The Slack workspace is an unparalleled collaboration and communication tool. This chapter concludes by highlighting two critical things to do after you've created your workspace. First, you should invite others to join it. Second, you'll want to let your future Slack-mates know a bit about you.

Expanding your existing workspace

A recurring theme in this part of the book is that Slack is a team tool, not an individual one. In case you forgot, you can invite members to your workspace when you create it. (See the earlier section "Creating a new Slack workspace.")

Your Slack workspace(s) will likely morph in ways that you don't expect. At some point, adding new members will make sense. Invariably, others will need to join in your reindeer games.

Luckily, you don't have to put on your fortune-teller hat. You don't have to try to predict who'll benefit from your workspace in the future. Put differently, Slack makes it remarkably simple to add new members *after* your workspace is up and running.

Inviting others to your workspace

To invite others to your existing workspace, launch the Slack desktop app and follow these steps:

1. **Click People in the sidebar.**

2. **Click the white Invite People button.**

   Slack launches a new window.

3. **Select the person's role.**

   Note that the next steps vary a bit based upon the specific role. In this example, you'll add a member.

4. **Enter the email addresses and, optionally, the names of the people you'd like to invite.**

   By default, Slack provides lines for two new members. You can click Add Another or Add Many at Once to add more.

5. **(Optional) Set the specific channels that new members will join if and when they accept your invitation.**

6. **(Optional) Compose a personalized message.**

7. **Click the green Send Invitations button.**

   When adding either type of new guest, Slack prompts you with the dialog box shown in Figure 4-9.

8. **Select the desired type of guest account.**

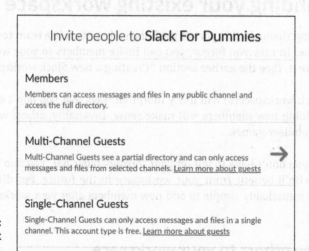

Invite people to **Slack For Dummies**

Members

Members can access messages and files in any public channel and access the full directory.

Multi-Channel Guests

Multi-Channel Guests see a partial directory and can only access messages and files from selected channels. Learn more about guests

Single-Channel Guests

Single-Channel Guests can only access messages and files in a single channel. This account type is free. Learn more about guests

FIGURE 4-9:
Slack guest account options.

TIP

In real life, you probably don't want your houseguests hanging around forever. Slack offers two options for deactivating guest accounts:

>> You can manually disable a guest account whenever you want.

>> You can automatically and preemptively deactivate a guest account after a fixed period of time or even on a specific date.

Restricting who can invite others to your workspace

Out of the box, Slack allows all members to invite others to join individual workspaces. (Guests lack this capability.) In October 2019, Slack smartly added some nuance to this feature: Workspace Owners and Admins can limit a member's ability to invite other members to their companies' workspaces.

Here are four reasons for adding a little friction to the workspace–signup process:

» An organization uses a number of different workspaces for different reasons. As such, it wants to ensure that its employees, partners, and vendors join the proper ones.

» A firm may operate in an industry and/or country whose government imposes strict privacy laws over which employees can view different types of information.

» A budget-conscious small business pays for Slack's Standard or Plus plan. As a result, it wants to monitor how many members are in its workspace to limit its monthly costs.

» A human resources department relies heavily upon a workspace. As such, its discussions typically involve sensitive information. The conversations are certainly not fit for public consumption, even in public channels. (Chapter 5 covers channels in far more detail.)

Regardless of your motivation, if you want to prevent existing members from adding others to your workspace, follow these steps:

1. **Click the main menu.**

2. **From the drop-down menu, select Settings & Administration and then Workspace Settings.**

   A new window or tab opens in your browser.

3. **Click the Permissions tab at the top of the page.**

4. **Look for the word *Invitations* and then click the white Expand button.**

5. **Check the box to require Admin approval for invitations.**

   Optionally, you can determine the channel to which Slack sends invitation requests.

6. **Click the green Save button.**

Configuring your member profile and key account settings

REMEMBER

Slack wants to be the place where work happens. It follows, then, that Slack needs to let members provide basic information about who they are and what they do.

Slack answers the call here by allowing members to create detailed profiles. Fields include email address, profile picture, phone number, and other key work-related information. Figure 4-10 shows the top part of a public workspace profile.

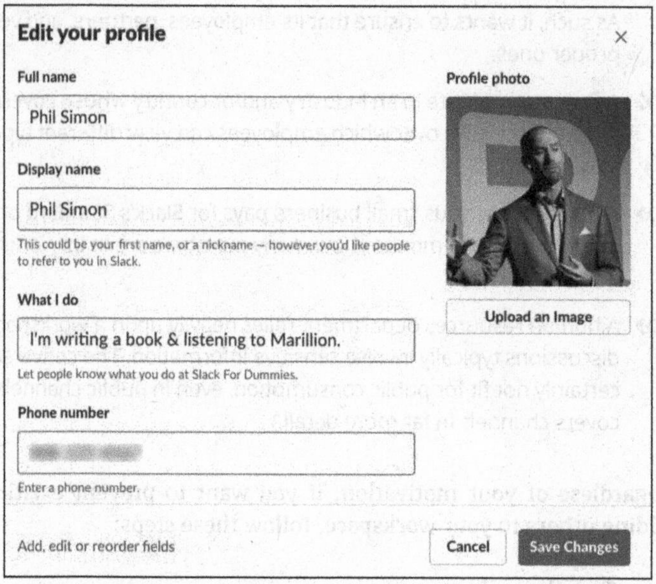

Edit your profile   ×

Full name   **Profile photo**

Phil Simon

Display name

Phil Simon

This could be your first name, or a nickname — however you'd like people
to refer to you in Slack.

What I do

I'm writing a book & listening to Marillion.

Let people know what you do at Slack For Dummies.

Phone number

Enter a phone number.

Add, edit or reorder fields   Cancel   Save Changes

FIGURE 4-10:
A Slack profile.

Note that more information exists under the buttons in Figure 4-10. To personalize your Slack profile, follow these steps:

1. **Click the main menu.**

2. **From the drop-down menu, select View Profile.**

3. **Click the green Edit Profile button.**

   - *Profile photo:* This option is self-explanatory.

   - *Email address:* This is the email address that you use to sign in to Slack. Based upon your role and permissions, you may not be able to change it.

- *Time zone:* Slack uses your time zone to send summary and notification emails (unless you've unsubscribed from them). With this information, Slack identifies times in your activity feeds and schedule reminders.

- *Language:* Choose the language that you want to use when interacting with Slack.

4. **Click the green Save Changes button.**

To be sure, you can customize your profile in many other meaningful ways. For instance, customers of premium Slack plans can add a slew of different fields, such as manager name and Twitter and LinkedIn profiles.

TIP

Make your profile as accurate as possible. Slack allows others to find you using the People view (see Chapter 6).

Chapter **5**

Targeting Your Communication with Slack Channels

Your relationship with email is likely complicated. You may lament the fact that you're always playing whack-a-mole with your inbox. At the same time, how else would you exchange messages with your colleagues, partners, customers, and vendors? Maybe you've wondered if there's a legitimate alternative to email.

If so, you're in luck, because Slack turns the traditional inbox model on its head. It offers superior options for communicating that leave email in the dust.

Slack does not portend the death of email. If used properly, however, Slack will reduce the size of your inbox and reduce the rate at which it grows. You may even break your email addiction!

This chapter introduces one of Slack's pillars for promoting effective business communication and collaboration: channels.

Introducing Slack Channels

Think of Slack *channels* as individual buckets that promote discussion about a particular topic or set of topics. (Workspaces are covered in Chapter 4.) Channels are big containers of information that you can make as specific or general as you like. Slack lets you customize channels to your heart's content.

At a high level, Slack users send and receive messages in two places:

» Within individual channels (the topic of this chapter)

» Outside channels via individual and group direct messages or DMs (see Chapter 6)

Forget Slack for a moment. When employees join a company, the IT department creates email inboxes for them to send and receive messages. If Derrick leaves for greener pastures, his inbox effectively dies.

Slack channels differ from email in this regard. They existed before Derrick arrived. Crucially, they continue to exist after Derrick leaves the company. Figure 5-1 shows how workspaces, channels, and direct messages all tie together.

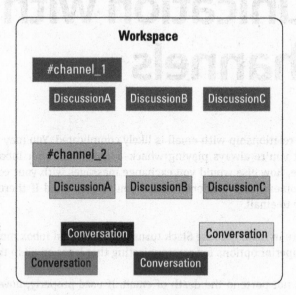

FIGURE 5-1:
The basic Slack workspace communication structure.

Discussions take place inside of channels — the topic of this chapter. However, you don't need to debate everything in a channel. You can exchange thoughts and ideas with your colleagues via DMs. Slack calls a string of DMs outside of channels *conversations*. Figure 5-1 intentionally omits shared and multi-workspace channels for the sake of simplicity.

REMEMBER

Slack channels allow you to keep discussions relevant to a particular topic. As such, you can accomplish a number of critical goals:

>> **Staying focused and organized:** Channels allow people to subscribe only to their areas of personal and professional interest. In other words, you can safely ignore topics that don't matter to you.

>> **Saving time:** Because Slack channels provide valuable context, you reduce the amount of time that you need to process each message. (Given how many emails people receive every day, even a few seconds per message helps.)

>> **Finding information:** By using channels, you make finding information much easier. Slack users can restrict their searches to specific channels, if they want.

When you create a new workspace, Slack automatically adds two public channels to it: #general and #random. By default, any member can post in #general. After that, as long as your role permits, you can set up and join as many or as few channels as you like. Slack roles restrict what users can do (see Chapter 4). You can also view the other members of public channels, and they can view you.

Exploring the Different Types of Slack Channels

As of this writing, Slack allows for four different types of channels, depending on your plan:

>> Public

>> Private

>> Multi-workspace channels (Enterprise Grid only)

>> Shared

Conceptually, each type of channel serves the same general purpose. In its simplest form, a channel represents a customizable container for discussions with others in the Slack universe. The differences are subtle but important.

For example, the primary differences between public and private channels lie in privacy settings and the ability for others to discover and join it.

REMEMBER

Regardless of the type of channel, only workspace members can access the information inside a channel. Put differently, even public Slack channels aren't available to the general public.

Public channels

Here's a simple introduction to the idea of a public channel:

» They generally exist within a specific Slack workspace. Exceptions to this rule occur when you share a channel with another organization (see "Shared channels," later in this chapter).

» Other than single-channel guests, by default, anyone in a workspace can join public channels. Of course, someone in an administrative role can disable this setting.

» Other than guests, anyone in a workspace can create public channels.

How can you use public channels? The applications are limitless. Figure 5-2 shows some channels for a fictitious company.

REMEMBER

The key point is this: Each channel serves a different purpose.

FIGURE 5-2:
A workplace with channels.

Private channels

Like public channels, private channels also exist under a specific workspace. Public and private channels fundamentally serve the same purpose: to share context-specific information with a group of people. Any member in a Slack workspace can join — and contribute to — a public channel. The only exception to the latter is if the Workspace Owner or Admin has limited channel posting rights.

For example, an organization may create public channels for #company_news or #system_issues. The rationale here is simple: All employees should be able to view this critical company information. For confidential discussions in #payroll_issues, #research, and #hr_staffing_plans, however, discussions probably aren't fit for public consumption.

Unlike public channels, private channels appear only in a user's channel directory if she's already a member of that private channel. Put differently, if you're not a member, in theory, you wouldn't know that a private channel even existed.

Unlike public channels, private ones require invitations to join. You can't browse private channels and join them.

WARNING

You can leave a public channel at any time and rejoin at your leisure. However, if you leave a private channel, an existing member will need to invite you back.

How do you know if a particular channel to which you belong is public or private? If you see a lock icon to the left of the channel name, it's private. Returning to Figure 5-2, notice how the #announcements channel is private, but the #supplies and #tips_slack channels are public.

REMEMBER

When you add users to private channels, they can see the entire history of all previous communications.

Multi-workspace channels

What if your organization uses Slack but different departments set up separate workspaces? Employees want to be able to send messages, share files, and collaborate within the same channel. Slack makes such scenarios possible though *multi-workspace channels* (MWCs).

TIP

You can skip this section if you're not using or considering Enterprise Grid.

Say that you work in your company's finance department. You want to share a channel with your peers in accounting, even though the two groups use different workspaces. Follow these steps:

1. **Click the channel name in the sidebar of the finance workspace.**

2. **Click the information (i) icon in the upper-right corner.**

   Slack displays a four-pane tab with the word *Details* above it.

3. **Click the More icon on the far right.**

   Slack displays a panel underneath the icon.

4. **Click Additional Options.**

5. **Select Add to Other [organization name] Workspaces.**

   Here you locate the accounting workspace.

   Slack presents a search box with default text that reads *Type a Team Name.*

6. **Type a few letters of the workspace name with which you want to share this channel; when the workspace pops up, select it.**

7. **Click the green Review Changes button.**

   Slack warns you if the same workspace name already exists in the "target" workspace. If that's the case, rename the channel. You can add an underscore when this happens. For example, @announcements becomes @announcements_.

   Slack confirms that all members of both workspaces will be able to join this channel. What's more, they'll be able to see the channel's history and files.

8. **Click the green Save Changes button.**

   Members of the finance workspace now may join the MWC, view its content, and contribute on their own.

TIP

Expect Slack to take a few minutes to make the channel available in the other workspace. The process isn't instantaneous. When Slack completes this process, you see an overlapping circles icon to the right of the channel. Everyone will know that the channel now effectively exists in *both* workspaces.

REMEMBER

MWCs work really well for organizations that meet two conditions: They've purchased Slack's Enterprise Grid, and they rely upon multiple workspaces.

REMEMBER

With Enterprise Grid, others can add you to an MWC without your consent at any point. If the MWC is public, you can leave it if you want and rejoin it later. If the MWC is private, you can leave, but you'll need another invite to rejoin.

Shared channels

At some point, you may want to use Slack to work with people from other organizations and third parties that also use Slack. Examples here include vendors, clients, and partners. What if you want to share a specific channel with them? Wouldn't doing so allow you to seamlessly collaborate?

Customers of premium plans can choose to share channels with external organizations. Slack now allows up to ten different organizations to share the same channel. Of course, all organizations need to belong to a premium Slack plan. To share a channel with an external organization, follow these steps:

1. **In the sidebar, click the name of the channel that you want to share with another organization.**

2. **Click the information (i) icon in the upper-right corner.**

   Slack displays a four-pane tab with the word *Details* above it.

3. **Click the More icon on the far right.**

4. **From the drop-down menu, click Additional Options.**

5. **Click Share with Another Organization.**

6. **Copy the link that Slack generates so you can share it with the person in the external organization.**

7. **Click the green Done button.**

   You can email that link to the contact at the other organization. Alternatively, you can share the channel with another workspace that you own.

8. **Paste the link into your web browser's address bar and press Enter.**

9. **Select the workspace with which you want to share that channel.**

   Slack asks you to review and accept the channel's invitation.

   If the "receiving" workspace is on the Slack Free plan, Slack will prompt you to start a trial to a premium plan. You'll have 14 days to kick the tires on this paid feature.

10. **Click the green Accept Invitation box.**

    Slack has now successfully shared your channel with another organization's workspace. Slack now places two overlapping diamonds to the right of the channel to indicate that it's shared. Also, Slackbot notifies all invitees that they now belong to the channel. Note that if the invitee doesn't belong to a premium plan, Slackbot will post a message with upgrade instructions.

TIP

If your organization is using Enterprise Grid, one of its Org Owners or Admins may need to approve your request to share a channel with an external organization.

Creating Public and Private Channels

You create as many channels as you like. Each channel requires a unique name. That is, you can't create two #development channels within the same workspace. Also, you'll want to give your channels descriptive names. For example, you don't want to christen your company's marketing channel #payroll. Put differently, there's a big difference between *can* and *should*. When naming channels, common sense goes a long way.

Next, understand that Slack bans certain words in channel names. Table 5-1 lists Slack's current reserved words by language.

TABLE 5-1 **Reserved Slack Words as of April 1, 2020**

Language	Forbidden Words
Brazilian Portuguese	*aquí, canais, canal, eu, general, geral, grupo, mí, todos*
English	archive, archived, archives, all, channel, channels, create, delete, deleted-channel, edit, everyone, general, group, groups, here, me, ms, slack, slackbot, today, you
French	*chaîne/chaine, général/general, groupe, ici, moi, tous*
Spanish	*aquí, canal, general, grupo, mí, todos*

If you try to create a channel using one or more of the terms in Table 5-1, you see the following message:

> That name is already taken by a channel, username, or user group.

TIP

If you create a Slack channel and carefully avoid the terms referenced in Table 5-1, and you still receive a similar message, chances are that Slack has added the word after this book's publication. You can view the most updated list of reserved terms, as well as banned Japanese symbols, by going to https://bit.ly/sl-ch-nm.

Creating your first public channel

When you know more about the concept of a channel and some restrictions on names, it's time to create a simple one. The following steps walk you through creating a public channel in your Slack workspace.

This section shows you how to create a basic channel. In reality, though, you'll want to put some thought into how you and others name and describe the channels in your workspace. (For more on this subject, see the later section "Building an intelligent channel structure.")

1. **Click the plus icon next to Channels in the Slack sidebar.**

Slack displays the window in Figure 5-3.

Create a channel ✕

Channels are where your team communicates. They're best when organized around a topic — #marketing, for example.

Name

e.g. plan-budget

Description (optional)

What's this channel about?

Make private
When a channel is set to private, it can only be viewed or joined by invitation.

ⓘ Learn more   Create

FIGURE 5-3:
The Slack prompt
for creating a new
channel.

2. **Enter a name for your channel.**

TIP

Keep the following rules and suggestions in mind:

- The current character minimum is 1; the maximum is 80.

- Consider using underscores to separate words. For example, #market-ing_team is a better channel name than #marketingteam.

- You can't use blank spaces and capital letters.

- Slack will gently suggest adding an existing prefix to your channel to help organize it. (For more on this subject, see the later section "Adding channel prefixes.")
- Remember that Slack restricts certain words (refer to Table 5-1).

As long as you adhere to Slack's naming conventions, you can proceed to the next step.

3. **(Optional) Add a description of your channel.**

   Ideally, the description illustrates the conversations that should take place here. In addition, the clearer the channel's purpose, the less likely people are to post inappropriate messages in it. For more information on this topic, see the later section "Defining each channel's purpose."

4. **Ignore the Make Private toggle.**

   After all, you're creating a public channel in this example.

TIP

   If Slack restricts you from creating a public channel, then it's because someone with higher privileges has restricted people in your role from doing so.

5. **Click the Create button.**

   Slack displays a screen that allows you to send channel invitations to current workspace members and user groups (see Figure 5-4).

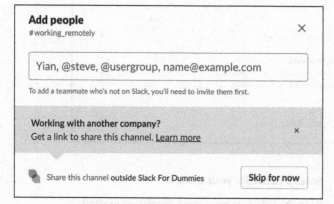

Add people
#working_remotely   ✕

   Yian, @steve, @usergroup, name@example.com

To add a teammate who's not on Slack, you'll need to invite them first.

Working with another company?   ✕
Get a link to share this channel. Learn more

🔗 Share this channel outside Slack For Dummies   Skip for now

FIGURE 5-4:
The Slack prompt
for adding
members to a
new channel.

6. **(Optional) If you want to invite others, do so and click the green Done button when you're finished.**

   Otherwise, click the white Skip for Now button. You can always add new members later (see the later section "Adding Members to Existing Channels").

After creating the new channel, Slack assigns a hashtag (#) to precede it. What's more, Slack automatically adds you to the channel (although you can easily leave it).

To create a private channel, simply follow the preceding steps with the exception of Step 4: You'll want to move the Make Private toggle to the right. It will then turn green. Beyond this, private channels operate in much the same way as their public brethren. Note, however, that Slack assigns private channels a special icon. Table 5-2 shows the icons associated with different types of channels.

TABLE 5-2 ## Slack Channel Icons and Descriptions

Type of Channel	Icon Position	Icon Description
Public (regular)	Left	Hashtag or number sign
Private (regular)	Left	Padlock
Multi-workspace	Right	Overlapping rings or circles
Shared	Right	Overlapping diamonds

Note that, depending on your type of channel, you may see more than one icon. That is, if you create a private shared channel, you see two icons: a padlock icon on the left and overlapping diamonds on the right.

TECHNICAL STUFF

If you're familiar with the programming language Python, you can write scripts that automatically create as many channels as you like. You don't need to create a bunch of channels individually. If you routinely need to create the same set of channels, this method can save you a great deal of time.

Building an intelligent channel structure

Slack won't prevent you from misnaming channels or entering inaccurate descriptions of the purposes that you want them to serve. As a result, you'll want to put some thought into how you structure channels in your workspace — and coach others to do the same.

Regardless of the type of channel that you create, each one should serve a different purpose. That's the whole point of channels. Trying to shoehorn every type of workplace message, question, poll, or announcement into a single channel or two just doesn't make sense. And forget cost, if that's what you're thinking; Slack charges by the user, not by the channel.

Defining each channel's purpose

The way you structure your channels hinges upon many factors. Perhaps most important are the types of communication that take place within your organization. Think about what each channel's purpose will be.

Large organizations typically create channels for #hr, #finance, #it, #development, and #marketing — and maybe multiple channels for each function. Others have created an #ask_the_ceo channel that apes Reddit's famous Ask Me Anything (AMA) feature, but an Italian restaurant won't need this structure. Unless you work in education, you probably won't create many #homework channels. Again, your channels will depend on your organization's and employees' specific communication and collaboration needs.

A little forethought about how to structure the channels in your organization's Slack workspace(s) will save you a good bit of time down the road. Beyond that, smart naming is less apt to confuse users — some of whom may not share your zeal for Slack. Constantly changing channel names and purposes is bound to wreak havoc throughout your organization.

WARNING

Be wary of channel overload, especially for new users. They may become confused, post information in incorrect channels, and/or eventually stop using Slack altogether.

TIP

Workspace Owners or Admins may want to create and promote a channel dedicated to gathering all users' requests for new channels. Think of it as a meta-channel.

Adding channel prefixes

If you're thinking that dozens or even hundreds of channels can become hard to manage, you're absolutely right. What's more, if your colleagues create new channels willy-nilly, your workspace's channel structure will start to become confusing. It's only a matter of time.

Fortunately, Slack channel prefixes can help in this regard. At a high level, they serve as internal guidelines for naming channels and help organize workspaces — especially large ones.

Slack provides a number of predefined prefixes, but you can create your own. By adding a set of standard prefixes such as help, team, news, tips, or class, workspace members can keep channel names descriptive and consistent throughout the organization.

The number of available prefixes hinges on your Slack plan. Workspaces on the Free plan create a maximum of six. For organizations on premium plans, that number is 99.

To add a new channel prefix, follow these steps:

1. **Click the main menu.**

2. **From the drop-down menu, select Settings & Administration and then Workspace Settings.**

    Slack displays a submenu on the immediate right.

3. **Select Customize [Workspace Name].**

    Slack launches a new window or tab in your default web browser.

4. **Click the Channel Prefixes tab on the far right.**

    You see Slack's predefined prefixes along with descriptions of them. If you want to delete an existing prefix, just click the X icon to its right.

5. **Click the Add Prefix button at the bottom of the page.**

    Slack launches a new window.

6. **Enter a prefix with a maximum of ten characters.**

7. **Enter a description that informs workspace members of how to use it.**

8. **Click the green Save button.**

    Slack now lists your new channel prefix with the rest of them.

You may be chomping at the bit to invite others to your channels. If so, jump to the later section "Adding Members to Existing Channels." However, you probably want to take the time to understand some of the specific features of Slack channels before blasting out invitations.

Viewing basic channel information

To see an overview of a particular channel, follow these steps:

1. **Click the channel in the bottom half of the sidebar.**

2. **Click the information (i) icon in the upper-right corner.**

    Slack displays the channel's Detail view, which are four icons in a new pane on the right-hand side:

    - **Add:** Invite others to a channel.

- **Find:** Search for information in the channel. (You won't find much material in a new channel, but that will change over time.)

- **Call:** Hold a call with channel members.

- **More:** Provides additional options to manage the channel.

Underneath the set of icons are collapsible elements:

- **About:** Provides the channel's current topic, description, creation date, and the name of the person who created it.

- **Members:** View existing members and easily invite more.

- **Shortcuts:** Create a channel-specific automation through Workflow Builder.

- **Pinned Items:** Pin a specific message to the top of the channel to maximize its visibility.

- **Shared files:** Displays files that channel members have uploaded for others to view. You don't need to scroll through dozens or hundreds of messages trying to find a file.

Note that Slack displays a number to the right of each item. As a result, you can quickly begin the process of absorbing information about the channel. Put all these items together, and you get something similar to Figure 5-5.

FIGURE 5-5:
Channel icons and containers.

TIP

New channel members should review this information to get a sense of what to expect from it. You don't want to appear foolish in front of your new channel mates.

Adding Members to Existing Channels

A channel with only one member serves no purpose. Slack is a group tool, not an individual one. To this end, Slack provides two ways to add members to channels: manually and automatically via default channels.

Manual additions

Channels are living, breathing things. Unlike email inboxes, they don't die when employees leave the company. At some point, you'll want to add workplace members to an existing channel. You don't want to wait for people to join specific channels on their own.

Here's how to add members individually:

1. **In the lower half of the sidebar, click the channel to which you want to add new members.**

2. **Click the information (i) icon in the upper-right corner.**

   Slack displays additional information in a new pane. Underneath About, you see Members.

3. **Click Members.**

4. **Click the white Add People button.**

   If you're adding a member to a private channel, Slack will display the following message:

   Anyone you add will be able to see all the channel's contents.

5. **(Optional) Click the green Continue button.**

6. **In the new pane, type a few letters of that person's name.**

   Repeat this process if you want to add more than one person to the channel.

7. **Click the green Add button.**

   Those members now belong to the Slack channel.

That's great, but what if you want to add hundreds or thousands of users to an existing channel? Selecting them individually would take far too long. In November 2019, Slack made it much easier to add users to channels *en masse*. Just follow these steps:

1. **Create a spreadsheet with the email addresses of each person you want to add to a channel.**

2. **Copy those email addresses.**

3. **In the lower half of the sidebar, click the channel to which you want to add new members.**

4. **Click the information (i) icon in the upper-right corner.**

   Slack displays additional information in a new pane. Underneath About, you see Members.

5. **Click Members.**

6. **Click the white Add People button.**

7. **In the window, paste those email addresses.**

   The current limit is 1,000 at one time. Slack verifies that those email addresses are valid and that they correspond to members in the existing workspace. If any issues crop up, you can simply delete the email addresses in question and proceed with the rest.

TIP

Say that you change your mind and no longer want to invite someone from your pasted list. Just click the X to the right of the person's name. Slack removes that member from the mass add. In other words, you won't have to start from scratch.

8. **Click the green Add button.**

   Those members are now part of the Slack channel.

Default workplace channels

You can always add new members to existing public channels, either via pasting email addresses or selecting them one by one.

What if you have public channels that you want all new workspace members to join? Slack makes these "auto-adds" simple. Owners and Admins can define default public channels that new workspace members will automatically join. This method represents the easiest way to add users to public channels *en masse*. Follow these steps:

1. **Click the workspace name in the upper-left corner.**

2. **From the drop-down menu, select Settings & Administration and then Workspace Settings.**

   Slack takes you to the first tab on the page, labeled Settings.

3. **Click the Expand button to the right of Default Channels.**

4. **Click the box that appears and select the public channels that all new workspace members will automatically join.**

5. **Press Tab and click the Save button.**

   Voilà! New Slack members now automatically join the channels that you just selected (see Figure 5-6).

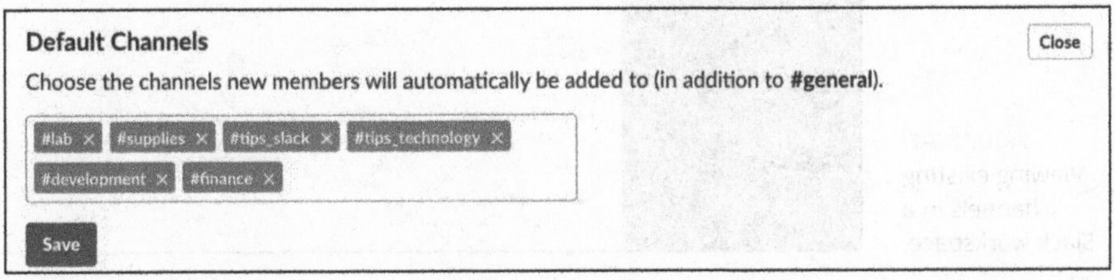

Default Channels   Close

Choose the channels new members will automatically be added to (in addition to **#general**).

#lab ✕ #supplies ✕ #tips_slack ✕ #tips_technology ✕

#development ✕ #finance ✕

Save

FIGURE 5-6: Setting default Slack channels for workspace members.

Exploring Existing Public Channels

If your organization has just started experimenting with Slack, your colleagues may not have created many public channels. Over time, however, that will change. People will create public channels devoted to different topics.

Say you're curious about what others in your organization are discussing. To browse existing public channels, follow these steps:

1. **Click the Channels view in the top of the sidebar.**

   You can now browse all available public channels, as well as the private channels to which you already belong (see Figure 5-7).

   The sheer number of channels may overwhelm you. Fortunately, Slack provides two useful ways to let users easily discover channels of interest:

   - *Sort:* Slack lets you filter by channel date, number of members, and alphabetical order.

   - *Filter:* Slack lets you restrict channel types: private and archived. You can also hide the channels to which you already belong (see Figure 5-8).

   Note that Slack won't let you browse and join others' private channels. By filtering on private channels, you can only view those to which you *already* belong.

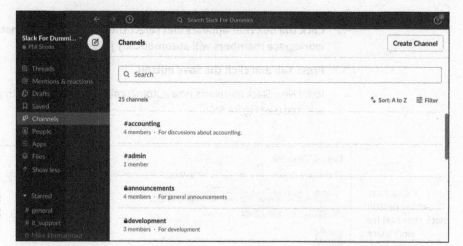

FIGURE 5-7:
Viewing existing
channels in a
Slack workspace.

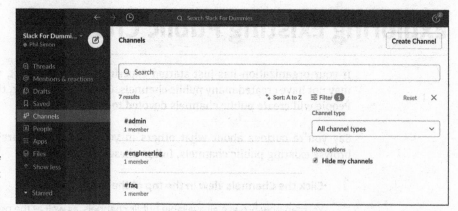

FIGURE 5-8:
Browsing a
filtered list of
public Slack
channels to which
you don't belong.

2. **(Optional) Click the channel that you want to preview before joining.**

    Slack displays four new icons in a pane on the right side:

    -   Preview

    -   Join

    -   Find

    -   More

    When you click the Preview button, Slack displays the messages in the channel. You haven't joined yet; you just want to kick the tires. Previewing a channel helps you get a feel for the types of discussions already taking place there. Click Find to search the channel for specific keywords.

3. **If you decide that you want to be a member of this channel, click the Join button.**

   You're now a member of this public channel. Access it in your sidebar.

TIP

Say that you already know the name of the channel you want to join. Go to any existing channel or send yourself a DM. (Chapter 6 covers DMs in much more depth.) Type **/join** followed by the channel's name and press Enter. For example, if you type **/join #marketing**, Slack skips the channel preview and automatically adds you to this channel. You can then read members' previous messages and post your own.

TIP

If you're joining an existing channel, take a few minutes to read its purpose, as well as a few topics. Also, if it's a relatively small or targeted channel, briefly introduce yourself to others in the channel.

Communicating via Slack Channels

Although a channel is a powerful tool, it's really only a means to an end — it allows you to disseminate information and interact with others. After you know more about channels, it's time to discuss sending messages in them. (Chapter 6 covers messages in more detail.)

REMEMBER

You'll likely spend far more time interacting with people in channels than creating and maintaining them.

Posting simple channel messages

To post a simple message in a Slack channel, simply go to the bottom of a channel and type whatever you like in the message prompt. Press Enter and you're done.

Figure 5-9 shows a simple message that I posted in the #tips_technology channel, along with Walter White's response.

REMEMBER

Messages and responses in Slack channels aren't private. Everyone in the channel can view the interaction. If you want to send private messages, you'll have to use direct messages (see Chapter 6).

You can mention your fellow workspace channel members by using the @ symbol. All other channel members can respond to any message that you post in a channel. They can include emojis, URLs, and even animated GIFs in their responses.

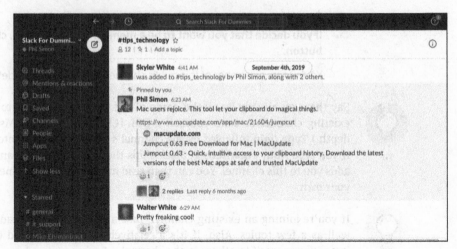

FIGURE 5-9:
A simple Slack
channel message
with a response.

TIP

Here are a few more tips:

>> If you want to alert every member in a channel that you've sent or responded to a message, simply type **@channel**.

>> Workspace Owners and Admins can delete others' messages in public channels. If you want to delete someone else's message, follow up with the offender and explain why his message was inappropriate. Ideally, this intervention will prevent a recurrence.

>> To guide the channel's discussion, set a topic. Find out more at `https://bit.ly/sl-topic`.

Understanding channel etiquette

In the rest of this chapter, you discover a great deal about how to create Slack channels and post messages and snippets in them. It's time to discuss Slack etiquette.

If you grab a drink or six with a group of long-time friends or go golfing, odds are that you're going to act in a certain way. Consider a different situation, though. Assume that you're out to lunch during a day-long job interview. You want to make a good impression with people you don't know — your potential future colleagues and bosses. As a result, you should overdress and behave in a more formal manner. Context matters.

The same holds true with Slack channels: Not all of them are created equal. What passes for acceptable behavior in one channel may be entirely inappropriate in another. For example, some good-natured banter or ribbing in the #humor channel isn't likely to ruffle your colleagues' feathers — especially if you've known them for a while. Routinely being a wiseacre and trolling others in #product_ideas, though, isn't likely to fly.

TIP

Here are some other tips to keep in mind:

>> Read the room. Err on the side of formality at first, especially if you're new to the company and/or channel.

>> The more members in a channel, the less frequently you should post in it.

>> Think before posting in a channel. Think about the channel's purpose.

Chapter **6**

Entering the Wonderful World of Slack Messages

S lack is a remarkably flexible and powerful tool on many levels. For example, Chapter 5 covers how you can use public and private channels to solicit information from — and provide targeted information to — others in your workspace. To be sure, that's useful. Still, you may be wondering if the channel is the only way to interact with your colleagues and partners in Slack.

The answer is a resounding no.

Slack's management understands that channels frequently don't represent the only (let alone the best) way for people to communicate with each other. To this end, and as this chapter demonstrates, Slack lets you send discrete, direct messages to individuals and groups. Even better, threads let you lump messages together into a single unit.

Understanding Slack Messages

Within a given workspace, you can send anyone a direct message (DM) about anything and respond. (Whether the recipient responds is another matter.) You can also post messages in channels. Slack lets users attach files to their messages, as well as share links, jokes, MP3s, videos, and whatever else they want.

Sending a message

To send a message in Slack, follow these steps:

1. **Click the message icon at the top of your workspace.**

    You can also click the plus sign next to Direct Messages in the lower part of the sidebar.

2. **From the drop-down menu, either type a few letters of the person's name or scroll down until you find him or her.**

    Slack displays a screen similar to Figure 6-1.

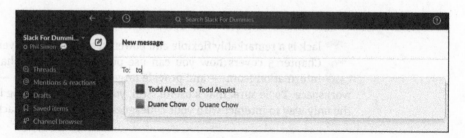

FIGURE 6-1:
Composing a simple DM to send to a colleague.

When you enter a person's name, press the Tab key on your keyboard. Your cursor begins blinking in the message line.

TIP

The process for posting a message to a channel is identical to sending a DM. The only difference is the recipient: a channel, not a person or group of people.

3. **(Optional) To attach a file to your message, click the paper-clip icon in the lower-right corner of the screen.**

    From there, you can attach a file in a way similar to how you add attachments to email messages. To easily share a file on your computer in a message, drag it from your desktop or a folder into Slack's message window. Either way, Slack attaches the file you chose or dragged to your message after you've clicked the green Upload button.

4. (Optional) Click the @ icon if you'd like to mention another workspace member in your message.

5. (Optional) Click the emoji icon and select one if you want to spice up your message or add a reaction.

6. Press the Enter key on your keyboard.

TIP

After you send a message, Slackbot alerts you if the recipient has paused notifications. If you click Notify Them Anyway, Slack attempts to alert the individual. (Chapter 7 covers notifications in more depth.)

By default, the bottom half of the Slack sidebar shows you the people with whom you've most recently interacted. Of course, you can send a message to any workspace member at any point.

You can also send DMs to multiple members. You follow the same process covered in the preceding steps. Instead of choosing one recipient in Step 2, though, select as many recipients as you like (see Figure 6-2).

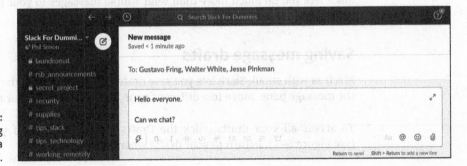

FIGURE 6-2:
Selecting
recipients for a
group DM.

Figure 6-3 shows the results of a group DM.

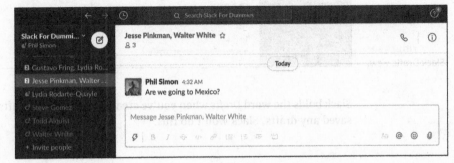

FIGURE 6-3:
A group DM.

After you send a group DM, the recipients appear under Direct Messages in the sidebar. What's more, Slack usefully displays a number to the left of the group to indicate how many members belong to your group DM.

If you want to leave yourself a note or just paste some text from another application, you're in luck: Slack lets you send yourself DMs as you see in Figure 6-4. Simply select yourself as the recipient in Step 2 in the preceding directions.

FIGURE 6-4:
An example of a
DM sent to
yourself.

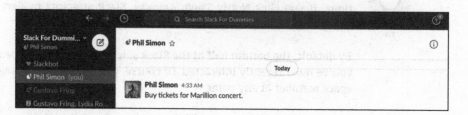

Performing basic message actions

Slack lets you do much more than send simple messages to your peers. You have plenty of tools at your disposal.

Saving message drafts

Much as with email, Slack lets you save drafts of DMs. Simply enter some text into the message pane. Move to a different pane, and Slack saves your text as a draft.

To access all your drafts, click the Drafts view at the top of your workspace (see Figure 6-5). Return to your drafts whenever you like.

FIGURE 6-5:
Slack Drafts view.

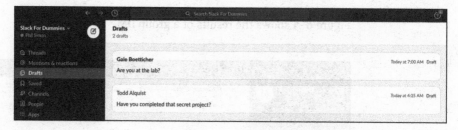

Slack bolds the word *Drafts* when you've created one or more drafts. If you haven't saved any drafts, Slack won't do this.

Marking messages as read or unread

At some point you've probably used your email program's Mark as Read feature. Slack offers the same ability in both channels and conversations. To mark a read message as unread, follow these steps:

1. Hover over the message.

Three dots appear next to the message along with the words *More Actions*.

2. Click Mark Unread.

When you mark a previously read message as unread, Slack bolds the name of the person or channel name in the sidebar. The visual indicator reminds you that the ball is in your court.

Understanding Slack conversations

Broadly speaking, *conversations* refer to a series of either individual or group DMs. Put differently, a conversation is an exchange of DMs with other workspace members that takes place outside of a channel. That last part is critical.

By default, Slack automatically creates a conversation when you exchange a DM with one or more workspace members. You can view all your conversations in the bottom half of the sidebar under the Direct Messages view.

Referencing public channels in direct messages

TIP

Although it's not a requirement, referencing public channel names in your DMs is a good idea. You can do this by including the hashtag before the channel name. Slack automatically creates a blue hyperlink to a *public* channel, but not a private one. Table 6-1 displays what happens when you use hashtags in Slack.

TABLE 6-1

Referencing Channel Names in DMs

Action	Results
Send a DM with a hashtag preceding the name of a public channel (for example, #finance).	The term #finance appears linked in blue. All members with access can click #finance to open it.
Send a DM with a hashtag preceding the name of the private channel (for example, #secret_project).	#secret_project won't appear linked in blue. Members can't click the channel's name to open it.

For example, Figure 6-6 references the #tips_technology channel. Following this practice makes it easy for the recipient(s) to navigate to the referenced public channel.

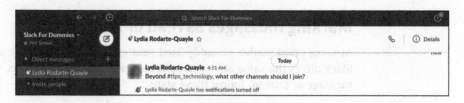

FIGURE 6-6:
A DM referencing
a public channel.

Formatting your messages

Perhaps you want to emphasize certain elements of your DMs to individuals or within channels. For instance, Elaine Benes of *Seinfeld* fame wants to go beyond merely inserting exclamation points to accentuate her points.

Fortunately, Slack offers plenty of options if you want to spice up the format of your message. Slack easily allows users to create numbered and bulleted lists, italicize and bold text, insert code from different programming languages, and more.

At a high level, Slack offers two options for sprucing up your messages: a visual or WYSIWYG editor and keyboard shortcuts. (*WYSIWYG* stands for "what you see is what you get.")

Using Slack's WYSIWYG editor

Prettying up your text is remarkably intuitive. In this vein, Slack resembles word-processing programs such as Microsoft Word. For instance, to bold a block of text, simply select the words and press the B icon underneath the text section and — *voilà!* — the text is bold. Ditto for italicizing text. Table 6-2 presents all Slack's visual formatting options from left to right.

TABLE 6-2 **Formatting Slack DMs via the WYSIWYG Editor**

Icon	Operation
Lightning bolt	Invokes a number of shortcuts not specific to formatting per se, but still useful.
B	Bolds the text.
I	Italicizes the text.
Strikethrough	Applies strikethrough to the text.
</>	Applies code style to the existing text.
Link	Hyperlinks text. That is, your text directs to a URL.
Numbers	Creates a numbered list.
Bullets	Creates a bulleted list.

Icon	Operation
Blockquote	Indents text to indicate that you're quoting another source or person.
Code block	Inserts an entirely new block of code.
Aa	Hides the text-formatting options.
@	Mentions someone.
⌣	Adds an emoji.
Paper clip	Attaches a file to a message.

Saving time with keyboard shortcuts

If you're more of a shortcut person, you're in luck as well. Slack lets you disable the rich-text formatting options by clicking the letter icon. Table 6-3 shows you how to format DMs using keyboard shortcuts.

You don't need to memorize these shortcuts if you prefer using the WYSIWYG editor.

TABLE 6-3 **Formatting Slack DMs via Keyboard Shortcuts**

Format	Keyboard Combination
Start a new paragraph	Press Shift+Enter as many times as you like.
Bold	Place asterisks at the start and end of the text.
Italics	Place underscores at the start and end of the text.
Strikethrough	Place tildes (~) at the start and end of the text.
Quoting one or more sentences	Place an angled bracket (>) at the start of the text.
Inline code	Place back ticks (`) at the start and end of the text. Three back ticks formats a block of text.
Bulleted lists	Press Shift+8 and then press Shift+Enter/Return. Also, you can press *+Space (an asterisk plus a space) or -+Space (a hyphen plus a space), and the formatting auto-adjusts to a bulleted list.
Numbered lists	Mac users: Press ⌘+Shift+7. PC users: Press Ctrl+Shift+7. Also, you can press 1+.+Space (the number 1 plus a period plus a space). Slack auto-adjusts the message formatting to a numbered list.

TIP

Regardless of whether you're a mouse or keyboard person, you can mix and match your styles in Slack messages. If you want to use bulleted lists, bold text, and a snippet of code in the same message, knock yourself out.

Finding people in your workspace to message

You'll send plenty of DMs in Slack to different people. This begs the question: How can you find your colleagues? You won't need to leave Slack and search your company's email directory. Slack conveniently lets you find fellow workspace members in several ways:

1. **Click the People view in the top half of the sidebar.**

Slack shows you something similar to Figure 6-7.

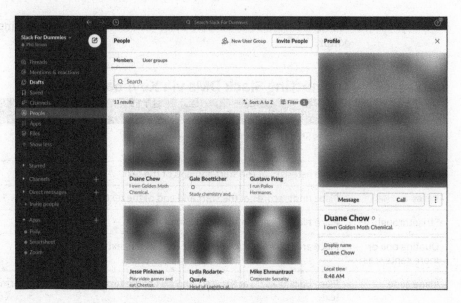

FIGURE 6-7:
Slack's People
view.

2. **Type some letters of the person's name in the search bar or just scroll down until you see the person's name or photo.**

When you click a person's name, Slack displays his profile and places a bar underneath his photo indicating his role (for example, Workspace Admin). Slack does this with all user roles save for member. (See Chapter 4 for more information on roles.)

TIP

The People view lets you sort by name, but there are plenty of other ways to quickly find the right person in your workspace. You can filter by role and even deactivated users by following these steps:

1. **Click the People view in the top half of the sidebar.**

2. **Click the filter icon next to the search bar and go nuts.**

You can filter by account type or whether the person uses Slack on a PC or a Mac. You can also hide deactivated accounts.

REMEMBER

Enterprise Grid workspaces work just a little bit differently than they do with other Slack plans. For example, in all other Slack plans, you see only the profiles of members in your individual workspace. That's not the case with Enterprise Grid, though. You can filter workspace members, as well as organization members.

WARNING

In large firms, being able to view all employees in the Slack workspace or organization is both a blessing and a curse. Just as with email, if you're not careful, you can send a DM to the wrong person. Before pressing Enter, consider double-checking the person's profile to ensure that you have the right recipient, especially if your query is sensitive in nature.

WARNING

Just because you find a colleague's name in the People view doesn't necessarily mean that the person uses Slack. This problem is particularly acute in big companies that pay for the Enterprise Grid plan.

Slack lets you do far more than send and read simple text DMs. You can edit DMs, delete them, set reminders, pin individual ones to conversations, and much more.

Editing messages

People send billions of emails every day and occasionally make mistakes. After you send an email, though, it's out there for good unless you catch the mistake quickly and try to recall it.

Compared to email, Slack wins here hands down. If you make a mistake, you don't need to send yet another message to everyone. Even after you send a DM, you can edit it. To do so, just follow these steps:

1. **Hover over a message from a colleague and three dots appear on the right in a pop-up menu.**

2. **Click Edit Message.**

3. **Make whatever edits to the message you like.**

4. **Click the green Save Changes button.**

   Slack saves your changes.

Note: Slack appends the text "(edited)" to the end of your initial message.

REMEMBER

For obvious reasons, Slack prohibits even Owners and Admins from editing other users' messages — anonymously or otherwise. Talk about opening Pandora's box!

Deleting messages

Who hasn't accidentally clicked Reply All on an email and regretted it five minutes later? Recalling a message may not work before others have seen it. Indeed, the mere fact that you try to recall the message may make others more inclined to read it. Slack again offers superior functionality to email.

To delete one of your messages, follow these steps:

1. **Hover your mouse over the message that you want to eradicate.**

   Three horizontal dots and the More Actions icon appear.

2. **Click Delete Message.**

   Slack confirms that you want to obliterate the message.

3. **Click the Delete button to complete the kill.**

   The message disappears from Slack for good.

Just because you delete a DM doesn't mean that someone else hasn't already seen it. Shaking your head? When it comes to deleting individual emails, Outlook's message-recall functionality is no fail-safe either.

Workspace Owners and Admins can delete others' messages in public channels. This feature comes in handy if someone posts an inappropriate message.

Muting conversations

Say that you want Slack to stop pestering you with notifications about an especially noisy individual or group conversation. You can easily mute it by following these steps:

1. **Click the conversation that you want to mute.**

2. **Click the information (i) icon in the upper-right corner.**

   Underneath the profile image of the person with whom you're conversing, Slack displays a three-pane tab below the word *Details*.

3. **Click the More tab on the right.**

4. **From the drop-down menu, click Mute Conversation.**

To restore proper notifications for the muted conversation, repeat this process but click Unmute Conversation in Step 4.

Say that you've muted a conversation with Lydia, and she sends you another DM. Slack won't notify you. It will, however, place a red numerical badge next to her name in your sidebar. If she sends you three messages, a red 3 will appear.

Setting message-specific reminders

Odds are that you use reminders in real life. Perhaps you use a sticky note or a full-blown reminders app on your smartphone. Regardless of your tool of choice, you don't want to forget critical things like anniversaries, paying taxes, or that Netflix premiere you've been waiting for.

Say you're working on a coding project. Gilfoyle sent you yet another DM. Unfortunately, you just don't have time to deal with him right now. To remind yourself about a specific DM, follow these steps:

1. **Mouse over a DM or channel message.**

2. **Click the three horizontal dots.**

   Slack displays the words *More Actions*.

3. **Click Remind Me about This.**

   Slack displays a pop-up window that offers you a number of options from 20 minutes to next week.

4. **Select the time and/or date that you want Slack to send you a reminder about the message.**

   Slack notifies you about the message with a notification at the time specified in Step 4.

TIP

Feel free to snooze a reminder when it goes off, just like your alarm clock.

Saving direct messages and channel messages

With so many messages in a workspace, are you skeptical about keeping tabs on the critical ones? Slack allows you to easily access your most important content. When you save a message, Slack places it in its Saved view. If saving in Slack seems similar to bookmarking websites and pages in your web browser, that's because it is.

TIP

It's a bit of a misnomer to call this process *saving*. Slack saves everything posted in your workspace by default unless you delete it.

To save a DM or channel message, follow these steps:

1. **Hover over a message that you'd like to save.**

Slack displays a menu with five icons.

2. **Click the white bookmark icon.**

It's the second one from the right.

Slack turns the bookmark icon red.

You can now find a shortcut to the item in your Saved view in the top half of the sidebar.

As Figure 6-8 shows, Slack's Saved view displays items in reverse chronological order from the date that you saved them. Slack does not sort these messages by the date that the sender originally sent or posted them.

FIGURE 6-8:
Slack saved a DM.

To unsave an item, click the red bookmark for the saved item. The message's bookmark icon returns to its original white color. Slack does *not* delete the message; it just ceases to appear in your Saved view.

Pinning direct messages to conversations

In any given Slack workspace, you'll mostly likely interact with some people more than others. Over the course of months or years, you may have hundreds or even thousands of conversations with your colleagues about many different things. All messages are certainly not created equal. For example, a major group or department decision counts more than a simple thank you to your peer.

Alas, Slack lets users easily identify key DMs within a conversation. You can pin DMs to conversations. As such, you'll be able to easily view the most important content in the conversation's details pane.

To pin a comment to a conversation:

1. **Hover your mouse over the DM that you want to pin to the conversation.**

2. **Click Pin to This Conversation.**

Slack automatically pins the message to the top of the conversation.

Slack lets you pin DMs to individual conversations. Figure 6-9 shows a pinned DM within a conversation.

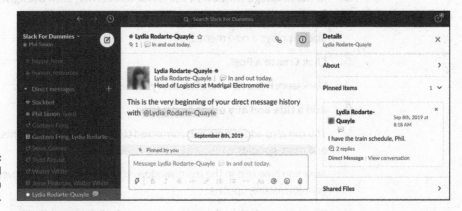

FIGURE 6-9:
Viewing pinned DMs in a conversation.

To unpin a message from the larger conversation, repeat the preceding steps, but in Step 2, click Un-pin from This Conversation. You can also click the X in the upper-right corner of the message. Note that removing the pin does not delete the DM.

Creating special types of messages

To be sure, you'll get a great deal of mileage out of sending simple DMs and posting comments to discussions in channels. However, Slack recognizes that sometimes users need to send something other than text-based responses.

Welcome to the world of posts and snippets!

Creating rich-text messages with posts

Slack posts are similar to simple messages, but they allow users to apply richer formatting. The post functionality lets users create, edit, and share fully formatted documents directly in Slack. Posts represent a great way to collaborate on relatively simple long-form content. To be fair, though, you won't be saying goodbye to Google Docs and Microsoft Word anytime soon. Examples of posts include project plans, meeting notes, articles, and drafts of blog posts. Slack posts show a green document icon to their immediate left after a user publishes one.

To create a proper post in a Slack channel, follow these steps:

1. **Click a channel in the sidebar.**

2. **In the message window in the lower-left corner, click the lightning bolt icon.**

    Slack displays a new menu.

3. **Click Create a Post.**

    Slack launches a new window that you'll use to create your post.

4. **Add a title and any other formatting.**

    You can also add simple and formatted text, headers, bullet points, URLs, code, and more goodies.

    After you type text in the main window, highlight it and mouse over it to see all your formatting options.

5. **When you're finished creating your post, click the white Share button at the top of the screen.**

    Slack displays self-explanatory options around sharing the post, letting others edit it, creating a link, and adding comments. Figure 6-10 displays those options.

6. **When you're finished, click the green Share button.**

    Your post looks something like the one in Figure 6-11.

FIGURE 6-10:
Sample post
options.

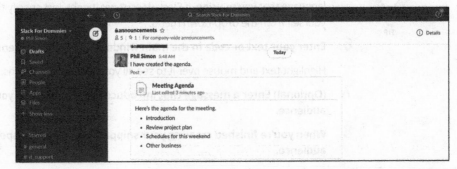

FIGURE 6-11:
A sample rich-text
post in Slack.

REMEMBER

You can view existing posts on your Slack mobile app, but you'll need to use Slack on a proper computer to create and edit them. You can view, create, edit, and delete regular channel messages, though, on any device you like.

Adding code and text snippets

In Slack, snippets represent a quick and simple way to share bits of code, configuration files, or log files with channel members. Slack's native ability to easily share code represents one of the major reasons that software engineers are so fond of Slack.

Creating both types of snippets is nearly identical to creating a rich-text message. To create a proper post in a Slack channel, follow these steps:

1. **Click a channel in the sidebar.**

2. **In the message window in the lower-left corner, click the lightning bolt icon.**

   Slack displays a new menu.

3. **Click Create a Code or Text Snippet.**

   Slack launches a new window.

4. **Use the new window to create your snippet.**

5. **(Optional) At the top of the page, add a title for your snippet and the type of snippet.**

TIP

   If you create a code snippet, Slack attempts to determine the programming language that you're using. If Slack doesn't get it right, just specify the language yourself from the drop-down menu.

6. **Enter your text or code in the main window under the Content heading.**

   Highlight text and mouse over it to see all your formatting options.

7. **(Optional) Enter a message that introduces your snippet to your intended audience.**

8. **When you're finished creating your snippet, enter your snippet's audience.**

   It may be a channel, an individual, or several folks.

   Slack displays self-explanatory options around sharing the snippet.

9. **When you're finished, click the green Create Snippet.**

   Slack automatically places line numbers to the left of each line in a snippet. Figure 6-12 shows an example of a code snippet.

You can download a text snippet, view raw versions, and/or leave comments. After creating one, Slack places a white icon with a capital *T* to its immediate left. When you click it, you can view the snippet's content.

FIGURE 6-12:
A sample code snippet in Slack.

Mouse over a current snippet in a channel. Slack displays these options:

» Collapse or expand (depending on the length of your snippet)

» Download

» Edit

» Share

Click the ellipsis icon, and Slack displays these options as well:

» View Details

» Copy Link to File

» Save

» View Raw

» Create External Link

» Delete File

REMEMBER

You can use posts and snippets as the basis for individual and group DMs. You don't need to confine snippets to channels.

Converting group direct messages into private channels

For lack of a better word, channels are more permanent than individual and group DMs. If you find that it makes sense to elevate your group discussion to a proper channel, you're in luck. As long as your conversation involves more than two people, just follow these steps:

1. **Click the group DM that you want to convert.**

2. **Click the information (i) icon in the upper-right corner.**

   Underneath the profile images of the people with whom you're conversing, Slack displays a three-pane tab.

3. **Click the More icon.**

4. **From the drop-down menu, click Convert to a Private Channel.**

5. **Confirm that you want to create the channel by clicking the green Yes, Continue button.**

   Slack creates a new private channel. Everyone in it can view the entire message history and all the shared files. You can't go back.

6. **Enter a name for the channel and click the green Convert to a Private Channel button.**

   Slack moves all the prior DMs into a new private channel.

REMEMBER

For privacy reasons, you can't turn a series of group DMs into a public channel.

Using threads to create topic-specific containers

A Slack thread represents a reply or series of replies *to a specific DM* or an in-channel interaction. Slack's rationale for threads is to allow users to engage in more focused discussions around a single topic — one that can take place separately from other messages in a conversation or channel. Although similar in concept, Slack *threads* operate a bit differently from DM-based conversations in a couple ways:

>> **Unlike in conversations, you can create threads from discussions that take place either within or outside of channels (see the earlier section "Understanding Slack conversations").** In other words, Slack allows users to create and view threads *regardless of where they take place*. When you start one, Slack provides notifications of new responses at the top of the workspace under the Threads header in the sidebar. If you're following ten threads from six channels and four different conversations, you can scan them all in one

place. Put differently, through threads, you don't need to hunt down each response in ten different places.

» **Threads are useful, but they're entirely optional.** Unlike conversations, Slack doesn't automatically start them for you.

Reviewing examples of threads

The types of threads run the gamut. Here a few:

» Tech-support teams may use the #hardware_issues channel to discuss a problem with a server or router. Rather than lump everything into that single channel, they thread the discussion within that channel about problems with a particular piece of equipment.

» HR folks often talk about company policies and the discussion sometimes gets into the nitty-gritty. A thread on the implications of offering paid family leave makes a lot of sense.

» Gus and Walt are having an animated discussion (outside of a channel) about a key business strategy. Each of them creates a thread in his Slack workspace to receive alerts about the other's latest response.

» Four partners in a consulting firm are providing specific feedback on a deck of PowerPoint slides. By creating a thread, you keep all comments organized.

» A college professor creates an #ask_the_professor channel for her classes every semester. That's a big bucket, to be sure. Students will usually ask her questions about the textbook that they're using, such as

- What version of the textbook do I have to buy?
- Can I share the textbook with my roommate?
- Can I buy the electronic version?

The professor turns each of these queries into a channel thread. For simple yes-or-no questions, a thread rarely makes sense. Still, there's really no downside to using them.

Creating, following, and viewing threads

To start a thread in Slack, follow these directions:

1. **Hover over a message.**

   Slack presents a floating menu with icons with the words *More Actions*.

2. **Mouse over the second icon from the left and click Start a Thread.**

TIP

Slack makes it easy to view threads in the full context of their channels:

1. **Hover over a message in the thread.**

   Slack presents a floating menu with icons and the words *More Actions*.

2. **Mouse over the second icon from the left and click the Open in Channel icon that appears.**

3. **To view all threads, click the Threads view in the top half of your sidebar underneath the workspace name.**

TIP

As you use Slack, you'll soon realize that not all discussions and content are created equal; you'll invariably view some discussions as more important than others. For example, a software engineer, VP of human resources, and finance manager will all keep their eyes on different discussions. Threads are invaluable in this regard.

Unfollowing threads

If you want to disengage from an individual thread, simply unfollow it:

1. **Hover over a message in a thread that you currently follow.**

2. **Click the three vertical dots on the far right.**

   Slack presents the words *More Actions*.

3. **At the top of the new menu, select Unfollow Thread.**

Note that you can't mute threads, nor can you delete them. After you unfollow a thread, Slack no longer shows you those red badges *for that thread* under the Threads header in the sidebar. Of course, you still may see badges from threads that you're following if someone calls you out.

TIP

Many people only use threads on a case-by-case basis. If the majority of your interactions are discrete, threads may not make sense for you. If, however, you find yourself routinely going back and forth with people about a specific topic, a thread is the perfect vehicle for tracking updates to a particular discussion.

Sharing in Slack

Slack is a group tool, not an individual one. Aside from sending DMs and posting messages in channels, you'll often share content with your colleagues. At a high level, Slack lets you share files and messages.

Sharing files

At some point in your Slack journey, you'll want to share documents that you've created in other applications with your colleagues and maybe even with yourself. Typical examples include spreadsheets, documents, photos, and presentations. Slack's Files view makes this a snap.

Uploading files to share

To upload a file that you intend to share, follow these steps:

1. Click Files in the sidebar.

2. Click the white Upload a File button in the upper-right corner.

Slack prompts you to locate the file on the computer.

3. Find the file and upload it.

You can do this in the same way as you do with email attachments. It's probably the Open button, but the exact name will hinge upon your computer's operating system.

4. (Optional) From the prompt, enter a message about the file.

5. (Optional) Click the blue Add File link to add another file.

Slack allows you to upload multiple files at a time.

6. (Optional) From the drop-down menu, choose the channel, group of users, or app with which you want to share the file(s).

Again, you can share file(s) with yourself — and no one else.

7. Click the green Upload button.

Play around with Slack's powerful search options here. Specifically, you can

>> Use the Files search bar to find specific documents.

>> Sort existing shared files by name and date.

>> Filter files by type, date range, and/or member who shared the file with you.

As Figure 6-13 displays, Slack's Files view allows you to easily access the files that you've shared — and that others have shared with you.

Note that you can also use Slack's main search bar at the very top of the workspace to find workspace files.

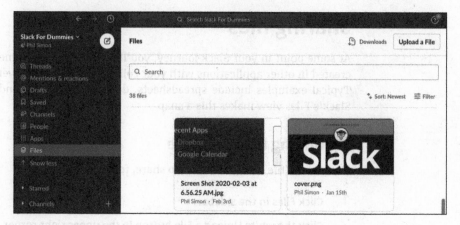

FIGURE 6-13:
Slack's Files view.

Copying links to existing Slack files

As another option, Slack allows users to create links to individual files that you've posted in public channels. Slack intends for you to share these links with existing workspace members. Follow these steps:

1. **Hover your mouse over the file.**

   Three horizontal dots and the More Actions icon appear.

2. **Click Copy Link to File.**

3. **Share the file link in a channel or direct message.**

REMEMBER

Note that this process creates a private link. Even outsiders who obtain access to that URL can't view the page. Only members of the Slack workspace can view the link.

Creating external links to files posted in channels

Say that you upload a file to a channel. Now you want to share a link to that file within Slack with someone who does not belong to the workspace. You can do so by following these steps:

1. **Hover your mouse over the file or message.**

   Three horizontal dots and the More Actions icon appear.

2. **Click Create External Link.**

3. **Share that link with another person via email, text, or another method you like.**

REMEMBER

Only you can create external URLs for files that you've shared. Other users cannot.

If you change your mind about letting others view this link, you can easily revoke it:

1. **Hover your mouse over the file.**
2. **Click View External Link.**
3. **Click the Revoke button.**

   Slack warns you that others are now unable to access the link.
4. **Click the Revoke It button.**

People who visit the now-disabled link will see a white page that reads, "The requested file could not be found."

TIP

Does an outsider's ability to view files in Slack scare you in general? Slack has you covered. Workspace Owners and Admins can disable members' ability to generate external links.

Sharing messages

You will frequently post messages to Slack channels. But what if you need to bring others into the loop? Fortunately, Slack allows you to reshare messages in a number of different ways.

Sharing messages from one public channel to another

For example, what if you spend half your time working in marketing and the other half in IT? In effect, you work as a liaison between the two departments. Not surprisingly, you belong to both the #marketing and #IT *public* Slack channels. This distinction is critical.

In this example, you want to let people from one department know about a decision that people in the other department have made. The following steps show you how to share messages from one public channel to another:

1. **Mouse over the message that you want to share.**
2. **Click the right-pointing arrow that appears.**

3. **Under Share With, search for the channel with which you want to share the message.**

   Optionally, you can add a few words about this DM à la forwarding an email with introductory comments.

4. **Click the green Share button.**

   You've now shared your message with members of the other channel.

You can share messages from public channels to private ones, but not vice versa.

Sharing files from existing messages

Along with messages, Slack allows you to easily reshare files — that is, to share a document that you've already shared with someone else. (Presumably, this document is yours.) Think of it as the equivalent of forwarding an attachment that you sent.

To share a file from an existing message that you've sent, follow these steps:

1. **Mouse over the file that someone has sent you in Slack.**

2. **Click the right-pointing arrow that appears.**

3. **Under Share With, click the destination for the shared file.**

   The destination can be a person or a channel. You see a familiar prompt.

4. **(Optional) Add a message to provide some context around the file.**

5. **Click the green Share button.**

Slack does not allow you to quickly share an attachment that someone has shared with you. Of course, you can always download the file and share it as your own.

Keep in mind basic workplace etiquette. Don't share messages or files with others unless your reason is legitimate.

Sharing private DMs

For obvious reasons, Slack doesn't allow you to share others' private messages. If you try, Slack displays a message like the one shown in Figure 6-14.

The same holds true for a message posted in a private channel. You can't share that message with other channels. You can only "share" it with the sender.

Share this message   ✕

> This message is from a private conversation, so it can only be shared with
> Lydia Rodarte-Quayle.

Add a message, if you'd like.

B

▌ **Lydia Rodarte-Quayle**
Thanks for sending that file! 😄

                                                              Share

FIGURE 6-14:
A Slack message
forbidding a user
from sharing a
private DM.

Forwarding Email to Slack

What happens if an internal conversation with your colleagues starts over email, but you'd like to move it to Slack? Through any number of third-party apps, as long as everyone on the email chain can access your workspace, you can effectively move any Outlook or Gmail message to Slack for good. Simply forward the message to a unique Slack-specific email address. Slackbot delivers the email to a designated channel or DM. From there, you can continue the discussion in Slack.

TIP

For more information about apps that support this particular feature, see `https://bit.ly/sfd-em`.

Communicating Outside of Slack

Here's a decidedly low-tech reminder about Slack: For two reasons, it's unlikely that you'll be able to use it exclusively and bid adieu to email forever:

>> **Not everyone in your organization may use Slack.** That goes double for a large organization.

>> **Even if everyone in your organization uses Slack, not every message or file necessarily belongs there.** It may not be possible or even wise to record all interactions in Slack. Potential exceptions may fall into the following buckets:

- Intellectual property

- Legal matters

- Confidential or highly sensitive corporate information

- Employee-discipline and health-related matters

Ideally, though, the percentage of messages that you send in Slack will increase over time as more people in your organization use it.

REMEMBER

Check with the powers that be at your organization about whether you should be documenting sensitive matters in Slack — or anywhere else for that matter.

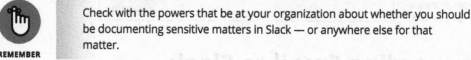

Chapter **7**

Staying Informed with Notifications, Statuses, and Feeds

O dds are, you'll spend a great deal of time in Slack writing messages and reading others' responses. You'll share files with your colleagues, make comments on them, and participate in internal polls. (Ideally, these activities collectively mean that you'll spend far less time in your inbox.)

But how will you know that someone needs your help or input? Slack sends workspace members notifications about individual and group direct messages (DMs), updates to channels, keywords, and more.

Perhaps you think an unfettered Slack will quickly become overwhelming. That is, you'll merely transfer your senses of information overload and constant distraction from email to Slack. You'll just go from chronically checking one application to checking another. What's the real benefit here?

To be sure, this position is an understandable and fairly common one. You're mistaken, though. Slack is the antithesis of email's never-ending, egalitarian inbox.

It allows you to prioritize the types of notifications you receive, when you receive them, and on what device. Take that, email!

This chapter covers how to configure notifications in Slack. In these pages, you discover how to customize your Slack alerts — even on different devices. If you want to go completely off the grid, that's easy to achieve in Slack, too.

Getting Your Arms around Notifications

At a high level, Slack notifications call attention to all the things in a workspace that interest you. To be fair, that's potentially a big bucket. More specifically, you can set notifications when any or all the following events take place:

>> Someone sends you a DM.

>> Someone mentions you in a channel by using @username.

>> Someone mentions @everyone in a channel.

>> Someone uses one of your keywords.

>> Slackbot reminds you to do something.

Of course, you can tweak all these settings. That is, when each of these five things happens, Slack doesn't have to notify you. Slack gives users unparalleled ability to control your alerts.

When you first install Slack and join a workspace, Slack notifies you only when someone sends you a DM or mentions you in a channel by using your username.

REMEMBER

By default, any unread workspace activity will cause Slack to display an indicator, or what Slack and other apps these days term a *badge.* The two types of badges in Slack are

>> **Dot:** Signifies general unread activity in one of your Slack workspaces.

>> **Number in a red circle:** Someone has done one of the following:

- Sent you a direct message

- Mentioned you or posted in a pubic channel to which you belong

- Used one of your keywords in a pubic channel to which you belong

Figure 7-1 displays a workspace with badges and unread activity.

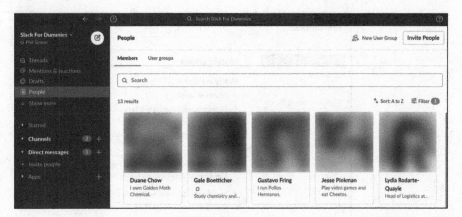

FIGURE 7-1:
A Slack
workspace with
badges and
unread activity.

If you belong to multiple workspaces, you may be worried about missing messages in one while working in the other. Don't be. As Figure 7-2 displays, Slack displays a numerical badge to the left of the sidebar indicating that new activity has taken place in the other workspace. (*Note:* Figure 7-2 displays Slack's previous UI.)

FIGURE 7-2:
A Slack badge
indicator from
another
workspace.

That's not to say that Slack will bother you if you want to be left alone. Later in this chapter, you see how you can easily pause workspace notifications at any point via Do Not Disturb (DND) mode.

In Slack, notifications represent an umbrella term covering a number of different types of alerts. At a high level, you can view the settings for your workspace notifications by following these steps:

1. **Click the main menu.**

2. **From the drop-down menu, click Preferences.**

    At the top of the screen, you see the word *Notifications* (see Figure 7-3).

By accessing this panel via a proper computer, you determine where all the magic happens.

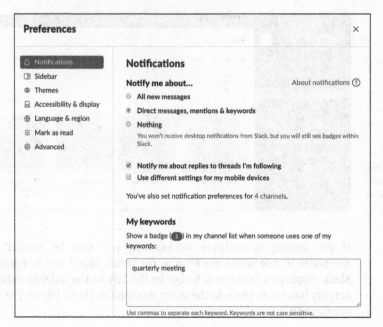

FIGURE 7-3:
The Slack
workspace
notification panel.

REMEMBER

Before going too far down the rabbit hole, keep this maxim in mind: There's no one right or best way to enable each of Slack's different notifications. Play around with them until you find a system that works for you. You want to balance receiving important alerts in a timely manner with keeping your sanity.

Channel-specific notifications

Say that you belong to a public or private channel, but you only want to check in it periodically. You don't need to receive regular notifications from the channel, but you don't want to leave it altogether. Fortunately, Slack provides two ways to control your notifications from a channel.

Muting a channel

If you'd like to remain in a channel, but you don't want to receive any notifications at all, this feature is just the ticket for you. Muting a channel is a particularly valuable feature.

To mute a channel, follow these steps:

1. **Click the name of the channel that you want to mute.**

   Slack displays a new pane on the right side of the screen.

2. **Click the More icon.**

Slack displays a number of options.

3. **Click the Mute #[Channel Name] button.**

TIP

Set regular reminders to check in on muted channels.

After you mute a channel, Slack grays it out in the sidebar and places it below the non-muted ones. That is, it will no longer be the color of the unmuted channels. In Figure 7-4, the #finance and #human_resources channels are muted.

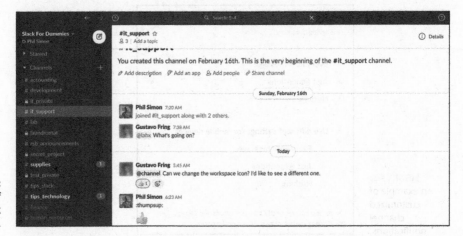

FIGURE 7-4:
An example of muted Slack channels.

REMEMBER

Muting a channel is not the same as muting a conversation with a person. A workspace member can still send you a DM or correspond with you in another channel. This action only applies to the activity that takes place within the channel.

REMEMBER

Say that you have muted a channel and someone mentions you in it. In this case, Slack displays a red badge in the channel. It's a subtle way of reminding you to check it. At the same time, though, Slack doesn't interrupt you with a notification.

Setting channel notifications

Slack lets you customize which channel alerts you receive and, even better, the devices on which you receive them. To tweak your channel notifications with a greater level of granularity than muting, follow these steps:

1. **In the bottom half of the sidebar, click the name of the channel whose notification settings you'd like to change.**

2. **Click the Details button in the upper-right corner of the screen.**

   Slack displays a new pane on the right side of the screen.

3. **Click Notifications.**

   From here, you can ignore additional mentions and tweak the channel's notifications on your desktop and mobile device. For example, say that you don't want to receive desktop notifications from a particular channel but you want to receive @mentions on your mobile phone. If that's the case, check the boxes in Figure 7-5.

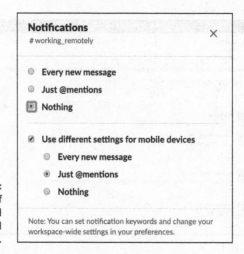

Notifications

\# working_remotely   ✕

○ **Every new message**

○ **Just @mentions**

◉ **Nothing**

☑ **Use different settings for mobile devices**

  ○ Every new message

  ◉ Just @mentions

  ○ Nothing

Note: You can set notification keywords and change your workspace-wide settings in your preferences.

FIGURE 7-5:
An example of customized channel notifications.

REMEMBER

If you don't enable notifications from the Slack app in your phone's settings, you won't receive them.

In a nutshell, you can configure Slack to send you different types of notifications from different channels on different devices. This is yet another example of how Slack leaves email in the dust.

Fine, but what if you want to view all your channels' notification settings in a single place? You don't have to hunt and peck. Again, Slack has you covered:

1. **Click the main menu.**

2. **From the drop-down menu, click Preferences.**

3. **Click Notifications and scroll down to the very bottom of the page.**

Figure 7-6 presents a composite view of channel notifications.

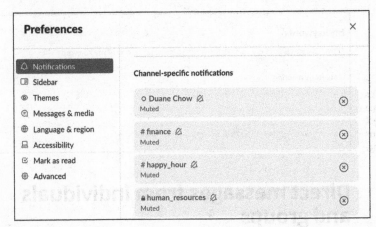

If you click the X next to a channel setting, Slack resets the channel's notifications to its default state.

Keyword-specific notifications

Keeping track of channel messages is one thing, but what if you want to follow a term or phrase across *all* channels? Setting up a keyword alert for every channel would be cumbersome. Slack couldn't agree more. To enable these notifications, follow these directions:

1. **Click the main menu.**

2. **From the drop-down menu, click Preferences.**

3. **Click Notifications and scroll down to My Keywords.**

4. **Enter the keywords for which you want to receive alerts.**

5. **Click the X in the upper-right corner of the screen.**

   Slack displays a red badge in your channel list when someone uses one of your keywords in that specific channel (see Figure 7-7). For example, you may want to know when anyone in your workspace uses the term *quarterly meeting*. In the notification preference panel, you simply enter that term.

When someone uses this phrase in a public channel of which you're a member, Slack notifies you. Note, however, that you won't receive notifications when others use that term in private DMs and private channels. This alert would be a clear violation of Slack's user privacy.

FIGURE 7-7:
A Slack
workspace
keyword alert
setting for
quarterly meeting.

My keywords

Show a badge (**1**) in my channel list when someone uses one of my keywords:

quarterly meeting

Use commas to separate each keyword. Keywords are not case sensitive.

Direct messages from individuals and groups

When a Slack user or group of users sends you a DM, Slack sends you a notification. You can view unread messages underneath the channels (see Figure 7-8).

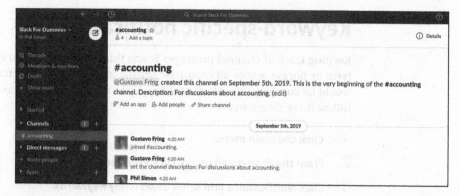

FIGURE 7-8:
Slack unread
DMs.

Missed calls

What if a colleague calls you but you aren't able to answer? In this case, Slack places a badge next to that person's name in the sidebar. If a colleague calls a channel and you miss it, Slack bolds the channel name in the sidebar. You see a notification that you missed a call.

DM reminders

Chapter 6 also covers reminders in more detail. For now, suffice it to say that you can easily set them. For example, at 3:51 p.m. on Friday, Steve sends you a DM but you're busy. You quickly set a reminder to see that message at 8:30 a.m. on Monday. At that point, Slackbot reminds you about his DM, such as the one in Figure 7-9.

FIGURE 7-9:
A simple Slack
reminder
notification.

Member join and leave messages

If you work at a big company, you probably want to disable Slack notifications when members join and leave company-wide public channels. If so, follow these steps:

1. **Click the main menu.**

2. **From the drop-down menu, select Settings & Administration and then Workspace Settings.**

   Slack launches a new window or tab in your default browser.

3. **Scroll down to Join & Leave Messages and click the white Expand button.**

4. **Uncheck the box next to the words Show a Message When People Join or Leave Channels.**

5. **Click the Save button.**

Depending on your individual and workspace settings, Slack may still display notifications in certain cases. Examples include

>> Small public channels

>> Private channels

>> When somebody accepts an invitation from a member of an existing private channel

Carefully think about the notifications that you need to receive. Ideally, each one really matters.

REMEMBER

Threads and notifications

The chief conceit of email at work is that all messages are equally important to all employees all the time. As you well know, nothing could be further from the truth; different things matter to different employees at different times. One size never fits all.

Chapter 6 describes how users can create threads that stitch together individual comments and questions into a cohesive entity. What's more, you can follow or unfollow them at your leisure. If you're keeping tabs on a thread, Slack places a red badge next to Threads at the top of your workspace (see Figure 7-10).

FIGURE 7-10:
A Slack notification of new activity in a thread.

Concurrently notifying multiple users

You probably receive mass emails just about every day at your job. Maybe a few of these messages really do apply to you. As for the rest, you rightfully dismiss them as irrelevant. Mass email blasts may only mildly annoy you. Still, you likely tolerate them because they represent the only way to alert everyone in a department or company of an announcement or event. After all, generally speaking, it's better to let too many people know than too few, right?

Slack makes it easy to alert both workspace and channel members en masse. Table 7-1 provides some quick tips to get the attention of a bunch of people. By using these handles, you don't need to look up everyone in the workspace and add them to a group DM — a major time-saver to be sure. What's more, you don't need to mercilessly pepper your colleagues with unrelated messages.

TABLE 7-1 ### @-Symbol Notification Tricks

Callout	Purpose
@here	Notifies only active channel members.
@usergroup	Notifies only the members of a particular user group.
@channel	Notifies all members of a channel, active or not.
@everyone	Notifies every person in the #general channel; as its name suggests, using this notifies everyone in the workspace.

WARNING

Say that you post a message in a channel with six or more members. What's more, your message includes @channel or @everyone. By default, Slack asks you to confirm your message before you send it unless a Workspace Owner or Admin has already disabled this warning.

In addition, keep the following pointers in mind:

WARNING

>> @channel does not work in a thread. If you want a bunch of people to see your response to a question, post a link to the message in the desired channel.

>> If you use one of the callouts in Table 7-1 in a thread, a red badge appears in the sidebars of relevant members with one caveat: Depending on how individual members have configured their device notifications, they may not receive alerts.

>> You can always call out a specific user by username. For instance, if you type **@ianmosley**, Slack shoots Ian a notification.

>> See https://bit.ly/sl-not for more information on Slack's desktop notifications. Slack allows you to customize their sounds, appearance, and more.

Letting Others Know Your Availability

Anyone in your workspace can call you or send you DMs at any point. Still, you'll want to let others know about availability. Put differently, just because others can contact you doesn't mean that you want to receive notifications from them.

For example, what if someone needs to go off the grid? Say that Skyler is out of the office because she's giving birth to her new daughter, Holly. Company president Ted is considerate. He doesn't want to send her urgent DMs and get upset when she doesn't respond. (Yes, these are all *Breaking Bad* references.)

Fortunately, Slack makes it easy and even fun to set your status — indefinitely or for a predetermined period of time. Slack statuses put the longstanding email "out of office" auto-response to shame. Note, however, that Slack can't stop someone from ignoring your status and peppering you with urgent queries if you're vacationing in Belize. No app can.

Setting your status

Set your status by following these steps:

1. **Click the main menu and then on Update Your Status.**

   You see something similar to Figure 7-11, which shows some default statuses that Slack easily lets you set, although you can customize these as needed.

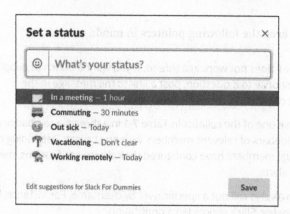

Set a status   ✕

☺ | What's your status?

📄 In a meeting — 1 hour
🚌 Commuting — 30 minutes
🤒 Out sick — Today
🌴 Vacationing — Don't clear
🏠 Working remotely — Today

Edit suggestions for Slack For Dummies   **Save**

FIGURE 7-11:
Slack default
statuses.

2. **Click Set a Status, which appears underneath your name.**

3. **Enter a custom status or select an existing one.**

   If you like, pick an emoji that describes your status. Now everyone in the workspace can view your status.

TIP

If you know the name of the emoji that you want to include in a message, you can also type **:[emoji name]:** and press Enter. For example, typing **:slack:** produces the Slack emoji.

If you do select an existing status, Slack inserts an icon to its left. You can override that icon with whatever you like.

4. **Click the Save button.**

By letting others know your status, you can start the process of maintaining your sanity. You can also opt not to receive notifications at all via Slack's Do Not Disturb mode, covered later in this chapter.

Viewing your colleagues' statuses

From time to time, you'll want to view your colleagues' statuses. To this end, do one of the following:

1. **If you've recently exchanged DMs with the person, click the member's name in the sidebar under Direct Messages.**

   If he has set a status, it appears at the top of the workspace to the immediate right of his name.

2. **If not, click People in the sidebar.**

   Slack displays the member's status underneath his name.

3. **If you see a white callout or emoji to the right of a person's name in the sidebar, mouse over it.**

   Slack displays the member's status.

Your custom status and icon appear to the right of your name in the sidebar. Ideally, users look at them before they send you DMs or call you.

Use a red stop sign as your status icon if want to emphasize the fact that you're unreachable. To change your icon and/or status, click the smiley-face icon and go nuts. For example, in Figure 7-12, the user has selected the red stop-sign emoji to indicate that he wants to be left alone.

FIGURE 7-12:
Slack status with a red stop-sign emoji.

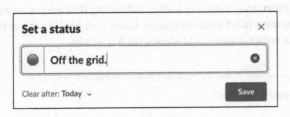

Set a status ✕

🔴 Off the grid.

Clear after: Today ⌄

Save

Editing your status

Slack recognizes that you do different things throughout the day or week, so your status often changes. As such, you can and should set different statuses. For example, you may not want to be disturbed if you're in an important meeting. On the other hand, you may be relatively free on Tuesday afternoon.

A Slack status is meant to be temporary. At some point, you'll want to change it. Follow these steps:

1. **Click the main menu.**

2. **Enter your new status in the white text box below your name.**

Clearing your status

To remove your status altogether, follow these steps:

1. **Click the main menu.**

2. **At the top of the drop-down menu, click Clear Status.**

Your status is now blank.

Setting yourself to away/active

When you indicate that you're away, Slack grays out your name in the sidebar. This way, your colleagues see that you're unavailable. Of course, just like email, they can still send you messages, but they shouldn't expect an immediate response.

To indicate that you're away, follow these steps:

1. **Click the main menu.**

2. **From the drop-down menu, select Change.**

If you're active, Slack flips your status to inactive and vice versa.

When you return to a workspace after indicating that you're away, Slack asks you whether you want to let your colleagues know that you're now available. Of course, the option is yours. Figure 7-13 shows such a screen.

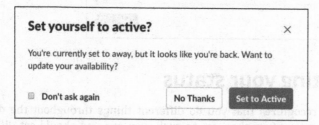

Set yourself to active?   ✕

You're currently set to away, but it looks like you're back. Want to update your availability?

☐ Don't ask again   No Thanks   Set to Active

FIGURE 7-13:
The Slack prompt
when returning
from away status.

Unplugging with Do Not Disturb mode

What if you worked at a software company called Initech? (Yes, this is an *Office Space* reference.) Your boss, Bill, has requested that you complete your monthly TPS reports. You start working on them, and you don't want anyone nagging you in Slack.

If you enable DND mode, Slack won't send you any notifications until you've disabled it or your DND period expires. Thanks to DND mode, you can keep Slack open and work without fear of Michael and Samir interrupting you. (Slack won't stop annoying colleagues from tapping you on the shoulder, though.)

If you attempt to call someone who's in DND mode, Slack displays a message that the person doesn't want to be disturbed. In other words, Slack nixes your call.

TIP

Think of DND as snoozing. You're taking a break for a predetermined amount of time and telling others as much.

Setting a DND schedule

Here's how you set your default hours during which you don't want to receive Slack notifications:

1. **Click the main menu.**

2. **From the drop-down menu, select Pause Notifications.**

   Slack displays a submenu to your immediate right.

3. **Select Do Not Disturb Schedule from the drop-down menu.**

4. **Pick the times during which you'd like Slack to disable notifications.**

5. **Press the Esc key on your keyboard or click the X in the upper-right corner of the screen.**

Manually activating DND mode

To pause notifications apart from your normal schedule, follow these steps:

1. **Click the main menu.**

2. **From the drop-down menu, mouse over Do Not Disturb.**

   Slack displays a submenu to your immediate right.

3. **From the available options, choose how long you want to be left alone.**

After you've done this, Slack puts a small *z* next to your name at the top of the workspace until your specified window elapses.

Deactivating or adjusting DND mode

If you want to deactivate DND mode, follow these steps:

1. **Click the main menu.**

2. **From the drop-down menu, mouse over Pause Notifications.**

   Slack displays a submenu to your immediate right.

3. **Click Resume Notifications now or, if you want to adjust your time frame, click Adjust Time.**

   Slack removes the small *z* next to your name at the top of the workspace.

TIP

DND works both ways. If you see a small *z* to the left of someone's name in the sidebar, that person has enabled DND mode.

TIP

As of this writing, Slack doesn't let users create separate DND schedules for weekends. Slack's customers have requested this feature for a while now, so the company will probably release it at some point in the future.

Sending urgent direct messages

Great, you're thinking. Thanks to DND, you can easily tell the world to bugger off. Still, crises may arise that require someone to reach you — even if you prefer not to be disturbed unless an emergency arises. Once again, Slack has you covered.

Slack lets users send urgent messages to folks who have enabled DND mode. Recipients receive notifications despite the fact that they're presumably busy.

What if Walt needs to send me a message, but I've enabled DND mode? I'm busy writing this book and rocking out to Marillion — both of which are important to me. Before sending me a message, Walt sees a green DND icon next to my name.

Ideally, my status deters him from interrupting me for the time being, but that's not necessarily the case. Walt types his message and presses Enter on his keyboard. Slackbot informs Walt that I don't want to be bothered right now (see Figure 7-14). Walt, however, is undeterred; he can't wait. Things are about to break bad, and he must reach me.

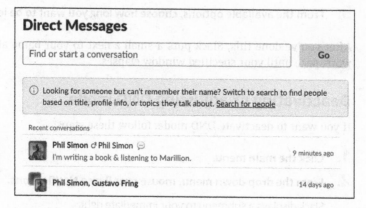

FIGURE 7-14:
The Slack DM options showing the member DND icon.

After seeing the message in Figure 7-15, Walt clicks Click Here. At this point, Slack sends me a notification. I can respond if I want.

Of course, I can always ignore Walt's messages. If I do, then Slack tells me that I missed critical messages while I had DND mode activated.

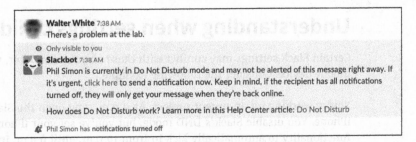

Walter White 7:38 AM
There's a problem at the lab.

Only visible to you

Slackbot 7:38 AM
Phil Simon is currently in Do Not Disturb mode and may not be alerted of this message right away. If it's urgent, click here to send a notification now. Keep in mind, if the recipient has all notifications turned off, they will only get your message when they're back online.

How does Do Not Disturb work? Learn more in this Help Center article: Do Not Disturb

Phil Simon has **notifications turned off**

FIGURE 7-15:
Overriding the DND status to send an urgent message.

What if I want to ignore all notifications — from Walt or anyone in the workspace? In other words, I want to ensure that no one bothers me for any reason. Maybe I'm trying to focus, or I'm on the golf course. My recourse is simple: I can quit the Slack app. Problem solved.

TIP

Don't be afraid to use DND mode or quit Slack altogether. Nowhere is it written that you have to immediately respond to notifications — in Slack or any other tool, for that matter. As Chris Hoffman astutely writes for *The New York Times,* "Slack shouldn't be ever-present in every minute of your life." (View the article at `https://nyti.ms/349ga07`.)

Configuring Device-Specific Notifications

Slack recognizes that you may want different devices to send you different notifications. For example, you may want to see a wider array of alerts on your desktop because you're working. (Of course, for that very reason, you may want to see fewer.) On your phone, you may elect not to be bothered at all.

Again, your configuration choices are your own. Customize to your heart's content.

Enabling notifications on mobile devices

Chapter 4 explains how you can access Slack on any device you like — although you can only perform certain functions while using a web browser. If you'd like to install Slack on your smartphone and tablet, have at it. You can also set notifications on the mobile app of your choice.

TIP

Visit `https://bit.ly/sl-mob` for far more information on mobile notifications.

Understanding when settings collide

Certain Slack settings may conflict with those on your computer, web browser, or mobile device. Consider the following example.

You're working on an urgent project. At 9 p.m., you open the Slack app on your iPhone. You disable Slack's DND mode, but you've set your iPhone's native DND functionality to automatically kick in from 10 p.m. until 6 a.m. In this case, your iPhone's DND mode beats its Slack counterpart. As a result, you won't receive DMs.

Here's another plausible scenario. Say that you're using a friend's computer. You log in to your Slack workspace via the web browser, but you don't enable the browser's desktop notifications. You then launch Microsoft Word and work on a document. Slack doesn't notify you of new activity in the browser.

REMEMBER

Implement a notification system that works for *you*. You don't want irrelevant alerts bothering you any more than you want to miss key ones. Play around. You'll land on your own Goldilocks principle.

Finding Other Ways to Stay Current

Here are two other useful, optional, and unobtrusive ways that Slack allows you to stay current.

Receiving emails on recent activity

What if you haven't accessed your workspace for a few weeks? (A pox on you, if you haven't.) By default, Slack sends you an email that summarizes the workspace messages and activity that you've missed if you've been inactive for 14 days (see Figure 7-16).

If you don't find these emails useful, you can opt out of them. Simply click the *unsubscribe* link at the bottom of one of the emails.

TIP

Reverting to email defeats the whole purpose of Slack. After all, one of Slack's chief benefits is that it reduces the time that you waste in your inbox.

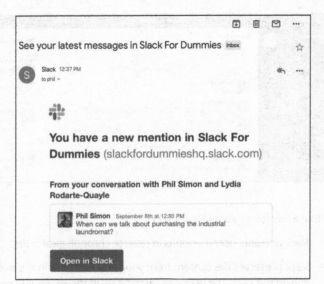

FIGURE 7-16:
A Slack email to
an inactive
member
summarizing
missed activity.

Viewing mentions and reactions

As an added tool to keep track of everything that's going on in a workspace, Slack provides the ability to easily view all your mentions in a single, consolidated view. These mentions include

» Your name

» Your notification keywords

» Your @channel mentions (optional)

» Your reactions (optional)

» Your user groups (optional)

Slack's feed eliminates the need for you to search individual channels and conversations for content related to you. At a high level, this stream is akin to the familiar news feeds of LinkedIn, Twitter, and Facebook. Even better, Slack lets you toggle this view on and off. To view your personalized mentions and reactions in Slack, follow these steps:

1. **Click Mentions & Reactions in the sidebar.**

Slack displays a pane on the right (see Figure 7-17).

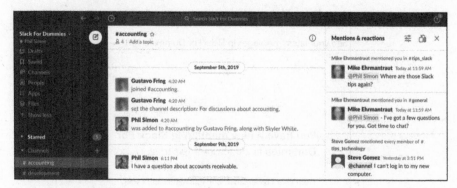

FIGURE 7-17:
Slack Mentions &
Reactions.

Note a few things about Figure 7-17:

- Slack presents user mentions in reverse chronological order.

- Slack preserves the content from your previous view in the middle of the app. In this case, the user was catching up in the #accounting channel before clicking Mentions & Reactions. That's why Slack displays that channel in Figure 7-17.

Say that you find the view in Figure 7-17 to be too busy. You'd prefer to see a dedicated screen of mentions involving you. No bother.

2. **Click the icon to the immediate left of the X in the upper-right corner.**

   Slack displays a full-screen view of your feed (see Figure 7-18).

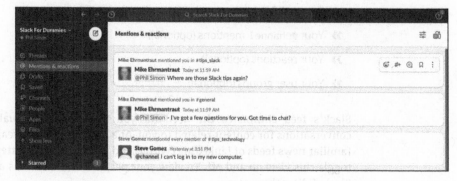

FIGURE 7-18:
The Slack
full-screen view
of Mentions &
Reactions.

TIP

Click the filter icon in the upper-right-hand corner to restrict the types of mentions that Slack shows.

3
Focusing on Zoom

Discover Zoom's core services and prepare to use them effectively.

Set up Zoom, familiarize yourself with its user interface, and start your first meeting.

Invite people to a meeting, join an existing meeting, and check out Zoom's calling features.

Connect with others using Zoom's channels and chats.

» Listing the benefits and features of Zoom's offerings

» Understanding the different plans and costs involved in each

Chapter 8

Getting to Know Zoom's Suite of Communication Tools

Z oom's tools let small and even enormous groups of people improve how they communicate. What's more, Zoom's offerings are flexible, powerful, affordable, and intuitive.

Of course, in order for you and your colleagues to reap the benefits of using Zoom's services, you must first understand them. Purchasing the wrong product altogether — or the right one but the wrong plan — will frustrate you and cost you time and money.

This chapter provides a high-level overview of each Zoom subscription. It covers the features, costs, and limitations of each core Zoom service.

Zoom's Core Services

Many people new to Zoom think of it exclusively as a communications or video-conferencing app. That belief is understandable, because Zoom has exploded in popularity. At the same time, though, it is not at all accurate.

As of this writing, Zoom's suite of videoconferencing tools consists of four core products and services. Two of them will run on just about any contemporary computing device — with or without a webcam — within a matter of minutes. In other words, they require neither special hardware nor elaborate setup.

The ready-to-go tools include

>> Zoom Meetings & Chat

>> Zoom Video Webinars

If you've purchased your computer, smartphone, or tablet in the last five years, odds are, you'll be up and running with each of these services within a few minutes.

Zoom's two other services are more intricate in nature. In order to work, they require a bit more setup and, in all likelihood, special hardware. That is, you won't be up and running in a few minutes. The following two Zoom services fall into the some-assembly-is-required bucket:

>> Zoom Rooms

>> Zoom Phone

These tools require more than just an individual device, such as a MacBook Air, a Microsoft Surface Pro 7, or a contemporary smartphone.

TECHNICAL STUFF

Note that your organization may not need to shell out beaucoup bucks to take advantage of Zoom Rooms and Zoom Phone. Your employer's IT folks may be able to configure its existing video displays, speakers, and the like.

WARNING

Zoom's hardware-intensive services can't perform miracles. Say that your company is located in an area with notoriously weak and spotty Internet connectivity. In this case, it's imperative to temper your performance expectations.

Regardless of the time and resources needed to get started, all Zoom products share some similarities, including the underlying technology behind them. What's more, in their own way, each helps the company achieve its lofty mission of "improving the quality and effectiveness of communications forever."

REMEMBER

An individual or large enterprise doesn't need to purchase or subscribe to every Zoom product. Each one works quite nicely on its own. To be sure, some organizations have gone all-in on Zoom and gladly subscribe to all its services. It's likely that the vast majority of Zoom's customers, however, opt for only a few of them.

Zoom Meetings & Chat

Zoom's most popular service is Meetings & Chat. (The nomenclature on Zoom's website is a bit inconsistent.) Regardless of its moniker, the product allows users to hold high-definition (HD) audio and video calls and send text messages. As such, Meetings & Chat is ideal for the simple one-on-one chat sessions, online training sessions, company announcements, calls to technical support to diagnose user issues (especially with screensharing), and many more.

If the concept of making audio and video calls over the Internet seems old hat to you, trust your instincts. In other words, it's not that Meetings & Chat does something fundamentally different than its predecessors did; it's that Meetings & Chat does the same thing much better. Think of it as a souped-up version of Skype.

Main features and benefits

Meetings & Chat is a robust offering that provides its users with an arsenal of potent bells and whistles:

>> **Built-in collaboration tools:** Many tools let users share their screens with others. Meetings & Chat takes this a step further. Multiple participants can concurrently share their screens, co-annotate their screens, and more. Ultimately, all these features provide for more interactive meetings.

>> **Device agnosticism:** In the past, mainstream videoconferencing tools tended to work well only on certain types of computers running specific operating systems. Not Zoom. Meetings & Chat lets you start and join meetings and collaborate across any device.

WARNING

That's not to say, though, that you can perform every task on every type of device.

>> **Easy scheduling:** Meetings & Chat integrates with popular calendar applications, such as Microsoft Outlook, Gmail, and iCal. As a result, you won't have to waste time synchronizing multiple applications. Third-party apps make this integration even tighter.

>> **Secure meetings:** No application is entirely safe from prying eyes, but Zoom has invested a great deal of resources in making Meetings & Chat as bullet-proof as possible. To this end, the product

- Encrypts all meetings
- Offers role-based user security
- Lets users protect their meetings with passwords
- Allows hosts to create waiting rooms for participants
- Lets users place attendees on hold

>> **The ability to record, store, and transcribe meetings:** Many previous videoconferencing tools required a third-party plugin or app to record meetings. Not Meetings & Chat. Depending on your plan, Zoom lets you

- Record and save your meetings locally or to the cloud
- Download searchable transcripts that improve in quality all the time

>> **The ability to send messages and files:** Sometimes you may not be in the mood for a video call. Maybe you haven't put your face on yet or your house is a mess. No bother.

As the second half of its name suggests, Meetings & Chat lets you communicate via text. That is, you can chat with groups of people just as you would with WhatsApp, Slack (see Part 2), and many more apps. You can search the history and upload files for others to view. Even better, Zoom maintains this archive for a decade.

Oh, and if you want to move your conversation from text to voice, that's easy to do as well.

Plans and costs

Zoom offers one free Meetings & Chat plan (Basic) and several paid ones:

>> Pro

>> Business

>> Enterprise

>> Enterprise Plus

Throughout the text, these options are collectively referred to as *premium plans*.

TIP

TECHNICAL STUFF

Date before you get married. As with any software plan or subscription, kick the tires before making a long-term commitment.

Zoom also offers specialized plans for organizations that must abide by specific legislation:

>> **Zoom for Education:** For more information, see `https://bit.ly/zfd-ed`.

>> **Zoom for Telehealth:** For more information, see `https://bit.ly/zfd-th`.

In both cases, you'll have to contact a Zoom sales rep to receive a proper quote.

Basic

Zoom's Basic plan for Meetings & Chat offers a great deal of functionality at zero cost. No, you can't take advantage of every Zoom bell and whistle. Still, the starter plan lets you do quite a bit. Here are some highlights:

>> Host meetings with up to 100 participants for a maximum of 40 minutes each. (Note that Zoom has waived this limit for teachers struggling to hold remote classes with their students in the wake of COVID-19.)

>> Host an unlimited number of meetings.

>> Chat with groups and send files.

>> Split your meeting into separate breakout rooms.

>> Brainstorm and take notes with a virtual whiteboard.

>> Share single or multiple screens with meeting attendees.

>> Call into a meeting via a phone.

Chapter 6 covers more of these features.

Pro

Zoom's first step up from the Basic plan is its Pro plan. The Pro plan delivers all the options of the Basic plan plus a bunch more. Here are some of the highlights:

>> Hold meetings for up to 24 hours.

>> Run a variety of reports on member usage.

>> Delegate your meetings. You can let someone else set up your meetings for you. (Note that your delegate also needs to subscribe to a Pro plan or above.)

>> Create and distribute a personal meeting ID (PMI).

>> Store up to a ridiculous 1 gigabyte (GB) of files in the cloud.

>> Grant different rights to different people (known as *user management*).

>> Control what other people in your organization can do. For example, you can enable and disable the others' ability to record calls, encryption, chat, and notifications.

For the Pro plan, Zoom charges $14.99 per month per host when billed monthly or $149.90 when billed annually.

Business

Zoom's Business plan delivers all the options of the Pro plan plus a bunch more. Highlights include the following:

>> Host meetings with up to 300 participants.

>> Receive dedicated phone support.

>> Access the Zoom Dashboard. Administrators on the account can view information ranging from overall usage to live in-meeting data.

>> Create a custom web address.

>> Automatically add users to your account via email-address domains.

>> Automatically generate call transcripts.

For the Business plan, Zoom charges $19.99 per month when billed monthly or $166.58 when billed annually.

Enterprise

Zoom's Enterprise plan delivers all the options of the Business plan plus the following:

>> Host meetings and webinars with up to 500 participants.

>> Receive unlimited file storage.

>> Work with a dedicated customer-success manager.

>> Talk to Zoom execs about Zoom's product road map and future direction.

>> Receive discounts on other Zoom products.

The Enterprise plan costs $19.99 per month per host when billed monthly. What's more, an organization needs to commit to a minimum of 50 hosts or software licenses. For a proper quote, you'll have to contact Zoom's sales staff. All else being equal, more licenses translates into a bigger bill — although the per-license fee is likely lower.

Enterprise Plus

Zoom's most expensive and robust Meetings & Chat plan delivers all the options of the Enterprise plan at a per-user discount. It allows you to host meetings and webinars with up to 1,000 participants. The Enterprise Plus plan requires

>> A minimum of 2,500 licenses

>> A two-year minimum commitment

To receive a proper quote for this plan, you'll have to contact Zoom.

Add-ons

Zoom realizes that one size does not fit all. To this end, it allows its customers to significantly customize their individual plans. Specific add-ons to its Meetings & Chat subscription include the following:

>> **Webinars:** See the next section.

>> **Zoom Rooms:** See "Zoom Rooms," later in this chapter, for a brief introduction.

>> **Large meetings:** This feature allows users to attend Zoom meetings with 500 or 1,000 participants, depending on the customer's license. Owners or admins of Pro accounts can simply add this feature to the monthly or annual tab.

>> **Audio conferencing options:** Maybe you want to make it easy for your employees, customers, and prospects — especially the international ones — to talk to you. To these ends, Zoom allows you to pay for toll-free numbers, fee-based toll numbers, and dedicated dial-in numbers.

>> **Cloud recording:** If your storage needs exceed those that Zoom offers under your current plan, you can upgrade as needed. You don't need to purchase a more expensive plan solely because you need to upgrade a single feature.

Zoom Video Webinars

Zoom's offering lets even the least tech-savvy person hold full-featured, intuitive, and engaging webinars. Webinar hosts can easily manage and administer the meetings thanks to Zoom's useful controls. As for size, you won't be lacking. As of this writing, up to 100 people can actively participate and 10,000 people can attend a single webinar.

Main features and benefits

Here are some of the most powerful and useful features of Zoom Webinars:

- » **Recording:** Zoom lets users easily and automatically record events for later publishing and viewing.

- » **Broadcasting to popular third-party sites:** Unless you live in a bubble, you're probably aware that untold millions of people view live-streamed videos on Facebook Live and YouTube Live every day. Fortunately, Zoom lets webinar hosts concurrently broadcast their events to those sites. Doing so often boosts user interest and engagement.

- » **Reporting:** Say that your organization sells widgets. To this end, it wants to use Zoom Webinars as a sales tool. Zoom lets users easily run reports on webinar registrants, attendees, polls, attendee engagement, and more. This information helps individuals qualify leads for their companies.

- » **Integrating with other enterprise systems:** Many organizations use webinars for lead-generation purposes. That is, by demonstrating the product or service, they hope to convert interested prospects into paying customers. To this extent, they need to easily integrate webinar-attendee data with popular marketing and customer-relationship management (CRM) applications, such as Marketo and Salesforce. Zoom makes this a breeze.

- » **Ensuring security:** Zoom safeguards all attendee login and webinar session data. As of this writing, version 5.0 of Meetings & Chat provides 256-bit Advanced Encryption Standard (AES).

Plans and costs

Zoom's plans are remarkably flexible: You don't need to pay for licenses that you don't need. (Years ago, companies often wasted bundles on unused software seats.)

Unfortunately, the company's flexibility makes understanding the pricing for Zoom Video Webinars a tad confusing in the following way: Zoom doesn't offer its webinars subscription on a standalone basis. (Zoom Rooms — discussed in the next section — is the only exception to this rule.)

To subscribe to the webinar plan, you first need to sign up for one of the premium Meetings & Chat plans listed in Table 8-1. In this sense, webinars represent an add-on to the core Meetings & Chat subscription. What's more, Zoom charges by the *host*. In this case, a host is a webinar emcee. More hosts means a larger monthly and annual tab. Ditto for increasing the cap on webinar participants.

Table 8-1 displays the Zoom Video Webinar offerings, as well as their costs as of this writing.

TABLE 8-1   Zoom Webinar Add-On Pricing Information

Plan Name	Host Minimum	Monthly Cost per Host	Annual Cost per Host
Pro	1	$40	$400
Business	10	$199.90	$1,999
Education	20	N/A	$1,800
Zoom Rooms	1	$40	$400

TIP

Note that Zoom does not provide add-on pricing for webinars for its Enterprise and Enterprise Plus offerings. In this way, webinars resemble the Meetings & Chat product. Contact Zoom's sales folks to negotiate a deal.

Zoom Rooms

Meetings & Chat and Video Webinars allow you to hold robust video-based meetings. Say that you're in Timbuktu, your boss Pete is in Montreal, and your client Ian is in Colombia. The three of you can meet online, but you won't feel as if you're in the same room.

But what if you and Pete are in the same physical location? Yep, as in an actual, brick-and-mortar room. What if you wanted to enter a souped-up conference room and share it with Mark in London, Steve H. in Gaza, and Steve R. in Warsaw, Poland? (These are the names of the insanely talented members of Marillion.) Collectively, you want to do more than host a simple teleconference from your homes or hotel rooms with basic screensharing and video feeds.

And what if employees at your firm regularly needed to conduct these types of high-end meetings from the same physical locations? That is, you want to fit a bunch of conference rooms with affordable hardware and software that really make an impression with your colleagues and prospects. Alternatively, what if your company routinely conducts remote training classes with new hires? In these cases, Meetings & Chat may not be sufficient for your needs.

Welcome to Zoom Rooms, a way of taking Meetings & Chat up a notch.

Main features and benefits

Zoom Rooms transforms normal conference rooms into something more powerful, interactive, and collaborative. With Zoom Rooms, you can do many of the same things as Meetings & Chat, but Zoom Rooms is a far more robust product. Here are some of the main things you can do with Zoom Rooms:

>> **Record meetings.** Just as with Meetings & Chat, Zoom Rooms lets users easily record what takes place in your company's conference and training rooms and with its virtual guests.

>> **Minimize maintenance.** Many IT departments and employees struggle to maintain their companies' legacy audiovisual systems. Compared to many of their predecessors, Zoom Rooms require very little software and hardware maintenance.

>> **Whiteboard and annotate.** Do you often brainstorm with others during meetings? Do you consider yourself a visual learner or thinker? Say that you're trying to nail that new product launch or find the best way to solve a vexing technical problem. Annotating a computer screen just doesn't cut it for you. You need something more.

Zoom Rooms allows for far more interactive whiteboarding than Meetings & Chat does. Meeting participates can

- Concurrently annotate across all devices and Zoom Rooms without everyone sharing the same virtual dry-erase marker

- Concurrently use up to 12 whiteboards

- Save and distribute their collaborative whiteboarding sessions

>> **Share content wirelessly.** Users can easily and concurrently share multiple desktops in the room. Meeting attendees and hosts can take advantage of a variety of simple wireless sharing options.

>> **Integrate with existing audiovisual systems.** Say that your employer already installed an expensive audiovisual system in its conference rooms. Depending on its current configuration, it may be able to integrate those devices with Zoom Rooms. That is, your company may not need to trash its current setup.

>> **Schedule easily.** To reserve a room for a given time and date, employees can simply tap a physical screen outside of a Zoom Room. From there, they can also view the scheduled meetings for that room. (Yes, they can do the same through Zoom software no matter where they are.)

>> **Guarantee system uptime.** The company guarantees its Zoom Rooms customers system uptime of 99.99 percent. This provision means that, in a given year, Zoom Rooms will go offline for a maximum of about nine hours.

TECHNICAL STUFF

To be fair, the 99.99 number is certainly impressive but not unique. That level has been fairly common in the tech world for years. For example, cloud-computing juggernauts Amazon Web Services (AWS), Microsoft Azure, and Google all guarantee similar uptime percentages in their end-user license agreements (EULAs). Ditto for the collaboration tool Slack (see Part 2).

Plans and costs

Subscribing to Zoom Rooms does not require the purchase of another Zoom product. It's a standalone solution — although you can certainly add on to it.

Zoom Rooms costs $49 per month per room. Organizations that want so save a few bucks can opt for the annual plan, which is $499 per month per room.

Note that there's no practical limit to the number of meeting participants under this plan. If you can cram 2,112 in a room for a single training session, have at it. Zoom won't be monitoring your meetings.

Supercharging Zoom Rooms

Depending on your organization's needs and its current videoconferencing hardware, you may want to consider two complementary products:

>> Zoom Conference Room Connectors

>> Zoom Rooms for Touch

Both work in conjunction with Zoom Rooms.

Zoom Conference Room Connectors

Say that you work at Gray Matter Technologies (GMT). Five years ago, it purchased and deployed expensive telecommunications equipment, like regular, speaker, and even video-enabled phones. Also assume that GMT contracted Cisco, Lifesize, Polycom, or another popular vendor. The implementation went fairly smoothly.

Today, those devices still function, but users wish that they could do more with them. Depending on their age, you find the devices a bit long in the tooth. The software isn't very intuitive and employees sometimes complain about audio call quality. Video feeds are sometimes choppy. Finally, you can't easily record conference calls, much less store them. But your audiovisual system still technically works.

You try making the case to GMT's chief technology officer (CTO), Elliot. He agrees with you, but he simply can't justify the cost of replacing all its videoconferencing hardware.

What to do?

Thanks to Conference Room Connectors, GMT can have its cake and eat it, too.

Companies can purchase Zoom Conference Room Connectors — devices that let their employees make Zoom video calls using their organization's existing conference-room hardware. Put differently, this fresh coat of paint allows employees to take advantage of Zoom's intuitive user interface (UI) while moving their existing, on-premises videoconferencing systems to the cloud.

Zoom Rooms for Touch

You've probably become accustomed to touchscreens over the past decade or more. In fact, you may chuckle when you see someone with a BlackBerry or an old-school flip phone. Odds are, though, that you don't touch your television or large computer monitor.

Zoom Rooms for Touch takes the core Zoom Room product to the next level. It turns a Zoom Room into an app the size of a television. Specific features include being able to do the following:

>> Instantly collaborate with others and share content over remarkably fluid video.

>> Brainstorm with your entire team on a massive digital video screen.

>> Easily share your screen and whiteboard with meeting participants.

Zoom Phone

Got a landline?

Fifteen years ago, you almost certainly did.

Data provider Statista reports that, in 2004, you could find a landline in nearly 93 percent of U.S. households. As of 2018, that number had declined to 41.7 percent. (See the chart yourself at `https://bit.ly/2004-zoom`.) Brass tacks: At home, hundreds of millions of people across the globe have dropped their landlines altogether.

At work, however, it may well be a different story. Traditional desk-based phones haven't gone the way of the dodo just yet. After all, do you want to give your personal cell phone number to every Tom, Dick, and Harry? We're talking about customers, colleagues, vendors, and partners. Plus, what about call centers? Millions of businesses still need to provide traditional desks and company-owned phones to their employees. Many organizations have discovered their answer in the form of Zoom Phone.

Main features and benefits

Zoom's final offering as of this writing is Zoom Phone — a high-tech version of a traditional business phone system. Its slick software and technical underpinnings (again, cloud computing) make it a vast improvement of early Voice over Internet Protocol (VoIP) efforts. Here are the main features:

>> **Centralized management:** Administrators can quickly provision and manage users. Zoom Phone dashboards allow administrators to easily view key information on the calls that employees are making. What's more, the visualizations allow for quick identification of call performance. As a result, the company can quickly identify any network-related quality issues before they mushroom.

>> **Security and reliability:** The company has taken great pains to ensure that users' Zoom Phone calls are both secure and clear.

>> **Traditional phone features:** You may not leave voicemails for your friends and family, but the feature remains important in many corporate settings. Ditto for call recording. Zoom Phone offers both of these essential features.

>> **Call routing:** Zoom Phone allows organizations to quickly and intelligently route queued calls to available agents and assistants. Without this essential functionality, modern-day call centers would cease to exist.

Plans and costs

Like Video Webinars, Zoom Phone is an add-on to its core Meetings & Chat plan. Table 8-2 displays the available types of Zoom Phone plans and their costs.

TABLE 8-2   Zoom Phone Plans

Plan	Number Locations	Cost
Unlimited Calling	U.S. and Canada	$15 per month per license
Metered Calling (ideal for infrequently used phones)	U.S. and Canada	$10 per month per license
Additional Phone Numbers	U.S. and Canada	$5 per month per number
Toll-Free Phone Numbers	U.S. and Canada	$5 per month per number
Metered calling options for calls placed outside of your designated calling plan	All	Variable

Chapter 9

Setting Up Zoom

Z oom allows people to easily hold high-quality videoconferences with their colleagues, partners, customers, families, friends, and students. You may be chomping at the bit to start one.

Your excitement is easy to understand, but hold the phone. It's essential to first cover a few foundational topics. Case in point: Before you can host a meeting, you need to take care of a few things.

This chapter explains the necessary housekeeping that you'll have to perform in order to start using Zoom in earnest. Don't worry. You'll be up and running with Meetings & Chat shortly.

Taking Your First Steps

The world is data driven. Rare is the company today that doesn't want to collect basic information about its users and customers. To this end, in order for you to host a Zoom meeting, you'll have to first create an account.

REMEMBER

Zoom labels all audio and video calls with others as *meetings*.

Creating a new Zoom account

Like many apps and web-based services today, Zoom requires users to establish accounts online if they want to host meetings.

REMEMBER

Someone in your organization may have already created a Zoom account for you. That is, management may have already subscribed to one of Zoom's premium plans (see Chapter 8) and registered you. In this case, you don't need to create a new account; you'll just log in with your existing email address and password. If you're not sure, just check with your employer's IT department.

To create a new Zoom account, follow these steps:

1. **Go to the Zoom web portal at** www.zoom.us.

2. **In the upper-right corner of the website, click the orange Sign Up, It's Free button.**

   From here, Zoom provides you with three signup options via

   - An email address
   - Google
   - Facebook

   If you select the second or third option, Zoom makes you authenticate your new account through that service. At a high level, you're granting Zoom permission to access some of the data that you've provided to Facebook or Google.

TECHNICAL STUFF

   Admittedly, this practice is quite common. For example, for years Spotify has allowed people to sign up for new accounts with Facebook. When they do, new users don't need to provide Spotify with their names, dates of birth, email addresses, and the like. Facebook already stores this information about its users — and plenty more, depending on how much they share on the social network.

   If that thought terrifies you or you don't use those popular services, simply select the first option and continue.

   The following instructions assume that you're signing up for Zoom with your email address, and not via Facebook or Google.

3. **Enter your email address and click the Sign-Up button.**

   Zoom informs you that an email confirmation is on its way (see Figure 9-1).

We've sent an email to ███████████████.
Click the confirmation link in that email to begin using Zoom.

if you did not receive the email,

Resend another email

FIGURE 9-1:
The Zoom browser message.

WARNING

To minimize spam and the impact of bad actors, Zoom blocks certain domains from registering new accounts. For example, Zoom rejected `heliyar802@ mailboxt.com` because people often use that domain to create disposable email addresses.

4. **Check your inbox and open the Zoom authentication email.**

   The message resembles Figure 9-2.

5. **Open the email and click the blue Activate Account button.**

   Zoom takes you to a new window or tab in your default web browser (see Figure 9-3).

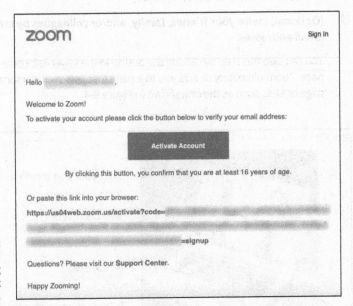

FIGURE 9-2:
A Zoom email requesting account authentication.

FIGURE 9-3:
Completing your
Zoom account.

6. **Complete your Zoom account by entering the required information.**

   Zoom requires you to enter your first and last name. You'll also need to create and confirm your password. When you click the password field, Zoom prompts you with guidelines about what your password can and cannot contain. For example, setting your password as *starwars* won't fly. Try again, young Skywalker.

7. **Click the orange Continue button.**

   The Don't Zoom Alone screen appears.

8. **(Optional) Invite your friends, family, and/or colleagues by entering their email addresses.**

   You can skip this step by clicking the button in the lower-left corner of the page. Zoom ultimately directs you to a page that lists your personal Zoom web page or URL, such as the one shown in Figure 9-4.

FIGURE 9-4:
The Zoom page
with a personal
meeting URL.

9. **Check your inbox again.**

Zoom sends you an email confirming your account and listing the features of your current plan (see Figure 9-5). (Chapter 8 explains more about Zoom's different plans.)

FIGURE 9-5: A Zoom email confirming a new account.

Congratulations! Your Zoom account is now active.

You're halfway home. To take advantage of the powerful features in Meetings & Chat, you'll want to install the Zoom desktop client. (For instructions, see "Downloading and installing the Zoom desktop client," later in this chapter.)

REMEMBER

Just as with many services today, you can create different Zoom accounts with different email addresses. In fact, you may want to create a personal Zoom account independent of your work account to separate church and state.

Modifying your Zoom plan

At some point, your business may expand, contract, or change. For example, maybe the sales folks begin to offer webinars and other customer-information sessions. Fortunately, Zoom allows its customers to easily upgrade, downgrade, cancel, and add on to their plans.

WARNING

Your current Zoom role may prevent you from upgrading yourself or your organization to a more robust plan. (For more on roles, see "Creating new user roles," later in this chapter.)

Upgrading from the Basic plan to the Pro plan

Say that you've kicked the tires on Zoom's Basic Meetings & Chat plan. You're impressed, and you want to take it to the next level. Follow these directions to upgrade to the Pro plan:

1. **In the Zoom web portal** (www.zoom.us), **under the Personal header, click Profile.**

2. **Scroll down until you see the User Type section.**

   Zoom displays your current plan. In this example, it's the Basic one.

3. **Click the Upgrade link to display a new page.**

4. **Click the orange Upgrade Account button.**

   A table that describes Zoom's different plans and features appears.

5. **Click the button corresponding to the plan you want to upgrade to.**

   In this case, it's the Pro plan.

6. **Select the number of meeting hosts you want to purchase.**

   Zoom's default is one. More hosts results in a larger bill.

7. **Select the length of your subscription.**

   Zoom defaults to annual (with a discount), but you can easily select monthly, if that's your preference.

8. **(Optional) Select your desired add-ons.**

   For more information on these options, see Chapter 8.

9. **Click the Continue button at the bottom the page.**

10. **On the page that appears, enter your contact information and payment method.**

11. **Confirm that you're not a robot and agree to the Privacy Policy and Terms of Services by checking the appropriate check boxes.**

12. **Click the blue Upgrade Now button.**

   Zoom displays an order summary.

13. **Look over the summary to ensure that you're subscribing to your desired plan and for the desired time period; if you're happy with what you see in the summary, click the orange Confirm button.**

Zoom displays a message confirming that you've upgraded your plan (see Figure 9-6).

FIGURE 9-6:
A Zoom message
confirming an
upgrade from the
Basic plan to the
Pro plan.

REMEMBER

Note that your specific upgrade steps may vary slightly based upon

» Your organization's existing plan

» The length of its current subscription

» Whether your organization had already upgraded

Canceling and making other changes to your existing plan

If you decide to cancel, change, or add on to your existing Meetings & Chat plan, follow these directions:

1. **In the Zoom web portal (www.zoom.us), under the Admin header, click Account Management.**

2. **Click Billing to display your current plans and add-ons.**

Zoom displays your current plans and add-ons. Figure 9-7 shows the Zoom account dashboard.

3. **Make your desired changes.**

From the Zoom dashboard, you can

- Downgrade your Zoom plan.
- Cancel your Zoom Meetings & Chat subscription.
- Update your credit card.
- Pay your bill.
- View your invoices.
- Add new features on to your existing Zoom Meetings & Chat subscription.

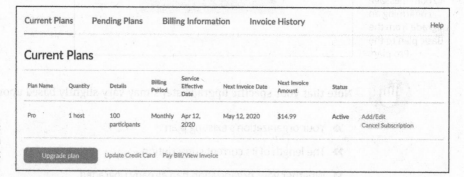

Plan Name	Quantity	Details	Billing Period	Service Effective Date	Next Invoice Date	Next Invoice Amount	Status	
Pro	1 host	100 participants	Monthly	Apr 12, 2020	May 12, 2020	$14.99	Active	Add/Edit Cancel Subscription

Current Plans   Pending Plans   Billing Information   Invoice History   Help

Current Plans

Upgrade plan   Update Credit Card   Pay Bill/View Invoice

FIGURE 9-7:
The Zoom
account
dashboard.

Downloading and installing the Zoom desktop client

To be sure, Zoom users and customers can participate in meetings no matter where they are as long as they can connect to the Internet. Again, Meetings & Chat runs on anything: smartphone, tablet, laptop, and desktop.

Still, to take advantage of all Zoom's robust functionality, you'll want to install the Zoom desktop client. Fortunately, if your computer runs macOS, Windows, or even Ubuntu/Linux, Zoom has you covered.

TECHNICAL STUFF

A *desktop client* is an application running on a desktop computer. Although purists will probably furrow their brows, this chapter uses the terms *desktop client* and *computer app* interchangeably. By the way, you can run that desktop client on your laptop.

To install the Zoom desktop client on your computer, follow these steps:

1. **In the Zoom web portal** (www.zoom.us)**, hover over the word** *Resources* **in the upper-right corner.**

   A drop-down list appears.

2. **Select Download Zoom Client from the drop-down list.**

   Zoom takes you to its Download Center, shown in Figure 9-8.

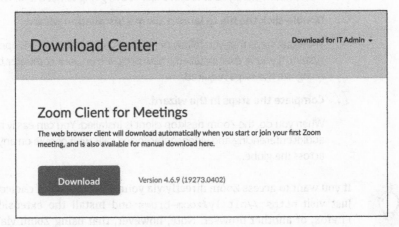

Download Center   Download for IT Admin ▾

Zoom Client for Meetings

The web browser client will download automatically when you start or join your first Zoom meeting, and is also available for manual download here.

Download   Version 4.6.9 (19273.0402)

FIGURE 9-8:
The Zoom
Download Center.

3. **Click the Download button.**

   Depending on your browser and how you've configured its settings, you may receive a warning that you're about to download a file. If you do, proceed.

4. **Save this file to your computer.**

TIP

   The specific location is generally a matter of personal preference, but it's wise to follow these common conventions:

   ● For PC/Windows users: `C:\Program Files`

   ● For Mac users: `Hard-drive name\Applications`

   Remember where you save this file.

5. **When the download completes, locate the file.**

The specific type of file hinges upon your computer's operating system. As of this writing, here are the filenames and extensions:

- **For PC/Windows users:** An executable file with an `.exe` extension, named `ZoomInstaller.exe`

- **For Mac users:** An installer package archive file with a `.pkg` extension, named `zoomusInstaller.pkg`.

Remember where you saved this file. You're going to need it for the next step.

6. **Double-click the file to launch Zoom's installation wizard.**

The exact steps that you follow depend upon your computer's operating system. If you've ever installed a new program on your computer before, you'll recognize the steps required.

7. **Complete the steps in the wizard.**

When you do, the Zoom desktop client is installed. You can easily host audioconferencing and videoconferencing calls with people on any device across the globe.

TIP

If you want to access Zoom directly via your web browser of choice, you're in luck. Just visit `https://bit.ly/zoom-brows` and install the extension for Chrome, Firefox, or another browser. Note, however, that using Zoom via a web browser means that you won't be able to do everything that you can on the desktop client.

Signing in to the Zoom desktop client

After you sign up for a Zoom account and download and install the desktop client on your computer (see the preceding section), you can sign in to the Zoom desktop client:

1. **Launch the Zoom desktop client.**

Zoom displays the window shown in Figure 9-9.

Note two things here:

- Zoom remembers who you are after you successfully log in.

- Figure 9-9 displays an option that this chapter hasn't mentioned yet: *single sign-on* (SSO). If you'd like to know more about it, read the nearby sidebar "Making life simple with SSO." For the purposes of these simple directions, however, you can ignore it.

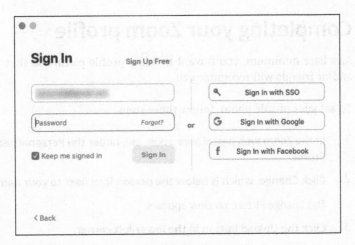

FIGURE 9-9:
Logging in to the
Zoom desktop
client.

2. **Enter your email address and password.**

3. **Click the blue Sign In button.**

   Zoom takes you to the main screen.

MAKING LIFE SIMPLE WITH SSO

Madrigal Electromotive is an international conglomerate with tens of thousands of
employees. Those workers need to access a wide variety of applications, web services,
and internal systems, including the following:

- Company email

- Productivity apps, such as Google Drive and Microsoft Office 365

- A slew of internal enterprise systems

- Collaboration applications, such as Slack (see Part 2) and Zoom

If you think that managing all these employees' usernames and passwords may be confusing, trust your judgment. In this vein, Madrigal has deployed SSO. Now, employees
can sign in to all these services using the same username and password. From the IT
department's perspective, SSO streamlines user administration and saves it mounds of
headaches.

Completing your Zoom profile

At a bare minimum, you'll want to add a profile picture so that your colleagues and/or friends will recognize you.

To set your profile photo, follow these steps:

1. **In the Zoom web portal** (www.zoom.us), **under the Personal header, click Profile.**

2. **Click Change, which is below the person icon next to your name.**

   The Change Picture window appears.

3. **Click the Upload button in the lower-left corner.**

   Zoom warns you that the maximum file size is 2MB.

4. **Choose the photo that you want to upload from your computer.**

5. **(Optional) Crop the photo.**

6. **Click the blue Save button.**

REMEMBER

From time to time, you may want to modify your Zoom profile. For example, perhaps you changed jobs or locations within your company. Zoom lets you make plenty of additional, self-explanatory edits in this part of its web portal. Note, however, that your role may limit the changes that you can make to your profile and account. (See the later section "Discussing the Importance of Zoom Roles" for more information.)

Getting to know the Zoom user interface

After you create your account and install the Zoom desktop client, you can explore Zoom's user interface (UI). Figure 9-10 displays the screen that appears when you log in to Zoom. Keep in mind that Figure 9-10 displays the UI for Zoom Meetings & Chat, not for its other offerings.

Think of the UI as a dashboard from which you can launch meetings, join existing meetings, tweak your settings, and do much more. After installing the Zoom app, the following icons and elements (from left to right) appear at the top of the screen:

» **Home:** Clicking Home always takes you back to this main screen. Think of Home as the equivalent of the home page in your favorite web browser.

» **Chat:** In Chat, you can start new text-based individual and group chats. You can also access your previous ones.

>> **Meetings:** In Meetings, you can find information on your previous and future meetings and view recorded meetings, among other things.

>> **Contacts:** You can access your directory of Zoom contacts and create *channels*, or containers for group-based text messages and file exchanges.

>> **Search bar:** You can search for messages, files, and contacts that exist within Zoom.

>> **Your Zoom Meetings & Chat profile:** You can set your status, edit your profile, check for app upgrades, and more.

>> **Settings icon:** You can control settings, such as video, audio, chat, and screensharing for Zoom meetings.

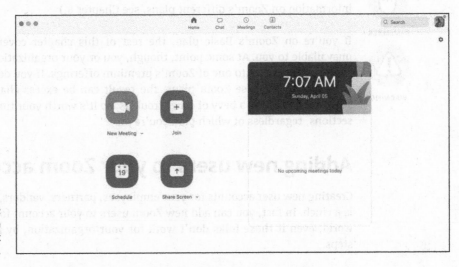

FIGURE 9-10:
The Zoom
Meetings & Chat
user interface.

The following four icons adorn the left side of the screen:

>> **New Meeting:** Start and host a new Zoom meeting.

>> **Join:** Join an existing Zoom meeting (that is, one that another host has initiated).

>> **Schedule:** Set up a future meeting and configure its settings.

>> **Share Screen:** Share your screen with other meeting participants.

Chapters 10 and 11 unpack these features and settings. For now, suffice it to say that you'll frequently return to the home screen of Zoom's desktop client. In other words, you won't just set it and forget it.

Reviewing Zoom Account Management

Think about your colleagues for a moment. How many of them are relatively new to your group or organization? How many have been there for a decade or more?

Zoom understands that organizations are living, breathing things. Things change. Maybe the president hires a new VP of finance and five programmers. Conversely, Travis's bad behavior finally caught up with him, and management has shown him the door. Your crosstown rival poaches a few of your rock stars.

Fortunately, Zoom makes account management a breeze.

REMEMBER

You must belong to a premium plan to add users to your Zoom account. (For more information on Zoom's different plans, see Chapter 8.)

WARNING

If you're on Zoom's Basic plan, the rest of this chapter covers functionality unavailable to you. At some point, though, you or your organization may upgrade from the Basic plan to one of Zoom's premium offerings. If you don't understand the features on these Zoom plans, the result can be excess charges, lost data, security issues, and a bevy of other troubles, so it's worth your time to read these sections, regardless of which plan you're on.

Adding new users to your Zoom account

Creating new user accounts for your employees, partners, vendors, and customers is a cinch. In fact, you can add new Zoom users to your account for anyone in the world, even if those folks don't work for your organization, by following these steps:

1. **In the Zoom web portal** (www.zoom.us), **under the Admin header, click User Management.**

2. **Click Users to see a list of your organization's current Zoom users.**

3. **On the right side of the page, click the Add Users button.**

   The Add Users window appears, as shown in Figure 9-11.

4. **Enter the email address for the user you want to add.**

   If you're adding multiple users, use commas to separate their email addresses.

FIGURE 9-11:
The Zoom
prompt to add
new users.

Add Users

Add users with their email addresses

Use comma to separate multiple email addresses.

| User Type | ○ Basic   ● Licensed ⑦   ○ On-Prem ⑦ |

Feature
☐ Large Meeting
☑ Webinar
☐ Zoom Phone

Department   e.g. Product

Job Title   e.g. Product Manager

Location   e.g. San Jose

Add   Cancel

5. **Select the type of user that you're adding.**

   Your choices are

   - **Basic:** Zoom lets these users ride for free, but they aren't able to access any of your plan's premium features.

   - **Licensed:** Zoom's default option results in account charges, the extent to which hinge upon your organization's plan.

     - **On-Prem:** These users can host meetings with unlimited minutes only if they use a Zoom Meeting Connector.

WARNING

     Pay attention here. Some people have neglected to check this option only to find unexpected charges at the end of their billing cycles.

6. **Select the features that you want to assign to the user.**

   Note that Zoom restricts you based upon your existing plan. For example, if you're currently not paying for webinars, Zoom forbids you from adding a user with the ability to host them. In this case, you have to subscribe to webinars as an add-on first.

7. **(Optional) Enter the new user's department, job title, and/or location.**

8. **Click the blue Add button at the bottom of the screen.**

   Zoom displays a temporary message at the top of the screen that lets you know the user has been added.

Deactivating existing accounts

Say that John has stepped on a bunch of shattered glass and has to take a two-month medical leave. (He wasn't wearing shoes. It's a long story.) Here's how you can deactivate his Zoom account:

1. **In the Zoom web portal** (www.zoom.us), **under the Admin header, click User Management.**

2. **Click Users to see a list of your organization's current Zoom users.**

3. **On the left side of the page, select the check box to the left of the name of the person whom you want to deactivate.**

4. **On the right side of the page, click the three horizontal dots that correspond to his name.**

   Zoom displays three options:

   - Deactivate

   - Delete

   - Unlink

5. **Choose Deactivate from the menu that appears.**

   Zoom asks you to confirm the deactivation. The user will no longer be able to access any Zoom service.

6. **Click the blue Deactivate button.**

REMEMBER

A few months later, John has healed and wants to return to work. Reactivate him by following the same steps with one exception: Choose Activate in Step 5.

Deleting existing users from your Zoom account

Sometimes deactivating an employee's user account isn't enough. Perhaps an employee did something unconscionable, such as stole company secrets. Maybe an employee passed away.

In either case, you want to permanently eliminate the person's Zoom account. Follow these steps:

1. **Follow Steps 1 through 4 in the preceding section.**

2. **Choose Delete.**

   Zoom displays a window asking whether you want to transfer the data associated with the current user's account. This step is optional, but your choices are

   - All upcoming meetings

   - All upcoming webinars

   - All cloud recording files

3. **Select your desired data transfer options by selecting the appropriate check boxes and entering an email address when prompted.**

   Zoom assigns all the current user's data to the account associated with the email address that you enter here.

4. **If you selected data transfer options in the preceding step, click the Transfer Data, Then Delete button; otherwise, click the Delete Now Without Data Transfer button.**

   Either way, you need to click a red button to proceed with the account deletion. Zoom displays a message at the top of the screen indicating that it has processed the account deletion. That account no longer appears in the list of users.

   WARNING

   This step is permanent. You can't undo it.

Unlinking users from your Zoom account

Zoom offers one final option for managing accounts, one slightly less draconian than deletion. By unlinking an account from the mother organization, the account continues to exist — just under a different, unaffiliated email address. Think of it as a divorce.

Follow these steps to remove a user account from your organization in Zoom:

1. **Follow Steps 1 through 4 in the "Deactivating existing accounts" section, earlier in this chapter.**

2. Choose Unlink.

Zoom displays a window asking whether you want to transfer the data associated with the current user's account. This step is optional, but your choices are

- All upcoming meetings
- All upcoming webinars
- All cloud recording files

3. Select your desired data transfer options by selecting the appropriate check boxes and entering an email address when prompted.

Zoom assigns all the current user's data to the account associated with the email address that you enter here.

4. If you selected data transfer options in the preceding step, click the Transfer Data, Then Unlink button; otherwise, click the Unlink Now Without Data Transfer button.

Either way, you need to click a red button to proceed to unlink the account.

WARNING

Note that the email address must correspond to an active and existing Zoom account in your organization.

Zoom displays a message at the top of the screen indicating that it has unlinked the account. That user account no longer appears in your Zoom web portal.

Unlocking the power of Zoom user groups

Zoom offers customers on premium plans a particularly valuable and time-saving feature: user groups. At a high level, user groups grant admins and owners the ability to manage user settings at the group level. In other words, they can concurrently change or lock the settings for multiple users. If that seems a bit abstract, consider one of the many potential applications of user groups.

The fictitious Octavarium University has subscribed to Zoom's Education plan for years. To build camaraderie and minimize misunderstandings, the school encourages its employees to enable their video when holding remote meetings. (See Chapter 10 for more information on this subject.)

At the same time, its administrators are justifiably concerned about student privacy, especially during the pandemic. They want to ensure that students don't join their professors' Zoom meetings with their video automatically enabled. In other words, undergraduates can activate their webcams if they want, but the choice should ultimately be theirs to make.

Jordan is Octavarium's Zoom admin. To make this change for all university professors, he follows this three-step process:

1. Create a new user group.

2. Populate the user group.

3. Apply the relevant Zoom account setting for that user group.

You can also restrict apps to specific user groups.

Creating a new user group

Jordan first creates a specific Zoom user group for professors by following these steps:

1. **In the Zoom web portal** (www.zoom.us), **under the Admin header, click User Management.**

2. **Click Group Management.**

3. **On the right side of the page, click the white Add Group button.**

4. **From the prompt, enter the name of the user group.**

   In this case, he calls it Professors.

5. **(Optional) Enter a description of the group.**

6. **Click the blue Add button.**

   Zoom displays a brief message in green at the top of the screen that the group is created.

Populating a user group

Jordan has created a new user group, but by itself, it's useless. In order to customize users' settings, he needs to place existing Zoom members into these groups — specifically, all Octavarium's professors.

You can populate a user group by following these directions:

1. **In the Zoom web portal** (www.zoom.us), **under the Admin header, click User Management.**

2. **Click Group Management.**

3. **On the right side of the page, click the name of the group to which you want to add members.**

   In this case, it's the Professors user group.

4. On the right side of the page, click the white Add Members button.

5. From the prompt, select as many users as you want by entering part of their email addresses into the text box.

6. Click the blue Add button.

Zoom confirms that you successfully added the group members.

Now that Jordan has both created the user group and added professors to it, he can apply a specific change to all Octavarium professors in one fell swoop. At a high level, Zoom's options fall into three buckets:

>> **Meeting:** Chapter 10 delves into Zoom's robust meeting options.

>> **Recording:** Chapter 10 delves into this subject as well.

>> **Telephone:** Zoom Phone is introduced in Chapter 8.

Changing a user group

Jordan is almost finished. He wants to allow group members to join meetings without enabling video, so he follows these steps:

1. In the Zoom web portal (www.zoom.us), under the Admin header, click User Management.

2. Click Group Management.

3. On the right side of the page, click the name of the group whose settings you want to change.

4. Find the setting that you'd like to tweak for this group.

In this example, Jordan wants to ensure that students can join meetings without enabling their video.

5. Click the Meeting tab on the right side of the page to enable members to join meetings without enabling videos.

6. Next to Participants video, slide the blue toggle switch to left.

It turns gray, indicating that it's now off.

Zoom displays a brief message in green at the top of the screen that confirms that the settings have been updated.

7. **As an added safety measure, click the gray lock icon to the right of the toggle switch so that no one can override this setting.**

   Zoom displays the same confirmation message at the top of the screen. *Voilà!* Now Octavarium students can join Zoom meetings with their professors via audio only if they desire.

For much more information on user groups, see https://bit.ly/zfd-groups.

TIP

Discussing the Importance of Zoom Roles

Zoom relies heavily upon user roles. In this way, Zoom resembles most powerful systems and applications. The basic premise behind roles is straightforward: In any organizations, users' needs and responsibilities will differ. As such, they require the ability to perform certain actions. Just as important, certain users should not be able to do specific things. It's not hard to imagine the chaos that would result if everyone in Zoom could perform every task.

Like users (the topic of the previous section), Zoom roles apply only to its premium plans: Pro, Business, Enterprise, Enterprise Pro, and Education. If your organization is currently a member of Zoom's Basic plan, it will have to upgrade to take advantage of the considerable flexibility and functionality that roles provide.

REMEMBER

Reviewing Zoom's default roles

Zoom has three default user roles:

>> **Owner:** This role grants full privileges to access and manage the organization's Zoom account. No one outranks the owner. For example, an owner can invite others to the Zoom account and downgrade, upgrade, or cancel a Zoom subscription altogether.

>> **Admin:** An admin technically sits underneath an owner, but the admin's privileges run the gamut. The admin can perform a number of essential tasks, both for themselves and others. For example, an admin can add, remove, and edit users.

>> **Member:** Members operate largely within the boundaries that owners and admins have set for them. Many times, they can change their individual settings, but they generally can't alter Zoom settings that affect others in the organization.

Creating new user roles

If the roles of owner, admin, and member seem a bit confining to you, you're in luck. Say you want to create a new role specifically for Roger, the head of marketing. Roger frequently hosts webinars for prospective customers. As a result, he needs to be able to do a few things that regular members can't. At the same time, though, you don't want to give him the keys to the kingdom.

Zoom lets admins and owners create new roles as needed. Just follow these steps:

1. **In the Zoom web portal (www.zoom.us), under the Admin header, click User Management.**

2. **Click Role Management to see the current roles in your organization.**

   By default, they are owner, admin, and member.

3. **On the right side of the page, click the Add Role button.**

4. **Enter a name for the role.**

5. **(Optional) Enter a description for the role.**

6. **Click the blue Add button.**

   Zoom displays a boatload of options.

7. **Select the specific options that you want to grant to the new role.**

   At a high level, Zoom lets you determine what the people in the role will be able to do. Options include

   - View the setting or output.

   - Edit the setting.

   - Do both.

   - Do neither (the default).

8. **When you finish, click the blue Save Changes button at the bottom of the screen.**

   Zoom displays a temporary message in green at the top of the screen that confirms that your settings have been updated.

Your custom role is created, but it isn't assigned to anyone in your organization.

WARNING

Tread lightly when creating new roles. Zoom grants users assigned to these new roles the power that you grant them. For example, in the preceding example, if you mistakenly allow Roger to delete users' accounts, he'll be able to do exactly that.

Changing an existing user's role

Employees and companies part ways. New hires come aboard. People transfer from one department to another. Don't worry, though. Zoom recognizes that things change.

To assign someone in your organization a new Zoom role, follow these steps:

1. **In the Zoom web portal** (www.zoom.us)**, under the Admin header, click User Management.**

2. **Click Users to see a list of users in your organization.**

3. **Click the Edit button next to the name of the person whose role you want to change.**

   Zoom displays a new window that allows you to edit the user's information.

4. **Next to User Role, choose the user's new role from the drop-down menu.**

5. **Click the blue Save button.**

   Zoom displays a temporary message in green at the top of the screen to confirm that you successfully changed the user's role.

TIP

Common courtesy dictates that you alert people when you've changed their roles.

For much more about Zoom roles, see https://bit.ly/zmroles.

Chapter **10**

Connecting with Others via Zoom Meetings

S ome people eschew actually talking to others at all costs. Others need to talk about everything — even when sending a quick message would do the trick.

Ideally, you don't fall into either category. You understand that when it comes to communication, one size doesn't fit all. Sometimes firing off a quick message is easiest. In other cases, hashing out a nuanced issue at work requires a real-time conversation — not a flurry of emails. Aside from business scenarios, people want to hear the voices and see the faces of the most important people in their lives: friends, family members, and significant others. It's a basic human need.

This chapter details Zoom's most popular service: meetings. Zoom designed its flagship product from the ground up. The result is a modern, robust, convenient, consistent, reliable, intuitive, and user-friendly experience. As a result, Zoom makes holding single- and multi-person video and audio meetings a breeze. The phrase *ridiculously simple* comes to mind.

Bottom line: If you rue the very idea of a video meeting, Zoom's boatload of cool features may just change your mind.

Getting Started with Zoom Meetings

You may be eager to jump right in and hold a Zoom meeting. After all, Zoom has created a powerful, user-friendly, flexible, and downright cool product. But developing a base understanding of Zoom's core functionality will help you use the service intelligently. What's more, it minimizes your chances of committing a *faux pas* or, even worse, exposing yourself and others to security or privacy issues.

TIP

Zoom appropriately names its flagship service Meetings & Chat because it performs both functions — admirably. This chapter focuses on the first half of Meetings & Chat. Chapter 11 goes deeper into the second half.

REMEMBER

Because of space considerations, this chapter simply can't describe every meeting-related feature in Zoom. Zoom has packed quite a bit of functionality into its meetings. As a remedy (and to let you find out more about the specific topics that interest you), plenty of contextual URLs are sprinkled throughout this chapter. Visit them for more information.

Reviewing Zoom's meeting-specific roles

Just as in real life, different people do different things in meetings. Zoom recognizes this reality by formalizing its meeting roles.

REMEMBER

The roles in the following section pertain only to Meetings & Chat. (They differ from the proper user account roles discussed in Chapter 9.) What's more, the following roles also overlap to an extent with their counterparts in Zoom Video Webinars.

Host

By default, Zoom assigns the person who starts or schedules the meeting the role of host. Say that Mary starts a meeting. Meetings & Chat assigns her the role of host. As such, Mary can perform the following tasks, among others:

>> Start live streaming.

>> End the meeting.

>> Share her screen with attendees.

>> Delegate another participant as co-host.

>> Start a breakout room (see "Using breakout rooms during meetings," later in this chapter).

>> Enable waiting rooms (see "Enabling waiting rooms for all Zoom users in your organization," later in this chapter).

Co-host

Depending on the size of your meeting, you may want to appoint a co-host. For the most part, these folks can perform the same tasks as hosts can with one main exception: They can't start live streaming. They can, however, live stream after the host has started the meeting.

Zoom also lets meeting hosts designate surrogates. Visit https://bit.ly/2URmHcS for more information about what Zoom calls *alternative hosts*.

Participants

Say that you haven't scheduled the meeting; you just show up. In this case, Zoom refers to you as a meeting *participant*. Participants can perform tasks such as

>> View the list of the other participants in the meeting.

>> Share their screens, with the host's permission.

>> Start and stop their own video.

>> Mute and unmute themselves.

Visit https://bit.ly/3fs7qHt to view a comprehensive list of the tasks that participants in each role can perform in a Zoom meeting.

Locating your personal Zoom information

Say that you're fortunate enough to sit in your own private office at work. If so, your organization has effectively reserved space for you — whether you're at work or on vacation. For example, if you're traveling to Belize, you lock your office. No one else enters it without your consent. (Forget the janitorial staff for a moment.)

Zoom embraces the same general concept via what it calls a *Personal Meeting Room* (PMR). Think of the PMR as your very own, unique virtual meeting space. If Kramer wants to enter his PMR and host a meeting, he'll need a key of sorts. Zoom refers to this key as a user's Personal Meeting ID (PMI).

You wouldn't give your house or office key to any Tom, Dick, or Harry. By the same token, you should treat your PMI with the same care. When bad actors know your PMI, things can break bad. Specifically, if you're holding a meeting, others can join your PMR as uninvited guests, subject to the following two exceptions:

>> You lock the meeting.

>> You enable Zoom's Waiting Room feature to individually admit participants. (For more on this subject, see "Enabling waiting rooms for all Zoom users in your organization," later in this chapter.)

To view both your PMR and PMI, follow these steps:

1. **In the Zoom web portal** (www.zoom.us), **under the Personal header, click Profile.**

   On the right side of the screen, you see the PMI. By default, Zoom hides a few of its characters.

2. **Click Show.**

   Zoom shows your PMI (see Figure 10-1).

TIP

   If you frequently host public meetings, you should change your PMI every month or so.

FIGURE 10-1:
A Zoom Personal
Meeting ID.

Phil Simon

Account No. ▓▓▓▓▓

Change   Delete   Edit

Personal Meeting ID   ▓▓▓▓▓▓   Hide   Edit
https://zoom.us/j/******▓▓▓   Show

× Use this ID for instant meetings

3. **(Optional) If you'd like to change your PMI, click Edit and enter your new PMI.**

   Zoom places some restrictions around PMIs. If Zoom doesn't like your new PMI, it displays a red warning message.

TIP

   You don't need to use your PMI when scheduling a meeting (see "Planning a future Zoom meeting," later in this chapter).

4. **Click the blue Save Changes button.**

WARNING

Giving out your PMR and/or PMI willy-nilly maximizes the chance of others crashing your meetings — or *Zoombombing*, as the kids say.

Augmenting your Zoom meetings

Before hosting a single meeting, you may want to consider enabling three useful and underused Zoom options:

>> Waiting rooms

>> Breakout rooms

>> Audio transcriptions (if your organization's Zoom plan allows; see Chapter 8 for more about plans)

Using these features lets you get more out of your meetings.

Enabling waiting rooms for all Zoom users in your organization

Think about the last time you visited your doctor. You didn't just barge in. You sat patiently (or impatiently) in the waiting room until the person at the front desk called your name.

Zoom lets meeting hosts follow the same protocol. If you're an account owner or admin, you can enable waiting rooms for all users who fall under your organization's Zoom account. Follow these steps:

1. In the Zoom web portal (www.zoom.us), under the Admin header, click Account Management.

2. Click Account Settings.

3. In the Waiting Room section, click the toggle button.

The toggle button turns blue, and the circle moves to the right. Zoom displays a new window asking you to confirm your decision.

4. Click the blue Turn On button.

Zoom confirms that your settings have been updated.

Of course, following these steps only means that members can choose to use waiting rooms. Admins can't *force* people to use them.

TIP

Play around with Zoom's different waiting-room options. You can even customize your logo and the message that future meeting participants see by visiting https://bit.ly/2UPKD0a.

Enabling breakout rooms during your meetings

John Keating teaches poetry at the Welton Academy in Middletown, Delaware. (Yes, I'm going all *Dead Poets Society* here.) He wants his class of 30 students to concurrently discuss Lord Byron's "She Walks in Beauty" in small groups. Unfortunately, he has to conduct his class via Meetings & Chat. Creating five or six distinct Zoom meetings isn't feasible. What to do?

Enter breakout rooms, one of the most useful features of Meetings & Chat. Hosts can separate attendees into any number of smaller configurations during their meetings. The host can then drop in to each group and, in this case, bring the class back together — all without leaving the Zoom meeting or having to start a new one. If you think that feature would be beneficial in plenty of settings beyond classrooms, trust your instincts. Even better, Zoom enables this feature on all plans, including the Basic one.

To enable breakout rooms for all members in an organization, an admin or owner needs to follow these steps:

1. **In the Zoom web portal** (www.zoom.us), **under the Admin header, click Account Management.**

2. **Click Account Settings.**

3. **In the Breakout Room section, click the toggle button.**

   It slides to the right and turns blue. Zoom displays a new window asking you to confirm your choice.

4. **Click the blue Turn On button.**

   Zoom confirms that your settings have been updated.

Note that you need to enable breakout rooms only once. What's more, you can use them at your leisure. For more on how to enable breakout rooms for meeting participants, see "Using breakout rooms during meetings," later in this chapter.

TIP

As of this writing, Zoom lets hosts create up to 50 separate breakout sessions per meeting.

Enabling meeting audio transcriptions

Zoom lets customers on its Business, Education, and Enterprise plans create audio transcriptions of their meetings. Even better, Zoom displays these transcriptions as different attendees speak. Think of it as watching a movie with subtitles.

To enable this setting for all members in an organization, a Zoom admin or owner needs to follow these steps:

1. **In the Zoom web portal** (www.zoom.us), **under the Admin header, click Account Management.**

2. **Click Account Settings.**

3. **Click the Recording tab at the top of the page.**

4. **Under Advanced Cloud Recording Settings, select the Audio Transcript check box.**

5. **Click the blue Save button.**

TIP

Using breakout rooms is not a binary for all people under your organization's Zoom plan. For much more information on how you can configure them for different Zoom users and groups, see https://bit.ly/2Chtfvf and https://bit.ly/2AwU91D.

Hosting Zoom Meetings

Zoom calls its impromptu virtual get-togethers *Instant Meetings* or *Meet Now*. To start a meeting, launch the Zoom desktop client. Click the Home icon and then click the New Meeting icon.

You're now hosting a live, one-person Zoom meeting (see Figure 10-2).

Zoom displays a series of icons from left to right when meetings begin, whether anyone has joined the meeting or not. Table 10-1 displays the menu icons that hosts see during their meetings.

FIGURE 10-2:
The Zoom user
interface during
active meetings.

TABLE 10-1   **Zoom In-Meeting Menu Icons**

Icon	Description
Mute	Control the audio output from your computer. The arrowhead lets you tweak your computer's microphone and speaker settings for this meeting.
Stop Video	Let meeting participants see your visage. The arrowhead tweaks your computer's microphone and speaker settings for this meeting.
Security	Manage your meeting's security and privacy settings. Zoom added this icon in April 2020 to make these features more prominent and easier to access.
Participants	Determine who can do what during a meeting. For example, click here to quickly invite people to an existing meeting.
Share Screen	Minimize the main meeting window and share your screen with meeting participants. Stop sharing at any time by clicking the red Stop Share button that appears. You can also momentarily stop sharing by — wait for it — clicking the Pause Share button. The arrowhead lets you invoke additional screen-sharing options.

Icon	Description
Record	Record your meeting. You can also stop or pause recording after you've started recording.
Reactions	Add simple emojis for all other meeting attendees to see.
End	Terminate the audio or video meeting for everyone.

Note: Table 10-1 intentionally omits two icons that you may see in the future, depending on how you configure Meetings & Chat:

>> **Polling:** See "Collecting participant input through polls," later in this chapter.

>> **Breakout Rooms:** See "Using breakout rooms during meetings," later in this chapter.

REMEMBER

You can host only one meeting at a time per device.

Inviting others to your current meeting

Unless you have split personalities or imaginary friends, you've probably never held a meeting with yourself. Instead, you need to talk with your boss or some colleagues about an issue. Maybe you want to catch up with your friends via a virtual happy hour.

After starting your meeting, follow these directions to invite others:

1. Click the Participants icon at the bottom of the screen.

2. Click the Invite button in the right-hand corner.

3. Click the Email tab at the top of the screen.

In total, Zoom displays five options. The first three email-based invitation methods are as follows:

- **Default Email:** Launches your computer's default email client. It may be Microsoft Outlook or Mail.

- **Gmail:** Launches a Gmail window or tab in your computer's default web browser (see Figure 10-3).

- **Yahoo Mail:** Launches a Yahoo Mail window or tab in your computer's default web browser.

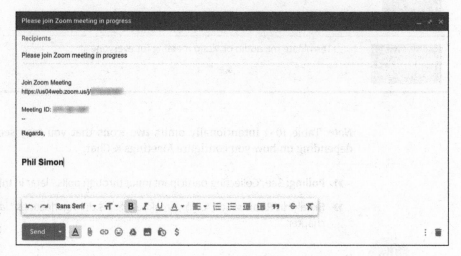

Please join Zoom meeting in progress

Recipients

Please join Zoom meeting in progress

Join Zoom Meeting
https://us04web.zoom.us/j/

Meeting ID:

--

Regards,

Phil Simon

Sans Serif

Send

FIGURE 10-3:
An automatically generated Gmail message with key meeting information.

After sending your email, wait for others to join. Say, however, that you don't want to use Outlook or Gmail to invite others to your little shindig. No worries. Zoom provides two options unrelated to email:

- **Copy Invite Link:** Copies the meeting's URL to your computer's clipboard.

- **Copy Invitation:** Copies the words *Join Zoom Meeting*, the meeting URL, and the meeting identification number.

If you choose one of the last two options, you can paste the copied text into a message in Slack (see Part 2), Microsoft Teams (see Part 4), WhatsApp, or just about any program or app that you can imagine.

4. **Send the message and wait for others to join your Zoom meeting.**

TIP

When three or more participants join a meeting, Zoom meetings default to what it calls its *Active Speaker* layout (the upper-right corner says *Speaker View*). In this mode, Zoom automatically switches the large video window based upon who is speaking. Go to `https://bit.ly/2Y51ZLi` to find out more about this layout.

Say that your meeting consists of just two people, though. Your friend Roger and you are just catching up. In this case, from your perspective, Zoom displays your video in a small screen at the top, while Roger's video takes a more prominent position below yours. (From his perspective, the opposite is true.) For more on the other in-meeting layouts in Meetings & Chat, see `https://bit.ly/37EQD15`.

TIP

It's even easier to hold audio and video meetings with people whom you've already added to your Zoom directory (see Chapter 11).

Planning a future Zoom meeting

As former president Dwight D. Eisenhower once astutely observed, "Plans are worthless, but planning is everything." In the context of Zoom, calling a spontaneous meeting makes sense in certain circumstances, especially when text-based communication just isn't working. Taken to the extreme, though, any given person's work life would be unmanageable and even downright chaotic if she couldn't at least *try* to plan her days.

To this end, Zoom makes it easy to schedule future meetings with others and to track attendee registration. What's more, by scheduling meetings, you unlock additional features that can make your meetings more valuable for all concerned.

Scheduling a Zoom meeting

To schedule a meeting with an individual or group of people in advance, follow these steps:

1. **Click the Home icon at the top of the desktop client.**

2. **Click the blue Schedule button.**

   Zoom displays the Schedule Meeting window (see Figure 10-4).

3. **Customize your meeting's settings.**

   You can change its

   - Topic and description

   - Date

   - Start and end time

   - Meeting ID

   - Audio and video options

   - Integration with third-party calendar tools, such as Microsoft Outlook and Google Calendar

   - Advanced options, including whether you've assigned any alternative hosts

REMEMBER

   Selecting Generate Automatically for the Meeting ID means that Zoom will produce and distribute a unique, disposable number. In other words, you won't be using your PMI for this meeting.

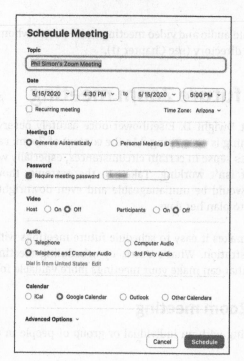

FIGURE 10-4:
Scheduling a future Zoom meeting.

4. **When you finish, click the blue Schedule button.**

   You've now scheduled your meeting. Zoom displays a meeting confirmation message with all the relevant information (see Figure 10-5).

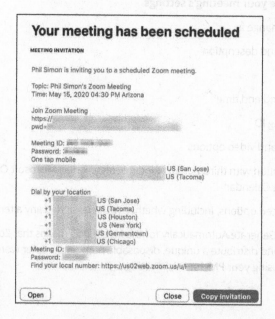

FIGURE 10-5:
Viewing a scheduled Zoom meeting.

From the meeting confirmation, you can perform the following actions by clicking the related buttons:

» **Open:** Opens the calendar in your computer's default calendar program.

» **Close:** Closes the window.

» **Copy the invitation:** Copies the meeting's information to your clipboard. From here, you can paste it into an email message or wherever you like.

View your scheduled meetings by clicking the Meetings icon at the top of the Zoom desktop client.

Although you can host only one meeting at a time per device, you can schedule as many as you like in advance.

Zoom also lets users schedule meetings via the web portal (www.zoom.us) and through different browser extensions. Go to https://bit.ly/2NgIruR for instructions.

Editing your scheduled meeting

Say you've successfully scheduled your meeting. After thinking about it, though, you decide that you'd like to make a few changes. Sure, you can junk your meeting and wreak havoc with others' calendars. A better way, though, involves editing your existing meeting — something that Zoom allows you to easily do by following these steps:

1. **In the Zoom web portal** (www.zoom.us), **under the Personal header, click Meetings.**

2. **Click the name of the meeting that you'd like to edit.**

   Zoom presents basic information about your scheduled meeting.

3. **Click the white Edit This Meeting button in the lower-right corner of the page.**

4. **Make whatever changes you like.**

   You can change the following:

   ● Topic
   ● Date
   ● Start and end time

- Meeting ID
- Audio and video options
- Advanced options, including whether you've assigned any alternative hosts

5. **Click the blue Save button.**

Collecting participant input through polls

Bruce has scheduled an upcoming meeting with members of his E Street Band. During the call, he wants to solicit everyone's feedback. Sure, attendees will be able to both chime in and enter text-based comments in the chat window. This type of unstructured data is often valuable, but collating it is typically messy and time-consuming, especially with larger groups. Structured data is far easier to collect and analyze. To this end, a better way in many cases is to conduct a poll — one that immediately displays results.

Zoom reserves polls for customers on premium plans.

To enable polling for all members in an organization, an admin or owner needs to follow these steps:

1. **In the Zoom web portal** (www.zoom.us), **under the Admin header, click Account Management.**

2. **Click Account Settings.**

3. **In the Polling section, click the toggle button on the right side of the page.**

    It turns blue. Zoom displays a new window asking you to confirm your choice.

4. **Click the blue Turn On button.**

    Zoom confirms that your settings have been updated.

You need to enable polls only once at the account level.

After you activate polls, you can create one or more polls for an upcoming meeting:

1. **In the Zoom web portal** (www.zoom.us), **under the Personal header, click Meetings.**

2. **On the left side of the page, under Upcoming Meetings, click the meeting for which you want to schedule a poll.**

3. **Scroll down to the bottom of the page and click the white Add button next to You Have Not Created Any Poll Yet.**

4. **In the window that appears, enter the title of your question.**

5. **(Optional) Select the Anonymous check box if you want to hide attendees' responses.**

6. **Type the name of your question.**

7. **Indicate whether the question is single or multiple choice by selecting the related check box.**

8. **Enter the possible responses in the text boxes.**

9. **(Optional) To continue adding questions, click + Add a Question and repeat Steps 4 through 8.**

10. **When you finish setting up your poll, click the blue Save button.**

   You can now view the poll (see Figure 10-6).

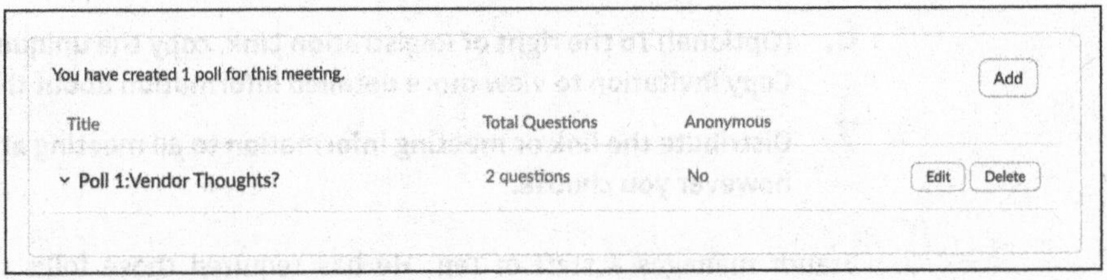

FIGURE 10-6:
A saved poll for a
future Zoom
meeting.

You have created 1 poll for this meeting.			Add
Title	Total Questions	Anonymous	
⌄ Poll 1:Vendor Thoughts?	2 questions	No	Edit Delete

Note that Zoom ties polls to specific users' PMIs, a minor but important point. Say that Hank needs to set up a meeting with the other Drug Enforcement Administration (DEA) agents in his office. He has read the earlier section on scheduling Zoom meetings. As such, he's weighing his options:

» **Using his PMI:** If he goes this route, he can access all the polls that he has created under his PMI.

» **Allowing Zoom to automatically generate a disposable meeting ID number:** If Hank selects this option, his poll applies only to that specific meeting. As a result, he won't be able to recycle them or transfer them to another meeting.

Either way, at some point during the meeting, hosts can launch their polls.

Handling meeting registration

Although it's optional, requiring participants to register for future meetings confers a number of obvious benefits, including counting the number of heads in advance. Beyond that, a company or your manager may mandate attendance at certain meetings.

Suppose that Brandt is holding an important department-wide meeting and wants to ensure that all employees attend. As such, he requires registration by following these steps:

1. In the Zoom web portal (www.zoom.us), under the Personal header, click Meetings.

2. Click the name of the meeting whose registration information you'd like to view.

3. Click the white Edit This Meeting button.

4. Scroll down to Registration, and select the Required check box.

5. Click the blue Save button.

   Zoom returns you to the main meeting page.

6. (Optional) To the right of Registration Link, copy the unique URL or click Copy Invitation to view more detailed information about the meeting.

7. Distribute the link or meeting information to all meeting attendees however you choose.

Brandt manages a staff of ten. He has required those folks to register for his monthly meeting. Plus, he has distributed the link to attendees, maybe even via Zoom Meetings & Chat (see Chapter 11). When others click that URL, they see a form similar to the one shown in Figure 10-7.

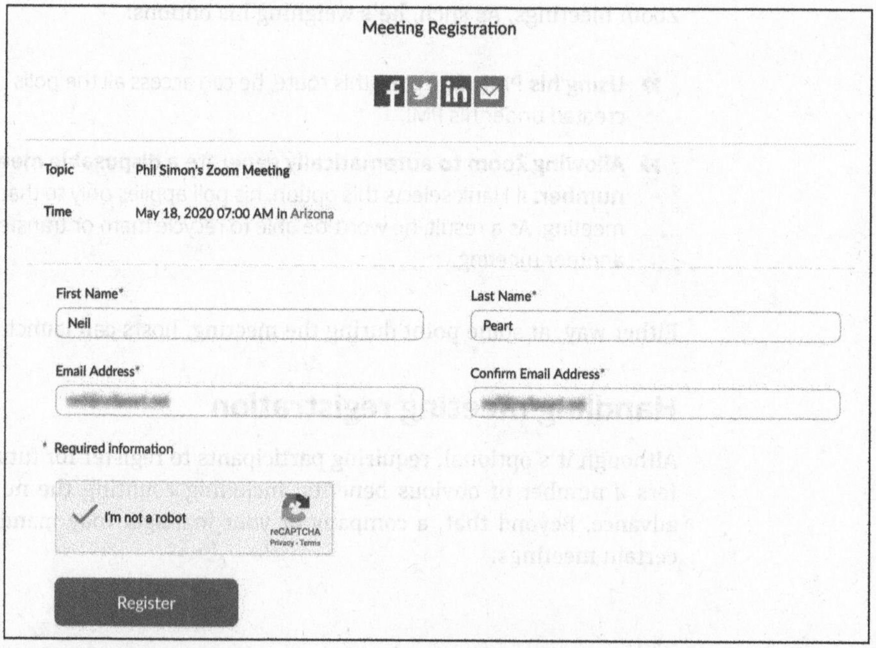

FIGURE 10-7:
A Zoom meeting registration form.

After attendees fill out and submit a meeting registration form, Zoom stores their information. You can access it by following these steps:

1. **In the Zoom web portal** (www.zoom.us), **under the Personal header, click Meetings.**

2. **Click the name of the meeting whose registration information you'd like to view.**

3. **Scroll down to the Registration tab; to the right of Manage Attendees, click View.**

   Zoom displays a window similar to Figure 10-8.

Registrants for 'Phil Simon's Zoom Meeting'   ×

	Registrants	Email Address	Registration Date	
☐	Neil Peart		May 16, 2020 07:00 AM	Copy

[Cancel Registration] [Resend Confirmation Email]

FIGURE 10-8: Viewing meeting registrants.

Click the Edit button to customize your registration options even more.

TIP

Letting others in to your current meeting

In the real world, a meeting's scheduled start time does not necessarily equal its *actual* start time. The same principle applies to Zoom meetings.

Earlier in this chapter, you find out how hosts can enable waiting rooms for their meetings (see "Enabling waiting rooms for all Zoom users in your organization"). Say you've enabled the waiting-room option. After folks have tried to join your meeting, Zoom displays the message in Figure 10-9 until you let them in.

If you're the meeting host, the Zoom desktop client notifies you with an orange blinking light on the Participants tab (see Figure 10-10).

Zoom provides meeting hosts with a number of options (see Table 10-2).

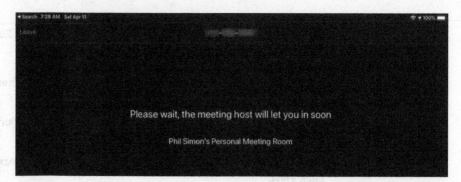

FIGURE 10-9:
Attendees' view
of the meeting
while they're in
the Zoom waiting
room.

FIGURE 10-10:
Participant
notification in the
Zoom Meetings
desktop client.

TABLE 10-2	**Zoom's Waiting Room Options for Meeting Hosts**
Action	Directions and Results
Admit a participant	Click the Participants icon and then click the blue Admit button to let them into the meeting.
Send message	Click to launch Zoom's in-meeting chat window. From here, you can send messages to everyone in the waiting room or single out a specific individual.
Do nothing	All attendees remain in purgatory.
Admit all participants	Click the Participants icon and then click the Admit All button in the upper-right corner. All participants enter the meeting.

Joining others' Zoom meetings

Just as in real life, you won't always host a meeting. Sometimes you'll participate in Zoom meetings with people from external organizations. Zoom makes it remarkably simple to join an existing meeting, whether you know the host's PMI or the meeting's URL.

Joining a meeting using the host's PMI

Walter invites you to a meeting via email. His message includes his PMI, as well as the meeting's password. You can join his meeting by following these instructions:

1. **Launch the Zoom desktop client.**

2. **On the Home screen, click the Join icon.**

3. **From the prompt, enter the host's PMI.**

4. **(Optional) Enter the meeting password.**

   By default, Zoom began enabling passwords for all meetings starting on April 5, 2020. (You can uncheck this box to disable this option, but leaving it enabled is a good idea for security purposes.)

5. **Enter your name or what you want others in the meeting to call you.**

6. **(Optional) Indicate whether you want to disable your audio by selecting the appropriate check box.**

   Zoom's default option connects you to the meeting with your computer's audio enabled.

7. **(Optional) Indicate whether you want to disable your video by clicking the radio button on the left.**

   Zoom's default option connects you to the meeting with your computer's video enabled.

8. **Click the blue Join button.**

   (Optional) If you chose to join with your video enabled, Zoom presents you with a prompt that allows you to preview what other attendees will see (see Figure 10-11).

9. **If you like what you see, click the blue Join with Video button; if not, click the white Join without Video button.**

   Assuming that the host hasn't enabled meeting waiting rooms, you'll join the meeting momentarily.

   You'll also have to enter a password if the meeting host required it.

   You've now joined the Zoom meeting.

Always show video preview dialog when joining a video meeting

Join without Video   Join with Video

FIGURE 10-11:
A Zoom video
premeeting entry
prompt.

Joining a meeting via a URL

Donnie invites you to a meeting by emailing you a URL. You can join him on Zoom by following these steps:

1. **Copy and paste the meeting URL into the address bar of your web browser and press Enter.**

    Assuming you installed the Zoom desktop client, your browser prompts you to open it.

2. **Click the Open or Allow button — or the equivalent button in your web browser.**

3. **Click the blue Join button.**

4. **If you like the video preview, click the blue Join with Video button; if not, click the white Join without Video button.**

Joining via a URL eliminates the need to enter the meeting's password because Zoom embeds the password in the link.

Waiting for hosts to begin their meetings

Say you've arrived early for James's meeting, or he's running late. If James has turned on waiting rooms for his meeting, you can expect to see a waiting room screen (refer to Figure 10-9 to see what it looks like).

Putting your best foot forward

No one forces you to enable video during your Zoom meetings. You can always join via audio only (see "Joining a meeting using the host's PMI," earlier in this chapter). Still, from time to time, you're going to want the world to see you.

Looking your best in Zoom

A seldom-used Zoom feature called Touch Up My Appearance purportedly helps smooth out the skin tone on your face. No, it won't transform you into Brad Pitt or Halle Berry, but think of it as the equivalent of putting on some digital makeup.

Follow these steps to enable this feature:

1. **Launch the Zoom desktop client.**

2. **Click the Settings icon in the upper-right corner.**

   Zoom displays your settings.

3. **On the left side, click Video.**

4. **To the right of My Video, select the Touch Up My Appearance check box.**

TIP

Refrain from looking at other devices and screens during your meeting, especially if you've enabled video. Others will quickly pick up on your lack of concentration. To enable video on Zoom's desktop client, you need to use your laptop's internal webcam or an external one.

TIP

Projecting a more professional visage isn't hard — in other words, to avoid the dreaded nostril-cam, just prop your laptop up on some books. If that doesn't work for you, consider purchasing a proper laptop stand.

Optimizing sound quality in Zoom

Of course, how you present yourself to others represents only part of the meeting experience. The other side is how you sound during your meetings — and, for that matter, how other participants sound to you. At a high level, a good deal hinges upon the quality of your computer's audio components. Contrary to what you may think, newer computers don't necessarily ship with better hardware in this regard than older ones did.

Plenty of folks aren't satisfied with the sound emanating from their computers' native microphones and speakers. If you find yourself in this boat, you can tweak your computer's audio settings. Still disgruntled? Consider purchasing an external microphone, like the Yeti Blue.

As for headphones and speakers, there is tremendous variation among Bluetooth devices. Some models work seamlessly, while others cut in and out throughout meetings.

TIP

Ask a trusted friend for honest feedback on your audiovisual situation.

Finally, don't expect first-rate audio and video quality during Zoom meetings if your Internet connection is spotty. Zoom can only do so much. If you're having a tough time hearing others and vice versa, consider disabling your video. Ask others in the meeting to do the same.

TIP

Your overall audio and video quality during Zoom meetings stems from a number of factors. If you're experiencing problems, use the process of elimination. For example, try to connect to a friend's network when taking Zoom meetings. Does performance improve? Use a family member's computer instead of yours. Eventually, you'll figure out what's causing your issue.

Performing Mid-Meeting Actions

After you start your meeting and let everyone in, you don't just need to sit back. On the contrary, Zoom provides a boatload of valuable options for hosts to interact with meeting participants and more.

Using virtual backgrounds

Musicians Jemaine and Bret need to take an early conference call in their studio apartment with their manager, Murray, to discuss band-related business. Unfortunately, the two of them haven't had time to tidy up. They prefer to let him see their faces, but they want to hide their unkempt environs during the meeting. What to do?

They can take advantage of virtual backgrounds — hands down, one of Zoom's coolest features and one that other vendors have copied. In other words, they can appear to join the meeting from the verdant fields in their home country of New Zealand, in space, or just about anywhere else they like. When they do, Murray won't know that their place is a mess.

Setting a virtual background

To use a virtual background for your meetings, follow these steps:

1. **Launch the Zoom desktop client.**

2. **Start a meeting and enable your video.**

3. **Click the Settings icon in the upper-right corner.**

4. **On the left side of the new window that appears, click Virtual Background.**

5. **Click the plus icon to the right of Choose Virtual Background (see Figure 10-12).**

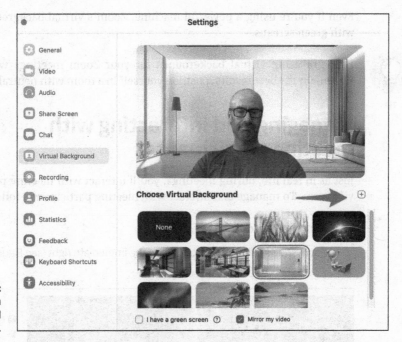

FIGURE 10-12:
Selecting a custom virtual background.

6. **Select an existing photo or video.**

    Zoom remembers this choice for your next video meeting.

7. **(Optional) If you're using a green screen, select the I Have a Green Screen check box.**

    This selection helps Zoom optimize video quality during your meetings. Ignore this selection if you're not using one.

8. **(Optional) Uncheck the Mirror My Video check box.**

    By default, Zoom displays the video as others see you, not as you see yourself.

9. **Close the screen and return to your meeting by clicking the red circle in the upper-left corner of the screen.**

Getting the most out of your virtual backgrounds

Virtual backgrounds don't work equally well on every type of computer. The computer's operating system needs to be current, and its processor needs to be sufficiently powerful. (Good luck if you're still running Windows 98.) If Zoom determines that your computer isn't up to snuff in either case, it displays a Computer doesn't meet requirements message.

Even if you're using a powerful machine, Zoom's virtual backgrounds work best with green screens.

TIP

If you're using virtual backgrounds for your Zoom meetings without a green screen, for the best results, position yourself in a room with neutral-colored walls.

Managing and interacting with meeting participants

Just as in real life, during meetings, you'll interact with meeting participants and vice versa. To manage and interact with meeting participants, follow these steps:

1. **Click the Participants tab.**

    Zoom shows a lists of Participants to the immediate right (see Figure 10-13).

FIGURE 10-13:
A meeting with the Participants panel displayed.

2. **Mouse over the name of the person with whom you want to interact and make your adjustments using the two blue buttons that appear.**

Clicking the Mute button temporarily disables the participant's ability to speak or generate sound. (In the case of the latter, perhaps ambient noise is making it difficult for others to hear.)

If you click the More button, Zoom provides you with the actions detailed in Table 10-3.

TABLE 10-3 **Meeting Participant Actions**

Actions	Description
Chat	Opens a new chat window that allows you to exchange private text messages with the participant. Participants can also use this feature to send private messages to each other during the meeting.
Ask to Start Video	Sends a notification to the participant that you want him to start his video.
Make Host	Promote the participant to meeting host.
Make Co-Host	Promote the participant to meeting co-host.
Rename	Edit participant names. For example, three people named Emily have joined the meeting. Adding their last names may help clear up any confusion. If people pose as others, though, bad things can happen.
Put in Waiting Room	Click here to temporarily remove someone from the meeting. From here, click the white Remove button to kick him out of the meeting altogether. Click the blue Admit button to let him back in.
Remove	Kick the participant out of the meeting. Note that Zoom displays a prompt asking you to confirm that you want to take this action. Click OK to proceed.
Report	Report a participant who is engaging in inappropriate behavior. (See https://bit.ly/2N6hYA2 for more on this subject.)

TIP

Zoom displays all these options for meeting hosts only. Put differently, these features are role-dependent. For example, Hans is a regular meeting participant, not a host. As such, he can't perform actions such as removing a colleague or promoting himself to co-host.

Using breakout rooms during meetings

You discover the benefits of Zoom's breakout rooms in the earlier section "Enabling breakout rooms during your meetings." To actually break meeting participants into different rooms, however, follow these steps:

1. **Launch the Zoom desktop client.**

2. **Start a new Zoom meeting.**

3. **(Optional) If you've enabled the waiting room, admit your participants.**

4. **Mouse over the menu and click the Breakout Rooms icon.**

   Zoom displays a new window.

5. **Enter the number of breakout rooms into which you want to separate participants.**

6. **Manually or automatically break out meeting participants by selecting the check box that reflects your preference.**

   Zoom displays the window shown in Figure 10-14.

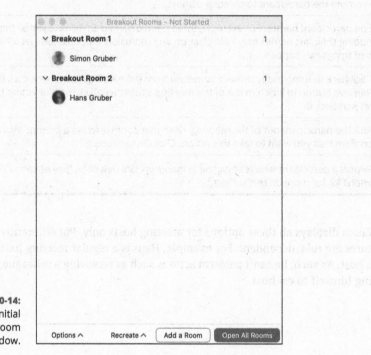

FIGURE 10-14:
The Zoom initial breakout room host window.

7. **Click the blue Open All Rooms button in the lower-right corner of the screen.**

   Zoom shows the meeting host a message indicating that you've now invited all participants into breakout rooms.

   Zoom prompts all meeting participants with an invitation to join the breakout room (see Figure 10-15).

8. **Wait for participants to join their breakout rooms.**

9. **Join participants in those individual rooms by clicking Join next to your desired room.**

   After you activate breakout rooms, Zoom displays Figure 10-16.

10. **To bring all meeting participants back together, click the red Close All Rooms button in the lower-right corner.**

Hosts can do a lot more with breakout rooms, including the following:

›› Renaming them

›› Creating new ones

›› Deleting them

›› Pre-assigning meeting participants to breakout rooms

›› Swapping meeting participants in and out of different rooms

›› Setting expiration times for them

If you're hosting a meeting and using breakout rooms, when you leave, breakout rooms end for everyone. To avoid this scenario, assign another participant the role of co-host before you bolt.

Go to `https://bit.ly/30NHHFp` to learn more about breakout rooms.

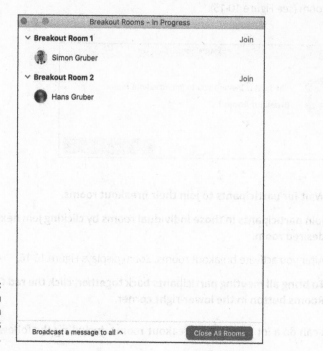

FIGURE 10-16:
The Zoom window with breakout rooms activated.

» **Understanding your status and basic notifications**

» **Chatting with your Zoom contacts**

Chapter **11**

Looking at Zoom Contact Management and Chatting

Sociologists will invariably look back at the early months of 2020 as particularly instructive. Near the top of the list of lessons learned is that video meetings fill essential professional and social needs. At a minimum, they allow untold numbers of people to quickly, easily, and reliably talk to individuals and groups no matter where they are. Make no mistake: This type of synchronous communication is often invaluable, especially when you consider the alternative. Imagine trying to brainstorm an idea or interview a job applicant via email. Plus, in many cases, a quick conversation obviates sending a bevy of perplexing emails.

That's not to say, however, that all communication needs to take place instantaneously. On the contrary, while on *and* off the clock, there remains a legitimate need to send asynchronous messages to others. Odds are that you use email or text messages for this very purpose, but Meetings & Chat performs admirably here, too. In fact, Zoom's functionality often makes it a superior alternative to the tried-and-true inbox.

This chapter explains how to perform many core functions in Meetings & Chat. It covers the Zoom directory, a simple way of managing the people with whom you frequently interact — whether they work for your organization or not. It also discusses setting your status, chatting with others, and customizing notifications.

Managing Your Zoom Contacts

Zoom lets people easily hold video and audio calls with others, whether they're paying customers or not. (Chapter 10 goes deeper into this topic.) Zoom also lets users store their contacts in a dedicated directory.

Although not required, adding contacts to your Meetings & Chat directory offers a number of significant advantages:

>> You can quickly call them and send them text messages, photos, and just about any type of file you want.

>> In a matter of seconds, you can elevate the conversation from one mode (text) to another (audio or video).

>> You can view their statuses to see whether they're busy (see "Understanding User Status in Zoom," later in this chapter).

>> All things being equal, you'll spend less time switching among different communications applications. Your brain will thank you.

Adding contacts to your Zoom directory

At a high level, Zoom's Meetings & Chat directory separates contacts into two buckets:

>> **Internal:** These folks joined as members under your organization's parent Zoom account.

>> **External:** These people have created Zoom accounts independently or through other organizations. Regardless, you can still add them to your personal Meetings & Chat directory.

Adding internal contacts

By default, and as long as your organization subscribes to a premium Zoom plan, your Meetings & Chat directory contains all internal users tied to your account. (See Chapter 8 for more information on Zoom's different plans.) Zoom makes adding external contacts to your directory a piece of cake.

Manually adding a new external contact to your directory

Say that you frequently email Richard, the founder of Pied Piper, a hot new startup in Silicon Valley, California. You're starting to sour on email as a communications tool, though. Because of this, you'd like to move your conversations from email to Zoom.

To add Richard to your Zoom personal directory, follow these steps:

1. Launch the Zoom desktop client.

2. Click the Contacts icon at the top of the screen.

By default, Zoom places you in your directory. Stay here.

3. To the immediate right of the word *Channels*, click the + icon.

4. From the menu that appears, click Add a Contact.

5. Enter the email address of the person you'd like to invite.

6. Click the blue Add button.

7. Click the blue OK button.

Meetings & Chat notifies you if and when the person accepts your invitation. Until then, Zoom displays the word *Pending* to the right of his name under My Contacts.

TIP

Say that you want to add Verna as an external contact to your Meetings & Chat directory. Years ago, she created her Zoom account under verna@bernbaum.net — her main email address. Make sure that you invite her using that one. If you send Verna an invitation to one of her other email addresses (such as verna@coen.com), she'll have to register again under that address to accept your invitation.

TIP

When an outside contact accepts your invitation, Meetings & Chat places the word *External* to the right of the person's name in the sidebar. You see it on the left under the Contacts icon at the top of the page. This label is a not-so-subtle reminder that the person doesn't belong to your organization's Zoom account.

REMEMBER

Just because you invite external contacts to connect with you via Meetings & Chat doesn't mean that they'll accept your invitation.

TIP

Zoom lets users on premium plans import their contacts from smartphones, tablets, or even spreadsheets into their directories. Regarding the latter option, you need to create a specific comma-separated value (CSV) file to import. For more information on this process, go to https://bit.ly/zfd-csv.

Removing an existing contact from your Meetings & Chat directory

Just as in real life, you may decide to break up with someone in Meetings & Chat. Say that you've had it with Jordan and you want to remove him from your directory. To do so, follow these steps:

1. **In the Zoom desktop client, click the Contacts icon at the top of the screen.**

   By default, Zoom places you in your directory. Stay here.

2. **Mouse over the name of the person you want to remove from your Zoom directory.**

   Zoom displays three new icons.

3. **Click on the ellipsis icon to the right of the person's name and choose Delete Contact from the menu that appears.**

   Zoom warns you that deleting the contact will also clear your chat history with that user.

4. **Click the Remove button.**

   Meetings & Chat dutifully banishes the user from your personal directory. If you want to reconnect, you need to re-invite him and hope that he accepts your invitation. The process resembles reconnecting with people on Facebook, LinkedIn, and other social networks.

REMEMBER

Say you're a regular Zoom member and you remove someone from your personal directory. This action is not the same as revoking or deleting that person's Zoom account. An admin or owner needs to do that (see Chapter 9). Only admins and owners can effectively banish others from their organization's Zoom account.

Inviting an existing Zoom contact to a new meeting

Although not imperative, adding Meetings & Chat contacts to your directory offers a number of advantages. For example, you can quickly invite them to meetings by following these steps:

1. **In the Zoom desktop client, click Contacts.**

2. **Right-click the name of the person whom you want to call.**

3. **From the menu that appears, choose Meet with Video or Meet without Video.**

   Zoom rattles off an email with a meeting invitation to that person.

Adding internal contacts to an existing meeting

Maude and Bunny are colleagues in the middle of an existing Zoom meeting. As the meeting host, Maude wants another one of her internal contacts to join the current meeting. To do so, she should follow these directions:

1. **Using the desktop client, click the Participants icon at the bottom of the screen.**

   Zoom displays a new window on the right side of the screen.

2. **Click the Invite icon at the bottom of the screen.**

   Zoom displays a new screen.

3. **Select the name of the contact in your Zoom directory whom you'd like to invite to the meeting.**

TIP

If you want to filter your contacts by name, simply type a few letters of the invitee's name. Zoom automatically restricts your results to people whose names contain those letters.

4. **Click the name of the invitee.**

5. **Click the blue Invite button in the lower-right corner.**

   Zoom indicates that you've successfully invited that person to your meeting.

TIP

Chapter 10 covers how to invite people who don't belong to your Meetings & Chat directory to your meetings.

Performing contact-specific actions

Over the course of sending messages to someone in Meetings & Chat, you may decide that it's time to move to a live meeting. Alternatively, you may want to bring others into the conversation or add the contact to your list of favorites.

Performing each of these actions — and many others — is easy. Just click the downward arrowhead to the right of the contact's name in the sidebar. Meetings & Chat displays the useful options in Figure 11-1.

Table 11-1 describes each of these options in more detail.

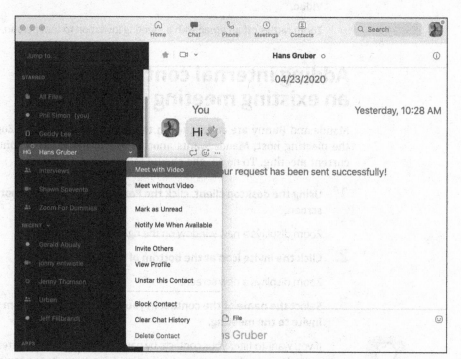

FIGURE 11-1:
Meetings & Chat
contact-specific
actions.

TABLE 11-1 ### Meetings & Chat Contact Actions

Name	Description
Meet with Video	Launches a video meeting and concurrently invites the individual to it. (See Chapter 10 for more information.)
Meet without Video	Launches an audio meeting and concurrently invites the individual to it.
Mark as Unread	Marks the last message that you received from the contact as unread. Zoom also places a numeric badge to the right of the person's name in the sidebar. (See "Chatting in Zoom," later in this chapter, for more on sending messages.)

Name	Description
Notify Me When Available	Alerts you when a person's status changes to active. (If you've ever used Skype, you'll recognize this feature.) Note that Zoom grays out this option if the contact's status is already available. (See "Getting familiar with Zoom's status icons," later in this chapter, for more information.)
Invite Others	Displays a window in which you can invite others to a group chat with the contact.
View Profile	Displays the information that the contact has provided for others to see.
Star/Unstar This Contact	Moves the starred contact to the upper part of your Meetings & Chat directory. Unstarring the contact reverses that action.
Block Contact	Prevents the user from contacting you in Zoom in any way. If you change your mind, you can unblock the user at a later point. Think of blocking as a trial separation, not a divorce.
Clear Chat History	Deletes your previous text-based conversations with the contact or group of contacts. Note that Zoom removes this information for you, but not for the other people participating in your chat.
Delete Contact	Permanently removes the contact from your personal Meetings & Chat directory.

Understanding User Status in Zoom

With a few mouse clicks, Meetings & Chat lets you hold calls and chat with the contacts in your directory. That's all well and good, but what if the person with whom you want to chat is offline or just plain busy?

Thankfully, Zoom lets users easily indicate their availability to everyone else — and vice versa. In this way, Meetings & Chat resembles many of today's popular collaboration tools. Notable examples include Slack (see Part 2) and Microsoft Teams (see Part 4).

Getting familiar with Zoom's status icons

When you look at your new contacts, you see different icons with different colors to the left of their names in the Meetings & Chat sidebar. These icons connote members' statuses. Table 11-2 presents the Meetings & Chat status icons as well as what they mean.

REMEMBER

Status icons are mere suggestions on availability; they're not absolutes. For example, just because Meetings & Chat shows that Steve is available doesn't mean that he necessarily is. He may have closed the Zoom desktop client because he's working on the new Marillion album. (Fingers crossed.)

TABLE 11-2   Meetings & Chat Status Icons

Icon Color and Type	Status	Description
Empty white circle	Offline	Contact has not signed in to either the Zoom desktop client or a mobile app.
Green solid circle	Online (desktop)	Contact has signed in to the Zoom desktop client.
Green outlined rectangle	Online (mobile)	Contact has signed in only to the Zoom mobile app.
Gray circular clock	Away	Contact has signed in to the Zoom desktop client, but either her computer is inactive or she has manually set her status to away.
Red circle with white horizontal line in center	Do Not Disturb (DND)	Contact has manually set his status to DND. He won't receive notifications of new chat messages or phone calls. (For more information on this topic, see "Enabling do-not-disturb mode," later in this chapter.)
Red video camera	In a Zoom meeting	Contact has started a Zoom meeting or joined one.
Red video camera	Presenting	Contact is sharing her screen while in a Zoom meeting.
Red telephone	On a call	Contact is currently participating on a Zoom Phone call.
Red calendar	In a calendar event	Contact is currently participating in an event on his calendar but is not in a Zoom meeting.
Red circle with white exclamation point	Chat error	Zoom failed to send the contact your chat message and/or file.

Figure 11-2 displays the current status icons for a user's internal and external Zoom contacts.

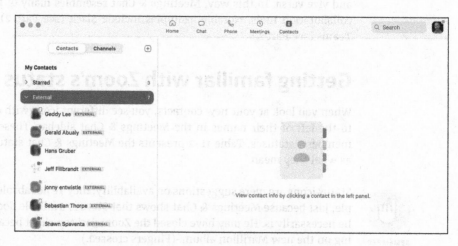

As you can see, Johnny and Gerald are free at the moment. For their part, Jeff and Shawn are currently in Zoom meetings.

REMEMBER

Contacts who are currently in Zoom meetings are almost always unavailable.

Changing your status in Meetings & Chat

By default, when you're logged in to the Zoom desktop client, Meetings & Chat sets your status as online. Your colleagues will certainly know as much if they bother to look at your status. If they do, they'll see a green solid circle appear in the upper-right corner of your profile image.

It's natural for others in your Zoom directory to assume that green means go. As a result, they may call you and/or chat with you. (The upcoming section "Chatting in Zoom" covers messages.) These actions will interrupt your flow.

Yes, you can quit the Zoom desktop client, but that extreme action comes with downsides. Most obviously, you can't use any of the features in Meetings & Chat. For example, you can bid *adieu* to accessing your prior conversations and finding valuable information.

What to do? Fortunately, Meetings & Chat provides a few options for people who want to keep the application open but, at the same time, don't want others pestering them.

Marking yourself as away

First, you can mark yourself as away. In theory, this status discourages others from pestering you in Zoom. In practice, though, your mileage here may vary.

To indicate that you're away, follow these steps:

1. **In the Zoom desktop client, click your profile image.**

   It lies to the immediate right of the search bar.

2. **From the menu, click Away.**

   When you're ready to indicate to others that you're available, simply click your profile image and then click Available.

Enabling do-not-disturb mode

Unfortunately, your away status may not deter your colleagues from calling you. They may still send you messages and expect an immediate response. When they do, Meetings & Chat promptly notifies you of these messages and calls.

To ignore them and focus, do you have to quit Zoom? You do not.

To prevent others from bugging you, just enable Zoom's DND mode. When you do, Meetings & Chat knows not to interrupt you. In this way, Zoom works just like the comparable functionality on your smartphone.

Enable DND mode by following these instructions:

1. **In the Zoom desktop client, click your profile image.**

2. **From the menu, click Do Not Disturb.**

3. **(Optional) Indicate the length of time that you want to be left alone.**

You're enabling DND mode here for a limited amount of time.

4. **(Optional) Select Set a Time Period to enable DND mode for daily intervals.**

Zoom launches a new window in which you can change many of your account settings and defaults.

5. **Scroll down to the bottom of the screen.**

6. **Select the Do Not Disturb From check box.**

7. **From the drop-down list, select the hours during which you want Zoom to leave you alone.**

WARNING

Meetings & Chat strictly obeys your preferences here. For example, say that you select 4 a.m. until 10 p.m. by mistake. Don't expect Zoom to send you any notifications during those 18 hours. Whether someone urgently tries to track you down by other means, however, is another matter.

8. **Close the Settings window by clicking the red circle in the upper-left corner of the screen.**

Regardless of how you've enabled DND mode, Meetings & Chat sends you notifications only when your period lapses.

Adding a personal note to your profile

You may find Zoom's current menu of statuses to be a bit limiting. (When it comes to user statuses, Meetings & Chat trails Slack, covered in Part 2, but that's neither here nor there.) At least Meetings & Chat lets you add a personal note to your profile. Follow these steps:

1. **In the Zoom desktop client, click your profile image.**

2. **From the drop-down menu under your email address, click the Add a Personal Note text box.**

   Meetings & Chat restricts you to 60 characters.

3. **Enter a few words, and then press Enter on your keyboard.**

Now the contacts in your directory can see a bit more information about you when viewing your profile.

Staying current with Zoom notifications

Unless you've enabled DND mode, by default Meetings & Chat notifies you when your contacts send you messages and try to call you. Still, it's not hard to envision other scenarios that warrant your attention — that is, apart from people trying to directly contact you.

Depending on how you use Meetings & Chat and the number of people in your directory, you may find its notifications a tad overwhelming. Here's one way that you can tweak them:

1. **In the Zoom desktop client, click your profile image.**

2. **Choose Settings in the menu that appears.**

3. **On the left side of the screen, click the Chat icon at the top of the screen.**

4. **Under Push Notifications, select the circumstances under which you want to receive notifications.**

   If you select Only Private Messages or Mentions, Zoom won't notify you when new activity in your group chats takes place. (You can still view related badges in the sidebar at your leisure, though.)

   If you select Nothing, you won't hear a peep from Zoom. The same disclaimer about badges applies, however.

5. **Close the Settings window by clicking the red circle in the upper-left corner of the screen.**

TIP

Say that you selected the Notify Me When Available feature for a contact who is currently in a Zoom meeting. Meetings & Chat displays a little red bell to the right of the contact's name in the sidebar.

Chatting in Zoom

Say you run into your boss, Kim, in the hallway. You start talking about a few things, but she's in a rush to get to a meeting. She asks you to shoot her a quick reminder of what you briefly discussed so that she can review it later.

For far too many people today, the message in that simple example reflexively takes the form of a proper email. Zoom provides users with another — and some would say better — option: Send that note via Meetings & Chat. Its rich message functionality makes it a valid email alternative, especially for internal company communications.

Exchanging messages with your individual Zoom contacts

Geddy Lee is the lead singer and bassist extraordinaire of the legendary Canadian rock group Rush. Say that you connect with Geddy on Zoom. (Dare to dream.) You'd love to congratulate him on the release of his first book, *Geddy Lee's Big Beautiful Book of Bass* (Harper Design), and give him a quick call. Chapter 10 describes how easy that is to do. Because you don't want to seem pushy, though, you hesitate. Ringing him — much less initiating a Zoom video call with him — out of the blue seems a bit presumptuous.

You decide you want to send Geddy a quick Zoom message. To do so, follow these steps:

1. **In the Zoom desktop client, click Contacts.**

2. **Click the name of the contact to whom you want to send a message.**

3. **Click the Chat button on the right side of the screen.**

    This button appears underneath the contact's profile picture, as Figure 11-3 displays.

    Zoom places the cursor in the text box at the bottom of the screen.

4. **Type your message.**

5. **Press the Enter key on your keyboard.**

    Figure 11-4 displays the message that you might send Geddy congratulating him on his new book.

Zoom often offers several ways to accomplish the same task. Don't be surprised if you stumble across one of them as you play around with Meetings & Chat.

TIP

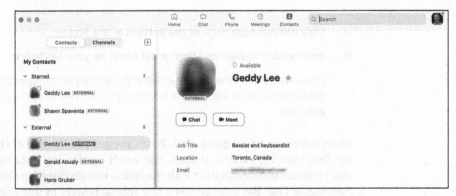

FIGURE 11-3:
The Chat button under a contact's profile picture.

FIGURE 11-4:
A simple Zoom message to an individual.

Holding group chats

To be sure, the idea of a one-on-one chat is invaluable. Zoom would be pretty limited as a communication medium, however, if it could accommodate messages only between two individuals. Fortunately, you don't have to worry. Meetings & Chat is more than up to the task.

Starting a new group chat

What if you want to concurrently exchange messages with David, Tim, and Gareth? Zoom's process for initiating a group chat is nearly identical to one covered in the earlier section "Exchanging messages with your individual Zoom contacts":

1. **In the Zoom desktop client, click the Chat icon at the top of the screen.**

2. **In the sidebar, click the + to the right of Recent.**

3. **Choose New Chat from the menu that Zoom displays.**

4. **At the top of the screen next to To, type a few letters of the names of the people you want to invite to the group chat.**

   Their names should automatically appear.

5. **Click the message pane at the bottom of the screen.**

6. **Enter your message and then press Enter on your keyboard.**

   Depending on whether they're active and how they've configured their notifications, Zoom alerts those folks that you're trying to start a group chat with them.

When you begin a new group chat, Zoom assigns you the role of chat administrator. Don't get too excited, though. You won't receive any gifts in the mail. Also, don't confuse this designation with the admin role discussed in Chapter 9. Instead, Meetings & Chat has granted you a few special powers in this group chat. You — and only you — can do the following:

» Delete the group chat altogether (see "Editing and deleting your messages," later in this chapter).

» Designate another participant as the chat admin if you decide to leave the discussion (see "Leaving a group chat," next).

Leaving a group chat

If you're like most people, you've become entangled in a few insufferable email threads over your career. After all, it takes inconsiderate or clueless people very little time to carbon copy (CC) you on their messages.

If this happens to you in Meetings & Chat, fret not. Zoom makes extricating yourself from pointless or low-priority group chats easy. Just do the following:

1. **In the Zoom desktop client, click the Chat icon at the top of the screen.**

2. **In the sidebar, click the existing discussion that you want to leave.**

   Zoom highlights it in blue.

3. **Click the arrow to display a drop-down list and then select Leave Chat.**

   If you're the chat admin, Zoom presents you with three options (see Figure 11-5):

   • **Delete Discussion:** You'll be removing the discussion for all current participants. If you select this option, Zoom prompts you with another window to ensure that you want to eradicate it. Click the red Delete Discussion button to finish the kill.

   • **Cancel:** You'll return to the previous screen. You can still participate in the group chat.

REMEMBER

- **(Optional) Assign New Admin:** You'll be delegating admin rights of this group chat to another current participant. If you go this route, you'll need to select that person in an additional next step. Finally, complete the process by clicking the blue Assign button.

  Zoom allows you to assign a new admin to the chat only if you started it or if someone else assigned you that role.

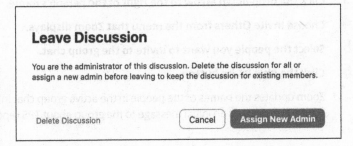

FIGURE 11-5: The Meetings & Chat prompt for leaving a group chat that you initiated.

Leave Discussion

You are the administrator of this discussion. Delete the discussion for all or assign a new admin before leaving to keep the discussion for existing members.

Delete Discussion   Cancel   **Assign New Admin**

4. **Select your desired option.**

REMEMBER

   Say that you're a regular participant in this group chat. That is, you're not the admin. In this case, Meetings & Chat offers you a more limited menu of options when you want to bolt: Cancel and Leave Discussion. Because of your limited role, this restriction makes complete sense.

   After you leave, Meetings & Chat removes your name from the group chat in the sidebar.

TIP

When you're in a group of people in real life (or IRL, as the kids say), it's polite to say goodbye prior to leaving. The same principle applies here: Don't just bolt from a group chat. It's best to send the group a message explaining why you're leaving.

Inviting others to an existing group chat

Conversations are sometimes like improvisational jazz. That is, they occasionally take unexpected turns. For example, Taylor, Nate, and Pat are chatting about hiring Chris as the band's new guitarist. Eventually, talks get serious, and it makes sense to bring Dave into the fold. Yeah, the three of them could forward Dave a bunch of separate chat messages, but that method is so 1998.

Fortunately, you don't need to create a new Zoom group chat and start from scratch. Meetings & Chat makes it insanely easy to add others to an existing discussion, allowing newbies to quickly catch up on all the previous back-and-forth. (Foo Fighters' fans will get that last reference.)

Just follow these steps:

1. **In the Zoom desktop client, click the Chat icon at the top of the screen.**

2. **In the sidebar, click the existing discussion to which you want to add another person.**

   Zoom highlights it in blue.

3. **Click the drop-down arrow to the right of the person's name.**

4. **Choose Invite Others from the menu that Zoom displays.**

5. **Select the people you want to invite to the group chat.**

6. **Click the blue Invite button.**

   Zoom updates the names of the people in the active group chat in the sidebar. Figure 11-6 displays an initial message to the group about TPS reports.

FIGURE 11-6: A simple group-chat message.

Creating threads in Zoom

You and your colleague Ricky have exchanged a series of ten discrete messages, but you want to respond to a specific one. Say that he made a comment a week ago that you let slide. Upon further reflection, however, something about that message confused you. Now you'd like to revisit it. Is there an easy way to refer to that prior message?

Like many modern communications tools, Meetings & Chat lets users create threads for specific messages. (If a Zoom thread sounds suspiciously like its email counterpart, trust your judgment.) This optional feature provides much-needed context to messages, especially if you and your colleague(s) have exchanged a bunch of them.

To create a thread on an existing message, follow these steps:

1. In the Zoom desktop client, click the Chat icon at the top of the screen.

2. Locate the specific message in the thread to which you want to respond.

As you hover over the message, Zoom displays a few icons.

3. Click the chat-bubble icon.

It's the first one.

4. Type your message and press Enter.

When you create a thread, Meetings & Chat indents your message and future ones in response to it. You and others can easily see that the thread stands apart from the other, unthreaded messages (see Figure 11-7).

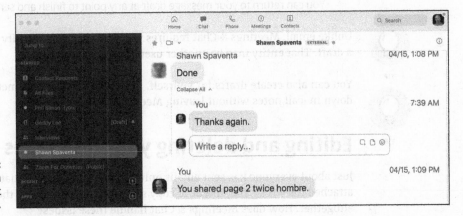

FIGURE 11-7:
An example of a
Meetings & Chat
thread.

TIP

Threads are über-useful. Used properly, they minimize confusion and save everyone a good bit of time.

Saving message drafts

Have you ever spent 30 minutes drafting a critical email, only to get distracted? Alternatively, maybe you've composed your message and want to send it. A voice inside you, however, is telling you to think long and hard about hitting Send on a message that slams some of your colleagues.

Just about every email program auto-saves drafts these days — and has for years. This feature allows users to return to email drafts when it's convenient for them. In a move that should surprise exactly no one, Zoom does the very same thing. Just follow these steps:

1. **In the Zoom desktop client, click Contacts.**

2. **Click the name of the contact to whom you want to send a message.**

   Zoom places your cursor in the message window.

3. **Type your message, but don't press Enter.**

4. **Click another contact name or icon at the top of the screen.**

   Zoom auto-saves your draft and even places the text *[Draft]* in red to the right of the contact's name.

   You can return to your message draft at any point to finish and send it.

TIP Unlike email, Meetings & Chat requires you to first select an entity before creating a draft. That entity may be another user, group, or channel.

TIP You can also create drafts for yourself. Some users prefer this method for jotting down in-call notes without leaving Meetings & Chat.

Editing and deleting your messages

Just about everyone has sent emails only later to have realized that they goofed — attached the wrong file, forgot to copy a key person, or emailed the wrong person altogether. How does Meetings & Chat handle these issues?

Say you sent Boris message by accident, and you want to take it back. No, Meetings & Chat won't erase Boris's memory if he has already read your message. You can't use it to summon hired goons to show up at his house. Still, you can delete it and minimize the chance that he views your errant note.

Delete a message that you previously sent by following these steps:

1. **In the Zoom desktop client, click the Chat icon at the top of the screen.**

2. **Locate the specific message that you want to remove.**

   As you hover over the message, Zoom displays a few icons.

3. **Click the ellipsis icon and then click the Delete button.**

   And like that, it's gone.

Perhaps your mistake is more benign, like typos or misspellings. Edit your sent message by following these instructions:

1. **In the Zoom desktop client, click the Chat icon at the top of the screen.**

2. **Locate the specific message you want to change.**

   As you hover over the message, Zoom displays a few icons.

3. **Click the ellipsis icon and choose Edit from the menu that appears.**

4. **Make whatever changes you like to your message.**

5. **Click the Save button.**

   Note that Meetings & Chat displays the text *(Edited)* to the right of your original message next to its date and time. In this way, Zoom lets everyone in the chat see that you've altered your original message. Zoom is nothing if not transparent.

For obvious reasons, Meetings & Chat prohibits users from editing and deleting others' messages.

Referencing other Zoom members in a group discussion

Say you're in a group chat with six other members, but you only want to ask Steven a question. It's best to specifically mention him using the @ symbol. This way, he'll likely receive a notification in Meetings & Chat.

To reference a specific member of a group chat, follow these steps:

1. **In the Zoom desktop client, click the Chat icon at the top.**

2. **In the sidebar, click a specific discussion.**

   Zoom highlights it in blue.

3. **Type @.**

   Zoom displays a list of the people involved in the current group chat.

4. **Select the name of the person you want to reference.**

   Zoom inserts that person's name in the message window in blue with the @ sign in front of it.

5. **Type the rest of your message and press Enter.**

Use @all to notify every chat participant.

Adding some flair to your messages

Sending a simple, format-free message often gets the job done. For example, when responding to a simple question of when today's meeting starts, you don't need to underline and bold your text. Sometimes, though, a little message styling does wonders. For example, bullet points often make sense for meeting agendas.

Table 11-3 lists the current rich-text formatting options that Meetings & Chat offers.

TABLE 11-3

Rich-Text Message Formatting Options in Meetings & Chat

Icon	Description
B	Bolds text
I	Italicizes text.
S	Applies strikethrough style.
* —	Creates a bulleted list.

Applying different formats to your text

To apply a style to specific text in your message, follow these steps:

1. **In the Zoom desktop client, create a new text message.**

2. **Type some text, but don't send the message just yet.**

3. **Highlight the text that you want to format.**

4. **In the formatting window that appears, click the format that you'd like to apply to the selected text.**

   Zoom applies that format to that text — and only that text.

5. **Press Enter to send your rich-text message.**

Figure 11-8 displays a simple agenda with bullet points.

TIP

Hold down the Shift key and press the Enter key twice to create new paragraphs in your messages.

FIGURE 11-8:
A Zoom message
with bullet points.

Adding emojis and animated GIFs

But what about emojis and animated GIFs? Surely Meetings & Chat lets its users add these modern staples to messages, right?

To add either one of these accoutrements to your message, follow these steps:

1. **In the Zoom desktop client, create a text message.**

2. **Click the smiley-face icon on the right side of the screen.**

Zoom displays the emoji and animated-GIF picker (see Figure 11-9).

3. **Select the emoji or animated GIF that you want to add to your message.**

4. **Press Enter.**

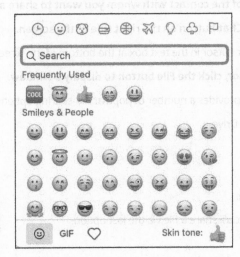

FIGURE 11-9:
The Zoom
emoji and
animated-GIF
picker.

Speaking of emojis, Zoom doesn't make you send new messages to use them. In fact, you can add one as a response to someone else's message as follows:

1. **In the Zoom desktop client, click the Chat icon at the top of the screen.**

2. **Locate the specific message to which you want to add an emoji.**

   As you hover over the message, Zoom displays a few icons.

3. **Click the smiley face.**

4. **Select your preferred emoji.**

Uploading and sharing files in Zoom

You run into your boss Kim in the hallway. She asks you to send her the latest version of your Microsoft PowerPoint deck. She'd like to review it and give you notes.

Fulfilling her request does not necessitate scheduling a meeting and discussing it for ten minutes. (Of course, an actual conversation may make sense down the road, but that's not important now.) In this scenario, you can certainly rattle her off an email and attach your file to it. You've probably performed that task hundreds or thousands of times. Again, though, a Zoom message also gets the job done.

Sharing files with other Zoom members

To send someone a file in Meetings & Chat, follow these steps:

1. **In the Zoom desktop client, click Contacts.**

2. **Click the name of the contact with whom you want to share a file.**

3. **Click the white Chat button on the right side of the screen.**

   Zoom places your cursor in the text box at the bottom of the screen.

4. **Above your cursor, click the File button to display a window.**

   Meetings & Chat provides a number of popular file-sharing options, including

   - Microsoft OneDrive

   - Google Drive

   - Box

   - Your computer

   In this example, you'll share a file via the last option.

5. Double-click the file that you want to share.

Zoom uploads the file to the chat.

Figure 11-10 displays a file sent to Geddy — a copy of the cover of *Slack For Dummies*.

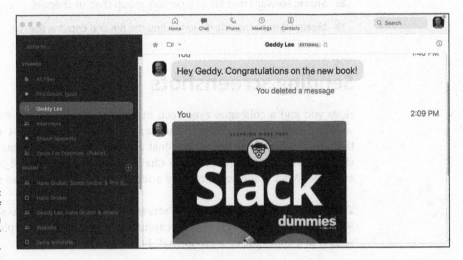

FIGURE 11-10:
An example of
a file shared with
a Zoom user
via chat.

You also upload files to channels in this manner.

TIP

Quickly accessing your Zoom files

Imagine having to track down all your files in different Zoom chats. The word *cumbersome* comes to mind. Thankfully, Meetings & Chat lets you access all your shared files in one place by following these steps:

1. In the Zoom desktop client, click the Chat icon at the top of the screen.

2. At the top of the sidebar, click All Files.

On the right, Zoom displays two tabs:

- **My Files:** Access all the files you've uploaded to Meetings & Chat.

- **All Files:** Access all the files that others have shared with you directly, via group chats, and via channels.

3. Click either tab to see related files.

4. (Optional) Double-click a file to open it.

Zoom launches the file's default program on your computer.

TIP

Meetings & Chat lets you do far more, however, than just open previously shared files. You can perform a number of other quick actions by mousing over them and clicking one of the following three icons that appear:

>> **Download:** Save this file to your computer.

>> **Share:** Forward that file to a person, group chat, or channel.

>> **More:** Options include downloading the file and copying the file.

Sending screenshots

Have you and a colleague ever been in separate places as you viewed the same website, code, or spreadsheet? She has identified an error. For the life of you, though, you just don't see it. You just aren't connecting the dots. Sure, you can share your screen via Meetings & Chat, but that only works if both of you are available. What if she could capture a screenshot, mark it up, and send it to you?

Truth be told, the idea of sending a screenshot isn't exactly earth-shattering. Still, Meetings & Chat makes it easy to capture your screen, add simple markups, and send it to a colleague or a group chat. Just follow these steps:

1. **In the Zoom desktop client, click the Chat icon at the top of the screen.**

2. **In the sidebar, click the person to whom you want to send a screenshot.**

    Zoom highlights the person's name in blue.

3. **Above the message prompt, click the Screenshot icon.**

4. **Zoom lets you crop the part of your computer screen that you want to share.**

5. **(Optional) Mark up your image by using the icons that appear below the screen:**

    - **Drawing:** Draw whatever you like on the screen.

    - **Arrow:** Easily point to specific areas by inserting an arrow.

    - **Box:** Insert a box.

    - **Circle:** Insert a circle.

    - **Text:** Enter whatever text you like.

    - **Download:** Download the screenshot to your computer.

    - **Undo:** Reverse your previous action.

    - **Cancel:** Abandon ship and abort.

6. **Click the Capture button (see Figure 11-11).**

   Zoom includes the screenshot along with your message.

7. **Press the Enter key on your keyboard to send the message.**

   Zoom includes the screenshot along with your message.

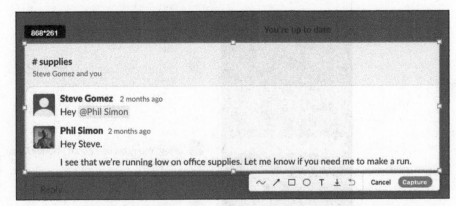

FIGURE 11-11:
Taking a
screenshot in
Zoom.

Performing message-specific actions

It turns out that you can do some other cool things with Zoom messages. Click the ellipsis icon to the right of a message. In turn, Meetings & Chat displays the useful options in Table 11-4.

TABLE 11-4 ## Zoom Message-Specific Actions

Name	Description
Share Message	Forward the message to another Zoom contact, group chat, or channel. This action resembles forwarding emails.
Copy	Copy the message's text to your computer's clipboard.
Follow Message	Ideal for messages in group threads and channels that don't specifically mention you with the @ symbol. Enabling it means that Meetings & Chat will send you a notification of new activity in the conversation.
Star Message	Places the message at the top of the Zoom desktop client in the Starred Messages container.
Mark as Unread	Much like email, restores the new message notification badge in Zoom in the sidebar next to the contact's name.

Figure 11-12 displays these actions in context.

TIP

For more information on Zoom's robust chat functionality, go to `https://bit.ly/zfd-chats`.

FIGURE 11-12:
Zoom
message-specific
actions.

4

Taking Advantage of Microsoft Teams

Chapter 12

Navigating Microsoft Teams

Opening Microsoft Teams for the first time can feel overwhelming. The reason for this is that Microsoft has added a jaw-dropping number of features to Teams over the last couple of years, bringing Teams to feature parity with Skype and Skype for Business. All this useful stuff is nice when you need it, but it can be overwhelming when you first start to use it.

In this chapter, you discover how to navigate the Teams app. You download, install, and open the app on your computer and then get a feel for the layout and how to navigate through the interface. You also look at how Teams can be used across multiple devices.

TIP

Visit `https://365trainingportal.com/teams` for helpful Teams training resources. To keep up with the ever-changing features of Microsoft Teams, check out the blog at `https://techcommunity.microsoft.com/t5/microsoft-teams-blog/bg-p/MicrosoftTeamsBlog`.

Downloading, Installing, and Opening Teams

You can use Teams in three primary ways: You can use the web-based app, you can install the client on your laptop or desktop computer, or you can install the Teams mobile app on your smartphone or tablet. Regardless of how you use Teams, the concepts remain the same. In this section, you first log in to the web-based app and then install the client on your desktop.

On the web

To log in to the web-based version of Teams, follow these steps:

1. **Open your favorite web browser and navigate to** https://teams.microsoft.com.

2. **Log in using the account credentials you created when you signed up for the Office 365 trial.**

   If you haven't yet signed up for the Office 365 trial and a Teams account, go to www.office.com. Click the Get Office button, and then click the For Business tab to see the available business plans. Scroll to the bottom of the page and click the Try Free for 1 Month link under the Office 365 Business Premium plan. Provide the requested information, and walk through the setup wizard to get up and running with Office 365.

3. **When presented with the option to download Teams or use the web app, click the Use the Web App Instead link.**

   After logging in, you're presented with the main Teams app running inside your web browser (see Figure 12-1).

Many people just use this web-based experience to use Teams. However, you may prefer the client that you can download and install on your PC (see the next section). It has much more functionality and integrates better with devices like a headset for making phone calls and a webcam for making video calls.

FIGURE 12-1:
Microsoft Teams
running in a web
browser.

On a laptop or desktop computer

To install the Teams client on your laptop or desktop computer running Microsoft Windows, follow these steps:

1. **Open your web browser and navigate to** https://teams.microsoft.com.

   If you haven't yet logged in to the web app (see the previous section), you're asked to log in. If you've already logged in, you see the Teams web app displayed in your browser (refer to Figure 12-1).

2. **Log in to the Teams site by entering the credentials you've set up, if you aren't already logged in.**

   When you first log in to the Teams site (https://teams.microsoft.com), you're presented with the option of installing the Teams client or continuing to the web app. In the previous section, you continued to the web app. Here, you install the desktop client.

3. **Click your profile icon in the upper-right corner and choose Download the Desktop App (see Figure 12-2).**

4. **Save the file to your computer.**

TIP

You can set the location on your computer's hard drive where your web browser downloads files. By default, files are usually set to download to the Downloads folder, which is where all downloads are stored. If you can't find the file you downloaded, check the configuration for your web browser to see where it places files it has downloaded.

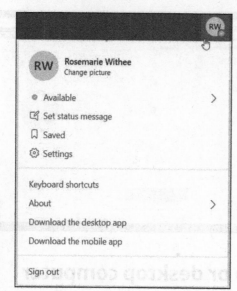

FIGURE 12-2:
Your profile
drop-down menu
has options to
install the
desktop and
mobile apps.

5. **After the Teams setup file has downloaded, open and run the file.**

   After a few moments, a dialog box appears asking you to sign in (see Figure 12-3).

FIGURE 12-3:
A sign-in dialog
box appears
when Teams first
installs.

6. **Enter your username and click Sign In.**

If you've already signed in to Teams using your web browser, you won't be asked for your password again.

The Teams client loads and lets you know that there is one last step to get Teams set up and connected to Microsoft Office (see Figure 12-4).

FIGURE 12-4:
A dialog box lets you know Teams will now be connected to Office.

One more step to set up Teams with Office

Click **Let's do it**, then click **Yes** in the next screen to get everything hooked up.

Let's do it

7. **Click Let's Do It to continue, and then click Yes to allow Teams to make changes to your computer.**

Teams works in the background to connect with Office on your computer and then loads the Teams application (see Figure 12-5).

Congratulations! You now have Teams running on your local computer.

FIGURE 12-5:
The Teams client running on your local computer.

Taking a Quick Spin around Teams

If you've been following along, you may notice that Teams running in the client on your computer (Figure 12-5) looks a lot like Teams running from within your web browser (Figure 12-1). Microsoft did this on purpose. This way, if you usually use Teams on your desktop computer at work and find yourself logging in to Teams using a web browser on your computer at home, you don't have to worry about learning a different interface.

Primary navigation appears on the left side of the screen and includes the following icons (refer to Figure 12-5): Activity, Chat, Teams, Calendar, Calls, and Files. Clicking one of these main options opens the associated screen in the main part of the app.

Activity

If you click the Activity icon in the navigation pane, you see your feed (see Figure 12-6). In the Activity feed, you find your notifications about things going on around Teams that you may find interesting. For example, if there is an unread message in a channel or someone sends you a chat message, it appears in your Activity feed. Think of the Activity feed as your one-stop shop for everything that has happened in Teams since you were last there.

FIGURE 12-6:
The Activity feed
in Teams.

TIP

Teams can get very noisy very quickly. Just a handful of people chatting and carrying on is enough to tempt you to ignore it entirely. Using the Activity feed, you can tune in to only the things that are important to you.

Chat

The Chat area is where you find all your personal and group chats. There is a subtle difference between conversations in chats and conversations in channels. You can think of chats as *ad hoc* messages to one other person or a few other people. Chats come and go and are spontaneous, whereas a channel is a dedicated area that persists and where people can communicate about a particular topic. (See Chapter 14 for more about channels and chatting.)

Teams

The Teams area is where you'll likely spend all your time. Yes, the product is called Teams and the navigation component is also called Teams (refer to the left side of Figure 12-5). And within the Teams navigation component you have individual teams called a *team*. Confused yet? It will become clear shortly.

Clicking the Teams icon in the left navigation pane opens all the Teams you're a member of. In Figure 12-5, you can see that Rosemarie is a member of only one team: Portal Integrators LLC. This is the team that showed up by default when she created the Office 365 subscription. Within the Portal Integrators team is a channel called General, which is the default channel that is created automatically when a new Team is created. If she were to click the General channel, she could see all the chats going on in the channel. In Figure 12-5, it's empty because she was the only person in the team and in the channel. (Chapter 13 covers working with teams, and Chapter 14 covers working with channels.)

Calendar

The Calendar area is focused on your calendar of events and meetings (see Figure 12-7). If you've ever scheduled a meeting in Microsoft Outlook, you'll be familiar with working with your calendar in Teams. The calendar area is where you can have real-time meetings (see Chapter 15).

WARNING

The Calendar is integrated with Microsoft Outlook. If you don't have Outlook installed on your desktop computer or laptop, you won't see the Calendar in Teams.

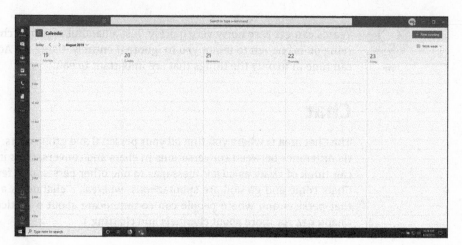

FIGURE 12-7:
The Calendar in
Teams.

Calls

The Calls area is where you can make and receive phone calls (see Figure 12-8). If you've ever used Skype, this area will feel familiar to you.

Files

The Files area is where you can save and share digital files (see Figure 12-9). If you've ever used SharePoint or Microsoft OneDrive, you'll be happy to learn that you're already ahead of the game. Teams uses SharePoint and OneDrive behind the scenes, and at any point you can jump out of Teams and open the same files in the SharePoint or OneDrive applications.

FAST AND FASTER

Microsoft moves fast with iterating on its software these days. In the past, you could expect a new version every few years. Now, a new version of software seems to be available every month. Most of the changes in new versions involve new features and bug fixes. But occasionally, the user interfaces change, too. For example, the Calendar section in the Teams navigation pane used to be called "Meetings." After the Teams software updated one night, it turned out that the underlying functionality of the Calendar section was the same as Meetings, but the name of the button to navigate to it had changed.

So, as you're reading and learning about Teams, keep in mind that although exact names and wordings of things may change, the concepts will remain the same. For updates, visit https://techcommunity.microsoft.com/t5/microsoft-teams-blog/bg-p/MicrosoftTeamsBlog.

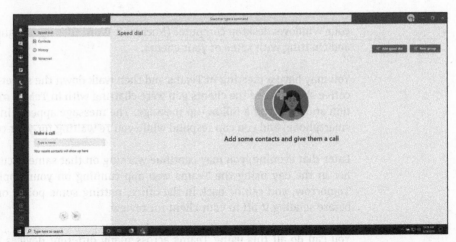

FIGURE 12-8: The Calls area of Teams.

FIGURE 12-9: The Files area of Teams.

TIP

In addition to SharePoint and OneDrive, you can also set up other cloud-based locations for your files and access them all from within Teams. Currently Teams supports Box, Dropbox, Google Drive, and ShareFile; others will likely follow in the coming days.

Using Teams across Many Devices and Platforms

One of the things people really enjoy about using Teams is that it doesn't matter what device they're using; they can instantly pick up where they left off. For example, you may be at your office working on a document inside of Teams on your Windows desktop computer (Microsoft Word files open right within Teams) and chatting with some of your clients.

You may have a meeting in Teams and then walk down the street to your favorite coffee shop. One of the clients you were chatting with in Teams may have a question and send you a follow-up message. The message appears in Teams on your smartphone, and you can respond while you're waiting for your coffee.

Later that evening, you may continue working on that same document from earlier in the day using the Teams web app running on your Apple MacBook Air. Tomorrow, you can be back in the office, putting some polish on the document before sending it off to your client for review.

You can do all this using Teams across many different devices and places, and because Teams is synced through the cloud (the Internet), you don't lose your train of thought and work that was in progress. Teams on all your devices are always in sync. That's one of the best things about working with an app born in the cloud, like Teams. Figure 12-10 illustrates a day using Teams.

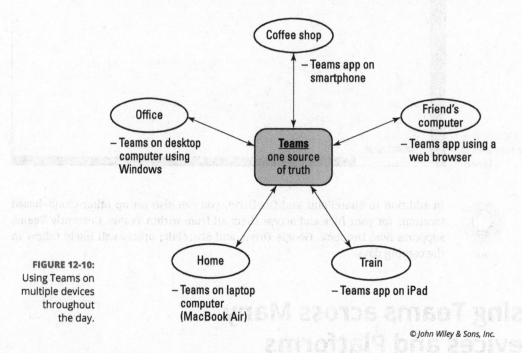

FIGURE 12-10: Using Teams on multiple devices throughout the day.

© John Wiley & Sons, Inc.

Chapter **13**

Starting Your First Team and Managing Your Settings

One of the nice things about Microsoft Teams is that the name of it says it all. Teams is about communicating and collaborating with other people as part of a team. At the heart of the Teams app is a team of people. A *team* in the context of Microsoft Teams consists of a group of one or more people (though a team of one is boring). Within a team is where you create channels to chat, share files among teammates, use apps, and do all sorts of other nifty things.

In this chapter, you find out how to create a new team and invite others to that team. You also discover how to manage the team you created and personalize each team's settings.

Creating a New Team

When you first log in to Microsoft Teams, you see that a default Team has been created for you automatically using the account information you provide when you first signed up for Microsoft 365, Office 365, or the stand-alone Teams app. (You can find a reminder on how to log in to Teams in Chapter 12.)

Many people may just use the default Team and don't realize they can create more teams. However, creating new teams involves only a few steps.

When you create a new team, you can customize it and build it out the way you want for your specific situation. For example, you may want the team to be private instead of the default organization-wide team that is created that everyone is automatically a member of. You may also want to create a team for a focus area, such as human resources or accounting. After you've spent a little bit of time in Teams, you'll find yourself creating new teams and trimming old teams as a regular habit.

To create a new Team, follow these steps:

1. **Open Microsoft Teams.**

2. **Click the Teams icon in the left navigation pane and then click the Join or Create a Team link that appears in the lower-left corner of the screen (see Figure 13-1).**

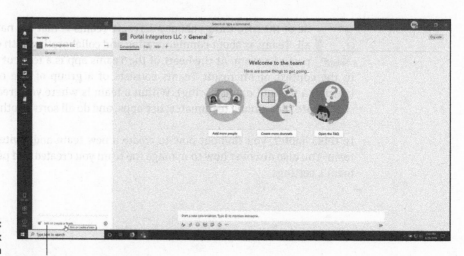

FIGURE 13-1:
Clicking the link to join or create a new team.

Click to create a new team

TIP

If you don't see the Join or Create a Team link, two situations may be at play. The first, and most likely, is that you're a guest user to Teams and, thus, have restricted access to the Office 365 and Teams products. If you're a licensed member of the organization but you still don't see the ability to create a new team, your administrators have likely locked down the Office 365 tenant your organization is using. If that's the case, contact your administrator in order to create a new team.

3. **Click the Create Team button (see Figure 13-2).**

The Create Your Team dialog box appears. You can choose to create a team based on an existing group of users in Office 365, or create a team from scratch. For this example, you create a team from scratch.

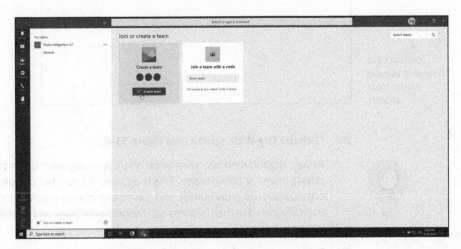

FIGURE 13-2: Click the Create Team button to start creating a new team.

4. **Click the Build a Team from Scratch option (see Figure 13-3).**

Next, you need to decide what type of team you want to create. You have three options:

- *Private:* A private team requires members to have permission to join.

- *Public:* A public team is one that anyone can join.

- *Org-wide:* An organization-wide team is one that everyone in the organization belongs to automatically when they log in to Teams.

For this example, you create an org-wide team that everyone belongs to automatically so that you don't have to worry about adding people. (Find out how to add members to your teams later in this chapter.)

Create your team

Build a team from scratch

Create from...
An existing Office 365 group or team

What's a team?

FIGURE 13-3:
Choosing to build
a team from
scratch.

5. **Click the Org-Wide option (see Figure 13-4).**

TIP

As your organization becomes larger, you'll probably want to start using either private teams or public teams. This is because the number of teams within an organization can grow quickly, and if everyone in your organization is automatically joined to them, Teams can become very noisy and people may start to ignore it.

6. **Enter a name and description for your new team and then click Create (see Figure 13-5).**

Teams takes a few moments and goes about its work of creating a new team for you. When it's done, the new team appears in your list of teams in the left navigation pane (see Figure 13-6). Notice that when the new team was created, a channel called General was automatically created. Chapter 14 covers how to create additional channels for your team.

As a user of Teams, you can be a team owner, a team member, or a guest. A team owner doesn't have to be the person who created the team. In fact, a team can have up to 100 team owners. Team owners can manage the team, which includes the ability to add members, approve or deny requests to join the team, create channels, change the team settings, view analytics, and add apps. A guest user is a nonlicensed user who has limited access and who must be invited to each team explicitly. A user can join a team either by receiving an invite to join or request to join an existing team. If a team is set up as private, new users will need to be invited because they won't be able to see the team and ask to join.

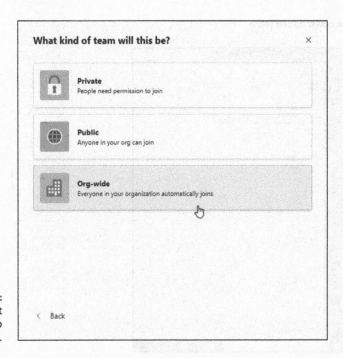

FIGURE 13-4:
Choosing what type of team to create.

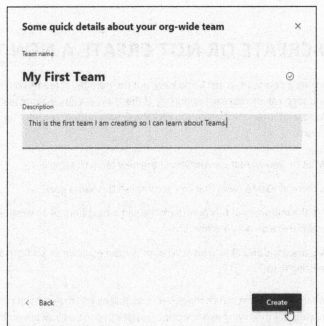

FIGURE 13-5:
Providing a team name and description when creating a new team.

The newly added team

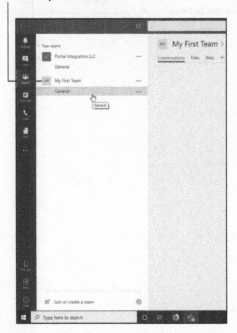

FIGURE 13-6:
Viewing your
newly created
team.

TO CREATE OR NOT CREATE A NEW TEAM

Setting up a new team is quick and easy, but the number of teams you have in your organization can increase exponentially. If there are already existing teams, think before you create another one. Before you click the Create button, consider the goals of the new team:

- What do you want the members of the new team to achieve?

- Is there already a team that can accomplish this same goal?

- Are the members of this new team the same members of an existing team, or will there be new members?

- Are the goals and objectives similar, or are the goals different from an existing team?

Membership to teams can change over time. Just as you may consider creating a new team, consider modifying existing ones and deleting teams that are no longer active.

Inviting People to Your Team

After you've set up your team, you can add people to the team. In the preceding section, you create an org-wide team so that everyone within the organization is automatically added to the team. In this section, you go through the same process to create a new team, but this time you create a public or private team, and you find out how to add members during the creation process and after you've already set up the team.

During the team creation process

To invite people to your team during the initial team creation process, follow these steps:

1. **Follow Steps 1–4 in the "Creating a New Team" section to create a new team.**

2. **When asked, "What type of team will this be?," instead of clicking the Org-Wide option (refer to Figure 13-4), choose Public or Private to create a new public or private team.**

   When you create a public or private team, you're also presented with a dialog box to invite people to join the team just after the team is created (see Figure 13-7).

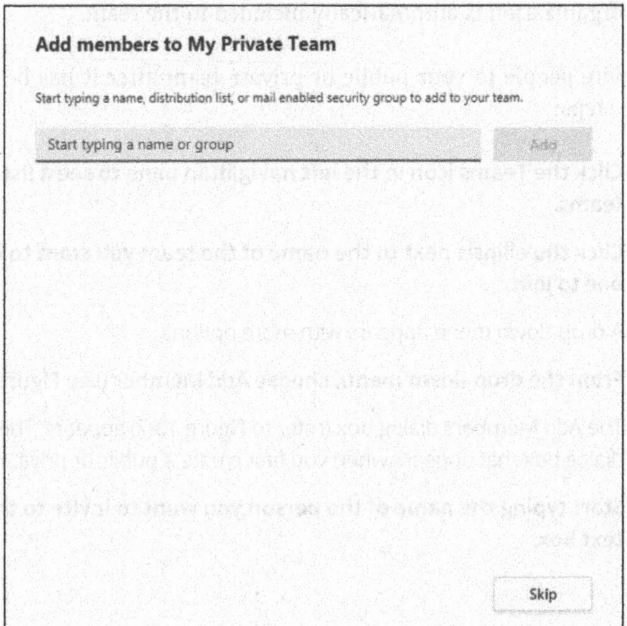

Add members to My Private Team

Start typing a name, distribution list, or mail enabled security group to add to your team.

| Start typing a name or group | Add |

Skip

FIGURE 13-7:
The dialog box to invite people to your team during the creation process.

3. **Start typing the name of the person you want to invite to the team in the text box.**

TIP

The search functionality automatically looks for and populates the text box based on the letters you're typing. This happens in real time so you can see the results of your search as you're typing. This feature is helpful if, for example, you only know the first part of someone's name or if you only know that the name starts with a certain letter.

4. **When you find the correct person, click that person's name, and then click Add.**

5. **Continue adding people until you've invited all the team members you want to add.**

   The users will be notified of their new team membership depending on how they've set up notifications.

After the team creation process

You can invite people to your public or private team after it's created, too. Suppose a new person joins your organization and you want to add that person to your team.

REMEMBER

The only way people can join a private team is if you invite them, whereas anyone in the organization can join a public team. With an org-wide team, everyone in your organization is automatically included in the team.

To invite people to your public or private team after it has been created, follow these steps:

1. **Click the Teams icon in the left navigation pane to see a list of your teams.**

2. **Click the ellipsis next to the name of the team you want to invite some-one to join.**

   A drop-down menu appears with more options.

3. **From the drop-down menu, choose Add Member (see Figure 13-8).**

   The Add Members dialog box (refer to Figure 13-7) appears. This is the same dialog box that appears when you first create a public or private team.

4. **Start typing the name of the person you want to invite to the team in the text box.**

Click the ellipsis to open a pop-up menu of options

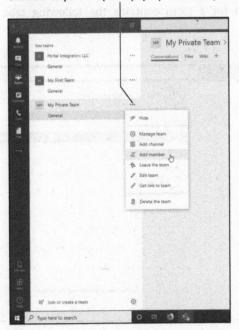

FIGURE 13-8:
Adding members
to a team already
created.

5. **When you find the correct person, click that person's name and then click Add.**

   The user will be notified of her new team membership depending on how she has set up notifications.

Managing Your Team Settings

You can control many different settings in Teams, such as adding and configuring channels, users, and chat behavior. The settings you'll likely use the most frequently are for your specific teams. These settings include adding and removing owners, members, and guests; adding and deleting channels; and working with apps.

To open the settings for a team, click the ellipsis next to the name of the team to open the drop-down menu (refer to Figure 13-8) and choose Manage Team.

The settings screen for a team contains the following tabs at the top (see Figure 13-9):

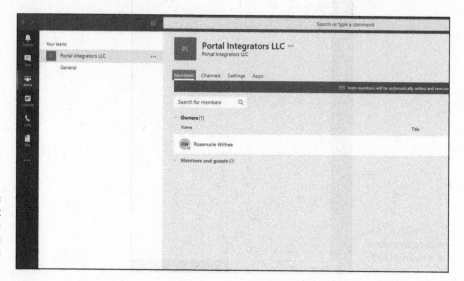

FIGURE 13-9:
The management screen for a team with the Members tab open.

>> **Members:** The Members screen is where you add new members to the team. You can add people as members of the team or as guests. A *guest user* is a user who has access to Teams and can chat with you but does not have access to the rest of your Office 365 ecosystem.

>> **Channels:** The Channels screen is where you can add a channel. A *channel* is an area of a team where you can chat about a common topic. For example, you may have a channel for accounting and a channel for clients. Find out more about channels in Chapter 14.

>> **Settings:** The Settings screen is where you manage the settings for a team, as shown in Figure 13-10. On the Settings screen, you can set the team picture, set the permissions of users (including what permissions you want to give to guest users), set how @mentions (pronounced "at mentions") work, get a link to the team that you can share so others can join the team, and other fun stuff such as adding virtual stickers.

TIP

An *@mention* is when someone uses the @ ("at") symbol followed by the name of a user in a message. It's essentially tagging the person so that Teams knows who the person is that's being mentioned. When your name is @mentioned, you get a notification that someone has mentioned your name in a message. This helps you scroll through and find messages that are pertinent to you.

>> **Apps:** The Apps screen is where you can add apps to the team. You can see that some apps are installed by default. You can also add more apps by clicking the More Apps button.

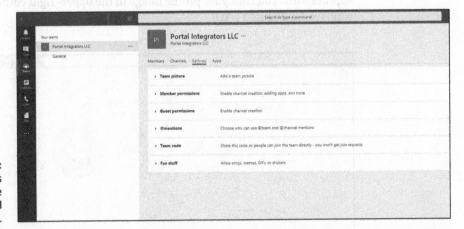

FIGURE 13-10:
The Settings screen is where you can control team settings.

FIGURING OUT SETTINGS THAT MATTER TO YOU

There are many different settings in Teams, and the ones you'll use the most will likely depend on the size of your organization and how you communicate and interact with each other. For example, if your organization is a two-person consulting firm, you may predominantly use Teams with guest and external users. If your org is a manufacturing company, you may mostly use Teams with people within your organization and prefer to focus on working with your feed to stay up to date with what's going on.

Just take it slow and see how Teams unfolds for you and your organization. What matters to one person may not matter at all to someone else. As you continue your journey with Teams, keep in mind that there are seemingly endless settings and features. You don't have to learn them all; you just need to be aware of what's available so you can get the most out of the product for your situation.

Managing Your User Settings

Several settings are unique to each individual Teams user. You can think of these as your user settings. These settings are found in the drop-down menu that appears when you click your profile image in the upper-right corner of the Teams window (see Figure 13-11).

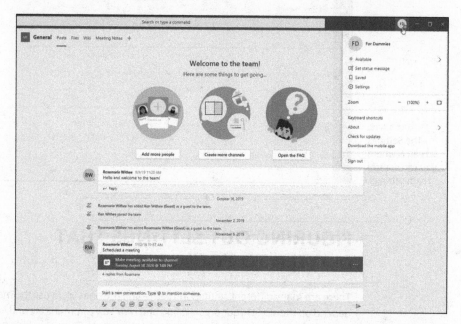

FIGURE 13-11:
The profile
drop-down menu.

You can use this menu to

>> Set your current status such as Available, Do Not Disturb, and Away. You may want to set your status to Appear Away so that you can get work done without people knowing you're busy on your computer.

>> Set your status message so that others see a message and know what you're up to or what you want people to know. For example, you can set it to the music you're listening to or a quote that captures your current mood.

>> View chats and messages you've saved throughout Teams.

>> Open your profile settings.

>> Adjust your zoom settings to zoom in and make items in your Teams window bigger or zoom out to make things smaller.

>> Change your keyboard shortcuts so you can maneuver around Teams with a few taps of your keyboard.

>> Learn more about Teams, such as the version number you're currently using and legal notices.

>> Check for any updates to Teams so that you can be sure you have the latest version.

>> Download the mobile app so you're never out of touch.

>> Sign out of Teams. You may need to sign out if you're a member of multiple organizations and you need to sign into one account or the other.

When you choose the Settings option from your profile menu, you can change several things that are specific to your account. The settings menu (see Figure 13-12) includes settings for six different categories: General, Privacy, Notifications, Devices, Permissions, and Calls. The following sections provide a brief overview of these categories.

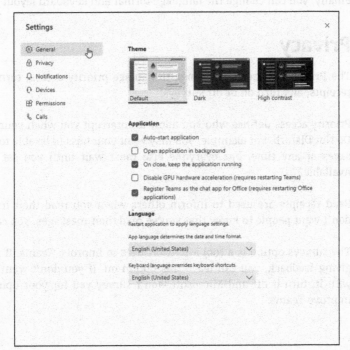

FIGURE 13-12:
The settings menu for a Teams user.

General

The General section includes settings for the theme you're using, how the application behaves, and the language you want to use.

You can change the way Teams looks by changing the theme you're using. For example, maybe you prefer a dark or high-contrast theme to the default.

In the application section, you can decide how you want Teams to behave on your computer. For example, do you want Teams to start up automatically when you boot up your computer? Or do you want it to stay running in the background when you click the X button to close the Teams app?

TIP

In this section, you can also associate Teams as the chat app of choice for the rest of your Office products. This option is useful when you're part of an organization that's moving from Skype to Teams. You can choose to use Teams instead of Skype by default using this option.

Finally, you can change the language format and keyboard layout you're using.

Privacy

The Privacy section has settings to manage priority access, turn on or off read receipts, and turn on or off surveys.

Priority access defines who you allow to interrupt you when your status is set to Do Not Disturb. For example, you may want your boss to be able to send you messages at any time, but everyone else must wait until you set your status to Available.

Read receipts are used to inform others when you read their messages. If you don't want people to know that you've read their messages, you can turn this off.

The surveys option is a tool Microsoft uses to improve Teams. If you don't mind giving feedback, you can leave this option on. If you don't want to be bothered with it, turn it off and Microsoft won't survey you for your opinion on how to improve Teams.

Notifications

The Notifications area is where you set your preferences for how Teams should notify you about things. You can set various events to show up in your *banner* (a pop-up window that appears in the lower-right corner of your computer) and through email, only in your Activity feed, or turn them off completely.

Devices

You configure the devices you're using with Teams in this settings section. A device includes things like your speaker, microphone, phone, headset, or camera.

Permissions

You can turn on or off permissions for Teams in this section. For example, do you want Teams to be able to use your location or be able to open external links in your web browser? You can configure those permissions here.

Calls

Teams provides a full voice solution. What does this mean? It means that Teams can replace your regular phone. In this section, you can configure how incoming calls are answered, as well as set up and configure your voicemail and ringtones. You can also set accessibility options such as using a teletypewriter (TTY) device for people who are deaf or hearing impaired.

Chapter **14**

Staying Connected to Others with Channels and Chat

Sending instant communication over chat has been around since the dawn of the Internet. You may remember back to the days of AOL Instant Messenger and Internet Relay Chat (IRC) — which was invented in 1988, by the way. The Internet has come a long way since then, but one thing hasn't changed: Most people still use the Internet to send communications back and forth in real time on a daily basis, and that capability is more valuable than ever. Have you heard of Slack? It relies on instant messaging. (See Part 2 for more about Slack.) Have you used Skype to send chat messages? That's instant messaging, too. Microsoft Teams just wouldn't be valuable if it didn't include instant messaging.

In this chapter, you discover how to send chat messages to others on your team via channels. You see how to create new channels and configure them. You also discover some of the cool features of channels beyond sending simple chat messages, such as tagging others, using emojis, and tracking activity. Finally, you find out how to turn down or turn off channels if they start becoming too noisy, and figure out the difference between chatting within a channel and private chats.

Chatting in Teams

You may be forced to use Teams because it's included with your organization's Microsoft 365 or Office 365 subscription, or you may decide to start using it on your own. Regardless of how you start using Teams, you'll likely spend your initial interactions sending messages to other people on your team.

Instant messages in Teams happen in *channels*. Channels are where people can type messages, add files, and share links. Think of a channel like a virtual water cooler — you go there to communicate with colleagues, learn and share gossip, and generally stay in touch with your social circle.

TIP

A channel lives inside of a team, and a team can contain multiple channels. You can name a channel anything you want. I recommend using a name that describes the purpose of the channel. For example, you can name your channels channel01, channel02, channel03, and so on, but these titles aren't descriptive. Do you want to create one channel for accounting and another channel for human resources? Name them Accounting and Human Resources, respectively. Or perhaps a group of people want to discuss the new policy of allowing pets in the office; create a channel called Pets. You get the point.

A channel can contain multiple conversations happening at the same time. To try to make these threads of conversation easier to follow, Teams groups them together in what are known as *threads*. A thread is simply a topic of conversation. When someone types a brand-new message, it appears in the channel, and any replies to that original message are placed underneath. If someone else types a different message for a different topic, it becomes its own thread and any responses to that message will be grouped under the original message. In Figure 14-1, you can see that someone is creating a brand-new topic of conversation ("Hello world!"). If you wanted to reply to the existing topic, you would instead click the Reply link at the bottom of the thread that starts with "Hello and welcome to the team!"

TIP

Replying to an existing topic of conversation (a thread) and creating a new topic of conversation are simply a matter of which Reply link you click and which text box you start typing in. One mistake many people make when first using Teams is to reply in the primary message box for the channel instead of in the reply message box for the thread. It can be confusing at first, but after you notice the two boxes, it quickly becomes second nature.

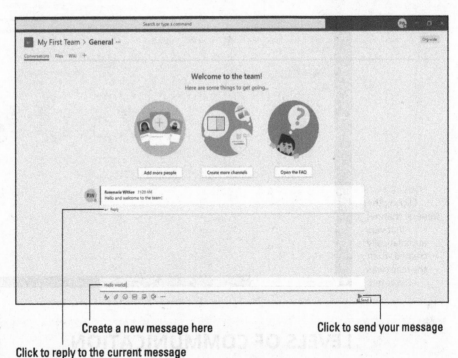

FIGURE 14-1:
Sending a new
message to the
General channel.

Create a new message here

Click to send your message

Click to reply to the current message

Sending Messages in Channels

Whenever you create a new team, a channel is created for that team automatically. Called "General," this channel is perfectly acceptable to use to start chatting with others on the team. (See Chapter 13 for a reminder on how to create your first team.)

To send a message in the General channel, follow these steps:

1. Click the Teams icon in the left navigation pane to view all your teams.

Under each team, you see a list of channels that are available to you. If this team is new, you only see the General channel until more channels are created.

TIP

In addition to the channels available to you, there may be private channels in the team that you don't have access to. There can also be channels that are public but that you have not joined. The list of channels you see under a team may not be inclusive of every channel that team contains.

2. Click the General channel, as shown in Figure 14-2.

When you click a channel, it opens in the main part of the screen.

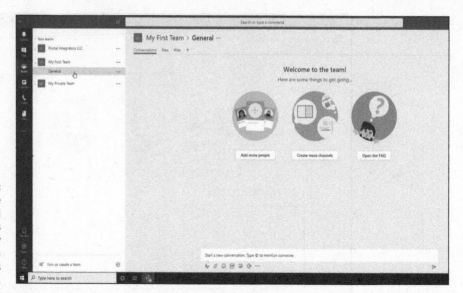

FIGURE 14-2:
Clicking the
General channel
that was
automatically
created when
the team was
created.

LEVELS OF COMMUNICATION

One of the reasons AOL Instant Messenger and IRC may have been so popular in the early days of the Internet is because chat fulfills a critical communications role when people are not located in the same room. I like to think of communications as existing on different levels. The first level of communication is being face to face in the same room. The second level is instant voice communication (think of using the phone). And the third level is instant digital communication (think of email or instant messaging).

Email was tremendously popular from the inception of the Internet as well, but it was not instantaneous. Even though it's a lot faster, email has more in common with sending a postal letter than it does with chatting with someone over the phone. Instant messaging, on the other hand, is similar to having a phone conversation with someone but in digital form, and it can happen asynchronously and with multiple people at the same time. Instant messaging doesn't replace email, just like sending a postal letter doesn't replace having a phone conversation. It's just a different form of digital communication.

A benefit digital communication has over both face-to-face and phone conversations is that it's inclusive. For example, if you have a colleague who is both hearing impaired and sight impaired, you can communicate with him just fine though digital communications. He can install software on his computer that turns your communications into braille, and you can stay in contact. This would not be possible without digital communications.

3. **Type a message in the text box at the bottom of the screen and click the Send icon (or press the Enter key), as shown earlier in Figure 14-1.**

   Your message appears in the General channel screen.

Congratulations! You're sending messages!

TIP

Notice that, above your message, Microsoft Teams is giving you some hints about adding more people, creating more channels, and opening the Frequently Asked Questions (FAQ). These buttons that appear in new channels are shortcuts for you. You can achieve these same tasks without using these shortcuts, and you find out how in the next sections.

Creating a New Channel

As you use Teams more and more, you'll likely want to create chat channels for other topics so that everything doesn't happen in one General channel. For example, you may want to create one channel for your team to discuss finances, another channel for human resources, and another channel for team-building events. Team conversations can be organized in seemingly endless ways. The only thing that matters is what works for your team.

To create a new channel in your team, follow these steps:

1. **Click the Teams icon in the left navigation pane to view all your teams.**

2. **Click the ellipsis to the right of the team to which you want to add a channel.**

   The More Options drop-down menu appears.

3. **Choose Add Channel, as shown in Figure 14-3.**

WARNING

   If this option isn't shown in the drop-down menu, you don't have permission to create a new channel. If you're a guest to a team, your ability to create teams and channels can be limited.

4. **Enter a name and description for the channel in the dialog box that appears and then click Add, as shown in Figure 14-4.**

TIP

   Note that you can also select the check box to have this channel automatically show up for every person in the team. If you don't select this box, the channel will show up as hidden, and people will need to click a button to see it in the list of channels in the team.

   The new channel appears under the team, as shown in Figure 14-5.

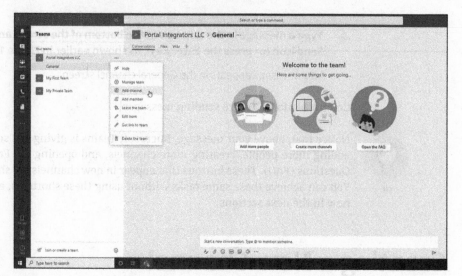

FIGURE 14-3:
Choosing Add
Channel from the
drop-down menu
for a team.

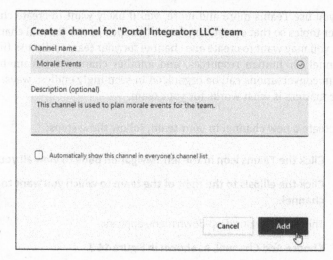

FIGURE 14-4:
Filling in the
dialog box to
create a new
channel.

You can create chat channels for any topic you want. Some teams have a lot of success breaking out core work-related channels from non-core work-related channels, such as team-building events in one channel and budget discussions in a different channel.

REMEMBER

A channel is part of a team. A team can contain multiple channels, and each channel can contain its own threads of conversation.

The new channel

FIGURE 14-5:
A new channel
in a team.

Configuring a Channel

You can configure many different settings for a channel via the More Options drop-down menu (refer to Figure 14-3). You access these additional options by clicking the ellipsis next to the channel you want to manage. Figure 14-6 shows the More Options drop-down menu that appears next to the new channel you created in the previous section. The options that appear for a channel you add include the following:

>> **Channel Notifications:** Configuring the notifications you receive for a channel is especially important as your organization's use of Teams increases. Teams can quickly become noisy with everyone chatting about all manner of topics. You can use this setting to turn down the volume for channels that are less important to you and turn up the volume for topics you need to pay close attention to. The channel notifications dialog box is shown in Figure 14-7.

>> **Hide:** Choose this option to hide the channel from the list of channels you have in the team. You can always unhide the channel at any time. You see a little message that lets you know how many channels you have hidden, and you can click it to see those hidden channels. Hiding and unhiding channels is something you need to become familiar with as the number of teams and channels grows and start to become overwhelming.

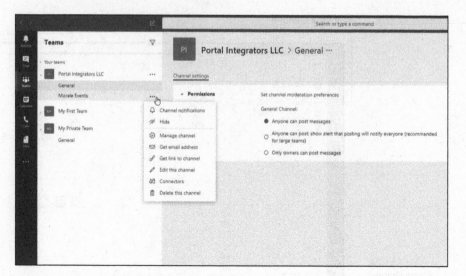

FIGURE 14-6:
The More Options menu for a team's channel.

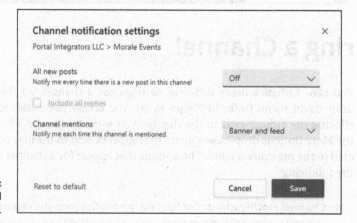

FIGURE 14-7:
Setting channel notifications.

>> **Manage Channel:** This option allows owners of the channel to manage the permissions for the channel, as shown in Figure 14-8. You can allow others to moderate the channel and control who can post new messages to the channel. For example, you can set whether you want bots to post messages to the channel with this setting.

>> **Get Email Address:** One cool feature is the ability to send an email message directly to a channel. You can configure the channel so that if you send an email, the message appears in the channel. Figure 14-9 shows the email address for the private channel created in Chapter 13. Whenever someone sends an email message to this address, it appears in the channel, as shown in Figure 14-10.

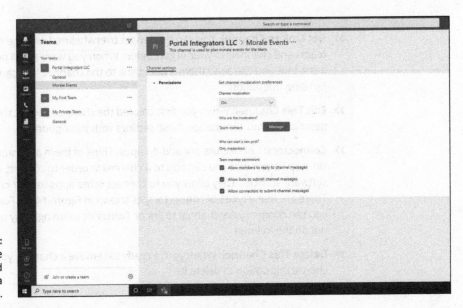

FIGURE 14-8:
Managing the
moderators and
permissions for a
channel.

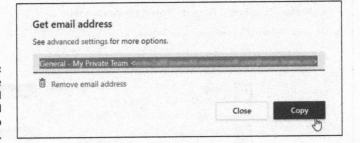

FIGURE 14-9:
Obtaining the
dedicated email
address to send
email directly to
the channel.

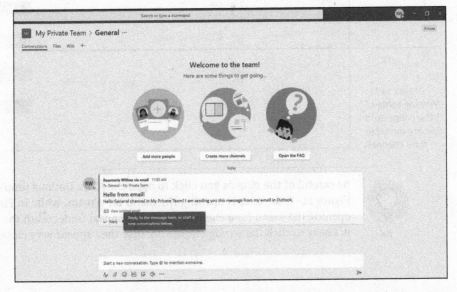

FIGURE 14-10:
Viewing an email
sent to the
channel.

>> **Get Link to Channel:** You can quickly get overwhelmed with the number of teams and channels in your organization. When you want to tell people about a channel, you can send them a direct link to the channel. You can get the link by using this option.

>> **Edit This Channel:** When you first created the channel, you set the title and description. You can change those settings with this option.

>> **Connectors:** Connectors are add-on apps. Think of them as custom extensions to Teams that you can add to a channel in order to connect with other software services. They allow you to connect other apps to your channel. There are many types of connectors, as shown in Figure 14-11. For example, you can connect your channel to Jira or Twitter or seemingly any other app out on the Internet.

>> **Delete This Channel:** When you're ready to remove a channel, you can choose this option to delete it.

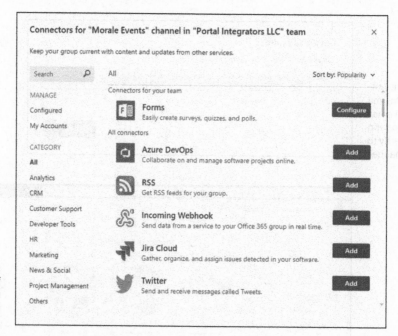

FIGURE 14-11:
Viewing some of
the connectors
that are available
for a channel.

TIP

Be careful of the ellipsis you click to open the More Options drop-down menu. In Figure 14-3, the user is opening the menu for a team, while in Figure 14-6, she's opening the menu for a channel. Channels appear underneath the team name, but it's easy to click the wrong ellipsis because they appear very close to each other.

Moving from a Channel to a Chat

The various ways you can communicate within Teams can quickly become confusing. As a quick recap, a *team* is a group of people, and a *channel* is an ongoing conversation within the team. You can be in multiple teams, and each team can have multiple channels.

The nice thing about this system of communication is that it has structure. You can always click a team in the left navigation pane and see the channels in that team. However, you may also need to just chat with someone or with groups of people, and you don't want to go through the process of setting up a new team or channel. Teams has you covered with a concept called *chat*. You find the Chat icon in the left navigation pane just above the Teams icon, as shown in Figure 14-12.

Chat icon

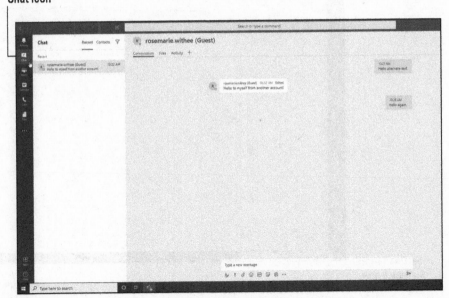

REMEMBER

A chat is an ad hoc conversation between two or more people.

Click the Chat icon to see a list of all your open chats. If you remember using AOL Instant Messenger, Skype, or most any other chat application, you may recognize that each chat item is like a window. However, instead of a new window for each chat, each chat appears as an item in the list. Click a chat, and you see the main window refresh to show that conversation.

Starting a private chat

You can start a private chat by clicking the New Chat icon, which is located just above the Filter icon at the top of the chat list. The new chat icon looks like a piece of paper with a pencil on it (see Figure 14-13). When you click the icon, a new chat appears on the right side of the Teams workspace. You type in the name of the person you want to send a chat message to in the To field, and then click that person's name to add that person to the chat. After you've added the person to the chat, you can send a message just like you do in a channel. You type your message in the text box at the bottom of the chat area and press the Enter key on your keyboard or click the Send icon, which looks like a paper airplane.

New chat icon   Adding a person to the chat

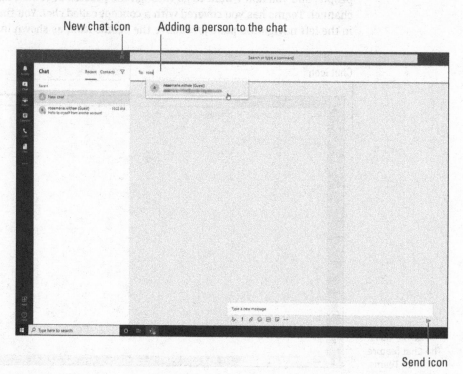

FIGURE 14-13:
Starting a new
chat in Teams.

Send icon

TIP

A recent addition to chats is read receipts. With this feature, you can tell whether people have read or seen messages you've sent. For details, check out `https://support.office.com/en-us/article/use-read-receipts-for-messages-in-teams-533f2334-32ef-424b-8d56-ed30e019f856`, or search for "Use read receipts for messages in Teams" in your favorite search engine.

Adding multiple people to a chat

The previous section covers how to start a new chat. You can chat with multiple people by adding them in the To line when you start the chat. However, you may find that you want to add more people to an existing chat.

To add more people to a chat that has already started, click the Add People icon that appears in the upper-right corner of the chat window (see Figure 14-14). Then, type in the names of the people you want to add in the Add dialog box. If you're chatting with only one person and you add another person, a new chat will appear with the three people in the chat. If you already have three people in a chat and you add a fourth person (or more), you'll be presented with the option of including the chat history for the new people you're adding, as shown in Figure 14-14.

Add People icon

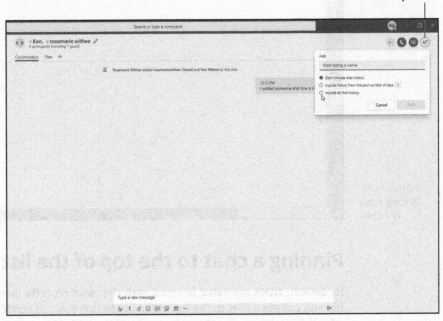

FIGURE 14-14:
Adding additional
people to a chat.

TIP

If you're chatting with one person, you can't add another person to the same chat and share the history of the personal chat with the new third party. The feature of adding people and keeping the history of the chat only appears when there are at least three people already in the chat. Microsoft has said that this is done for privacy reasons and the expectation that if there is a one-on-one chat happening, Teams should not allow one person to share that confidential chat with other people.

Giving a chat a title

By default, a chat is listed in your chat list with the names of the people in the chat. Often, a chat will take on a life of its own as more and more people are added, and the chat becomes the central point of communication for a topic. When this happens, you may want to give the chat a title so when you're looking through your list of chats, you can quickly remember the topic of that chat.

To add a title to a chat, click the pencil icon at the top of the chat and type in a name, as shown in Figure 14-15.

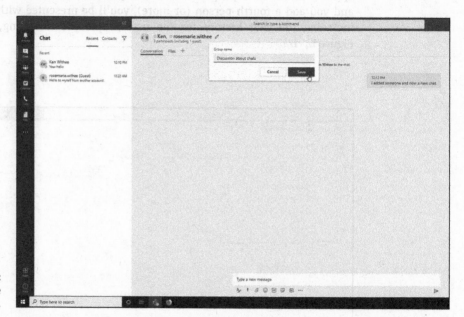

FIGURE 14-15:
Adding a title
to a chat.

Pinning a chat to the top of the list

By default, chats are listed in order with the most recently used chat at the top. But you can pin a chat to the top of the list so that you can quickly get to that chat even if it has been a few days since anyone has added a message to it.

To pin a chat, click the ellipsis next to the chat in the left navigation pane and choose Pin from the More Options drop-down menu, as shown in Figure 14-16.

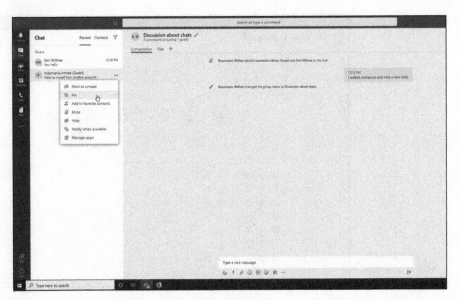

FIGURE 14-16:
Pinning a chat to
the top of the list
for quick access.

Sending More than Text When Chatting

Entering text into a channel or chat is the most common way of sending your message to others on the team. However, you can send more than just text. You can send emojis, GIFs, and stickers, and you can even attach files. These options appear at the bottom of the text box where you type in your message, as shown in Figure 14-17.

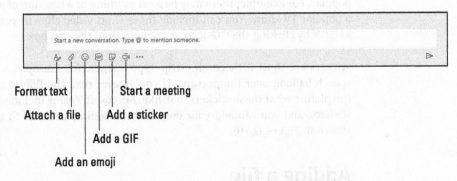

Format text

Attach a file

Add an emoji

Add a GIF

Add a sticker

Start a meeting

FIGURE 14-17:
Additional chat
options.

Adding emojis, GIFs, and stickers

Emojis are little icons that display an emotion. For example, a smiley face shows happiness and a sad face shows sadness. You find emoji icons of all shapes and sizes and meanings. You can send an emoji by clicking the emoji icon and then clicking the emoji you want to use (see Figure 14-18).

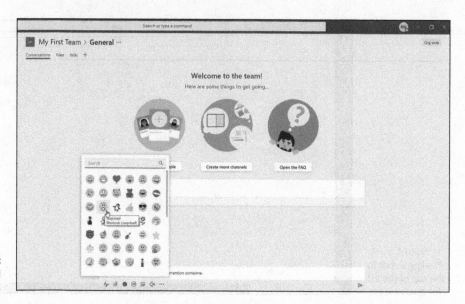

FIGURE 14-18:
Adding an emoji
to your message.

TIP

Teams includes text shortcuts you can type so that you don't have to click an emoji with your mouse from the list of options shown in Figure 14-18. For example, to send a happy face, you can type a colon (:) followed by a closing parenthesis ()]. When you type this sequence of characters, the happy-face emoji is automatically added to your chat. You can also type a keyword inside of parenthesis in order to create an emoji icon. You can find the entire list of emojis at https://365trainingportal.com/microsoft-teams-emoji-shortcuts/.

A GIF is an animated picture. Microsoft Teams includes several GIFs that are popular. For example, there may be a cat yawning or a reaction of a character from a popular TV show. You can include these short video clips in your chat message as GIFs by clicking the GIF icon at the bottom of the text box.

Stickers are short little comic-strip-type images (for example, a drawing with a speech balloon over the person). If you've ever read the *Dilbert* comic strip, you can picture what these stickers look like. Microsoft Teams includes a lot of popular stickers, and you can add your own as well. Adding a sticker to your message is shown in Figure 14-19.

Adding a file

In addition to fun emojis, GIFs, and stickers, you can also add a file to the chat message. For example, you may be working on a Microsoft Excel spreadsheet and you want to include it in the chat. You can add the file to your chat message using the paper-clip icon, as shown in Figure 14-20. You can choose a recent file you've been working on, browse the files already uploaded to Teams, choose a file from OneDrive, or upload a file from your local computer.

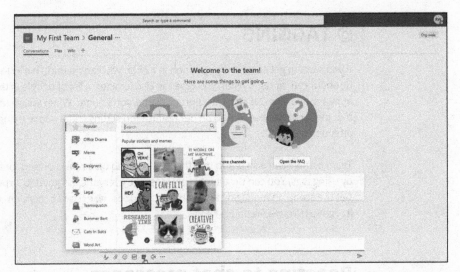

FIGURE 14-19:
Adding a sticker
to your message.

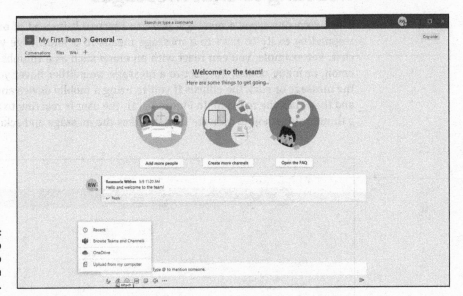

FIGURE 14-20:
Attaching a file to
a message to
send to a
channel.

TIP

When you attach a file to a channel, the file appears in the Files tab at the top of the channel. The Files tab is a SharePoint site behind the scenes. You can spot the Files tab at the top of Figure 14-20 in between the Conversations tab and the Wiki tab.

Reacting to chat messages

When someone types a message, you can react to it instead of or in addition to responding to it. To *react* to a message means to acknowledge you've seen the chat. For example, you can react with an emoji such as a thumbs-up, a surprise emoji, or many others. To react to a message, you either hover your mouse over the message or click the ellipsis if you're using a mobile device and touch screen, and then click the reaction. In Figure 14-21, the user is reacting to a message with a thumbs-up emoji to indicate that she likes the message and acknowledges it.

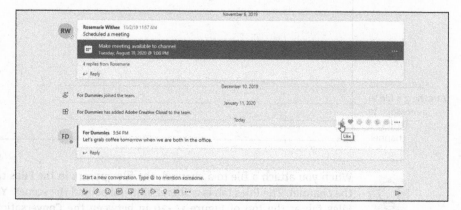

FIGURE 14-21:
Reacting to a message with a thumbs-up.

If someone else has already given a reaction, such as a thumbs-up, then your reaction will increase the number that appears next to the same reaction. For example, if your coworker gave a thumbs-up, and you reacted with the same thumbs-up, then a small number 2 will appear next to the thumbs-up emoji. Reactions can be an important way to acknowledge a message without having to type out a response.

Chapter **15**

Embracing Teams to Make Meetings Better

I f you're a veteran of Microsoft Office, you're surely familiar with Outlook. Microsoft Outlook is an app that's part of the Office suite of products that you can use to manage your email, calendar, and contacts. Microsoft Teams integrates with Outlook and shines when you use Outlook to manage and conduct your Teams meetings.

In this chapter, you find out about the different types of Teams meetings — scheduled meetings, ad hoc meetings, and private meetings. You discover how to schedule a new meeting in Teams and add Teams functionality to a meeting you schedule in Outlook. You also discover how to start a meeting and join an existing meeting. Finally, you explore the built-in conference call and video call capabilities of Teams, which enable you to meet with people from all over the world.

Getting Up to Speed with the Types of Meetings in Teams

A *meeting* is a general term that encompasses everything from a one-on-one chat with a friend to a presentation to hundreds of colleagues. Teams accommodates a variety of meeting types, and the way you set up a meeting in Teams depends on the frequency of the meeting and how many people need to be involved in the meeting.

Here are the three types of meetings:

>> **Regular or recurring meetings:** Think of this type of meeting as a traditional meeting in an organization. For example, you may have a recurring team meeting that happens every Monday at 11 a.m. Or your colleagues may have a regular meeting to go over the latest financial reports with various people throughout the organization. These types of meetings are meetings that are scheduled on your calendar.

>> **Instant ad hoc meetings:** This is a meeting that happens instantly. For example, you may be communicating with a group of people and someone decides that it would be better to call a quick meeting to decide on something.

>> **Private meetings:** A private meeting involves a discussion with another person. You can equate this meeting type to picking up the phone and calling someone.

As you work with Teams, keep in mind the type of meetings you can initiate. You can schedule a meeting, start an instant meeting with a group of people, or start a private meeting with another person.

TIP

Use the types of meetings in order to build your mental model of becoming more efficient with Teams. For example, if you need to meet with five people right away, you don't need to schedule a new meeting on everyone's calendar. You can use the Meet Now functionality to start an ad hoc meeting, which you find out how to do later in this chapter.

Viewing Your Calendar in Teams

Just as you can view your calendar in Outlook, you can view your calendar in Teams. Your calendar is where your meetings are scheduled and where you can view what meetings you need to attend. Click the Calendar icon in the left navigation pane, as shown in Figure 15-1, to open your Outlook calendar in Teams.

TIP

The Calendar navigational item only shows up as an option in Teams if you have Outlook installed on the same computer. If your Office 365 subscription includes the Office clients, you can install them by logging in at https://office.com. After you log in, you should see a button that says Install Office on the main landing page. The process is covered in detail in *Microsoft Office 365 For Dummies* (Wiley).

You can view your calendar in Teams in several ways. You can view by the day, by the week, and by the workweek. You can change the view with the selector in the upper-right corner of your calendar. By default, the view selector is set to Work Week.

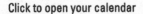
Click to open your calendar

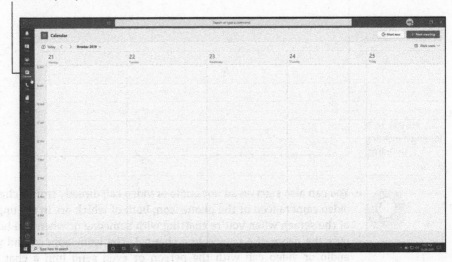

FIGURE 15-1:
Viewing your
Outlook calendar
in Teams.

Creating a New Meeting and Inviting People

With Teams, you can create an instant or ad hoc meeting to connect with someone right away, or you can schedule a meeting for the future that will appear as a meeting on the invitee's Outlook calendar. To create an ad hoc meeting, click the Meet Now button in the upper-right corner of your calendar, shown in Figure 15-2. When you click the Meet Now button, a meeting is created and you're instantly able to join it.

TIP

When you join a meeting in Teams, you have the option of turning on or off your video and microphone before you join.

When you first create a Meet Now meeting, you'll be the only one in the meeting. You can invite others to join your meeting by clicking Meeting Participants from the icons that appear in the middle of the meeting window and then typing the name of the person you want to invite.

Click to start an ad hoc meeting

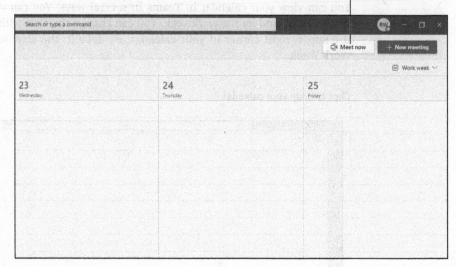

FIGURE 15-2:
Joining a meeting
in Teams.

TIP

You can also start an ad hoc audio or video call directly from a chat by clicking the video camera icon or the phone icon, both of which are in the upper-right corner of the screen when you're chatting with someone or when you hover your mouse over the name of a person in a channel. The icons appear, and you can start an audio or video call with the person or even send him a chat or email. (Chat functionality is covered in Chapter 14.)

Meeting instantly is a nice feature. But many of your meetings may also be scheduled in advance and booked on other people's calendars. This is a task you may be used to doing in Outlook, but you can use Teams to do this now.

To schedule a new meeting in Teams, follow these steps:

1. **Click the Calendar icon in the left navigation pane to open your Outlook calendar.**

2. **Click the New Meeting button, which is just to the right of the Meet Now button (see Figure 15-2).**

   The New Meeting dialog box appears (see Figure 15-3). Here, you can set up the meeting.

TIP

   You can also browse your calendar and click a day and time to open the New Meeting dialog box.

3. **Provide a title, location, date, time, and details for the meeting.**

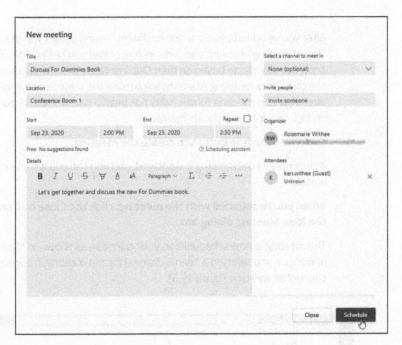

4. **Invite people to your meeting by typing the name of a person in the Invite People text box.**

   As you type, Teams offers suggestions of team members based on the name you start to type.

5. **Click the name of the person you want to invite from the list of team members.**

   You can also invite people who are external to your organization if you have that feature enabled. (See the later sidebar "The guest user experience in Microsoft Teams" for more information.)

   One nuance of a Teams meeting is that you can make the meeting available and open to anyone in an existing Teams channel. To do this, choose the channel you want to access from the Select a Channel to Meet In drop-down menu. When you do this, the meeting appears in the channel. When the meeting starts, anyone in the channel can join it. In addition, all the chat conversations of the meeting and recording appear in that Teams channel.

   Think of this option as a transparency feature. Even though you may only need to meet with three people, you can give everyone in the channel the option of joining the meeting. This also lets everyone in the channel view the recording, the chat logs, and any files that were shared. In other words, the meeting is transparent to everyone in the channel, even if only a few were invited.

After you've added people to the invitation, Teams shows you their availability. The scheduling assistant also kicks into gear and you see common times when people are available based on their Outlook calendars. To see more detail, you can click the Scheduling Assistant link to view the calendar availability for each attendee. This meeting functionality has been a part of Outlook for a long time, and it's now integrated with Teams.

6. **Click the Schedule button to create the meeting.**

   A summary of the meeting is displayed, and you can edit it if you made any mistakes.

7. **When you're satisfied with the meeting, click the Close button to close the New Meeting dialog box.**

   The meeting is now scheduled on your calendar, as shown in Figure 15-4. In addition, if you selected a Teams channel for the meeting, it appears in the channel as well (see Figure 15-5).

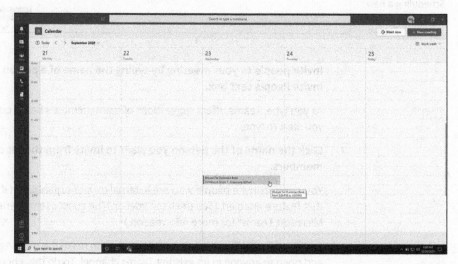

FIGURE 15-4:
A meeting on your calendar in Teams.

REMEMBER

The calendar in Teams is tied to Microsoft Outlook. If you open Outlook and look at your calendar, you see the meeting you just created in Teams, as shown in Figure 15-6. You can also schedule a Teams meeting directly from Outlook. When you're in Outlook, and you want to schedule a Teams meeting, click the New Teams Meeting button in the Ribbon in Outlook.

Outlook integrates with many different types of meeting software. Because Teams comes with many of the Office 365 subscriptions, I see most organizations quickly adopt Teams. However, if your organization uses other meeting software, such as GoToMeeting, you'll have a similar experience in Outlook.

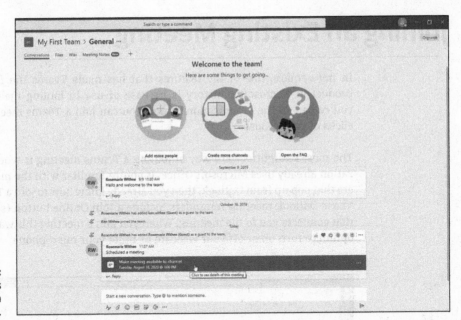

FIGURE 15-5:
A meeting that's
shared with a
Teams channel.

New Teams Meeting option

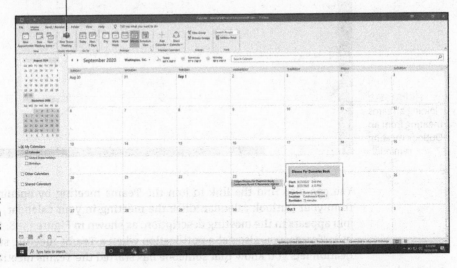

FIGURE 15-6:
Viewing a
scheduled Teams
meeting in
Outlook.

TIP

If you need to broadcast an event to many people, you can use a feature called Teams Live Events. This feature used to be called Skype Meeting Broadcast, and it's designed for presentations to a very large audience. If your Office 365 subscription includes Teams Live Events, you see the option to create a regular meeting or create a Teams Live Event when you click the Schedule Meeting button.

Joining an Existing Meeting

In my opinion, one of the features that has made Teams the fastest-growing product in Microsoft's history is its ease of use in joining meetings. Whether you're part of the organization or not, you can join a Teams meeting with a few clicks of your mouse.

The most straightforward way of joining a Teams meeting is when your organization already uses Microsoft Office. If you're familiar with the meeting reminders that pop up from Outlook, then you already know how to join a Teams meeting. Those Outlook meeting reminders include a Join Online button (see Figure 15-7) that connects you to the meeting. When you join a meeting this way, you have the option to turn on or off your webcam or mute your microphone.

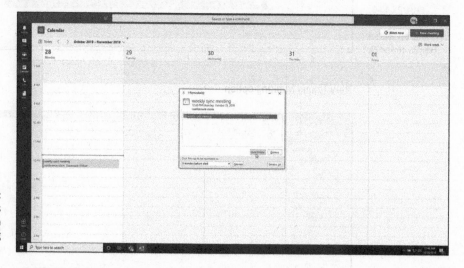

FIGURE 15-7:
Joining a Teams meeting from an Outlook meeting reminder.

You can also find the link to join the Teams meeting by opening the meeting from your Outlook calendar. Click the meeting in your calendar, and the link to join appears in the meeting description, as shown in Figure 15-8. If you're signed in to Teams, you also get a notification when a Teams meeting starts. The notification lets you know that someone has started the Teams meeting and that you can join.

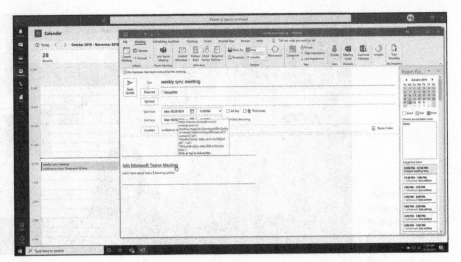

FIGURE 15-8:
Joining a Teams
meeting by
opening an
Outlook meeting
in your calendar.

REMEMBER

You can install Teams on Windows, Mac, and Linux. If you're using a temporary computer, you can use the web version of Teams. You can also install Teams on your mobile device running iOS or Android. However, attending meetings may be be more productive when you're sitting at a desk using a full keyboard, video camera, and microphone on a laptop or desktop computer. (Installing the Teams client is discussed in Chapter 13.)

TIP

Recent (and handy!) additions to meetings in Microsoft Teams include the following:

>> An increase in the number of people you can view at the same time from four to nine (you can see an example of a larger meeting in Figure 15-9)

>> A "raise hands" feature that lets you notify other attendees that you would like to speak (especially useful for large meetings)

>> The ability to customize your video background from a list of selected images, in addition to the ability to blur your background

>> The ability to blur your background on a mobile device, not just a desktop

>> Live captions that let you read and follow along with what's said during meetings

>> The ability for a meeting organizer to end a meeting for all attendees simultaneously

TIP

You can keep up with changes to meetings and more at https://techcommunity. microsoft.com/t5/microsoft-teams-blog/bg-p/MicrosoftTeamsBlog.

Using Teams for Conference Calls

If you expect people to call into the meeting using a traditional phone number, you can set up Audio Conferencing, which requires you to obtain a phone plan. When you set up the Audio Conferencing feature in Teams, a traditional phone number is assigned to the meeting. Participants are then able to dial into the audio portion of the meeting using a traditional phone. However, these attendees won't get the full meeting experience of sharing files and video.

MEETING CHATTER

Often a Teams meeting will have a chat going during the meeting, and everyone in the team can enter messages and follow along. The presenter can review the chat conversations and answer questions as time permits. In addition, people can share links and files in the chat portion of a meeting. One of the nice things about the chat portion of Teams is that you can always catch up later and see any of the discussions and chatter you may have missed if you're late to a meeting. If you miss the entire meeting, you can review the recording and catch up.

The chat portion of a Teams meeting is a great way to communicate information that is relevant to the meeting. For example, if someone is talking about a specific Excel spreadsheet, he can paste a link to that document in the chat so that everyone can access it immediately.

WARNING

The Audio Conferencing feature is not available in every country. You can check whether it's available in your country by using your favorite search engine and searching for "Audio Conferencing in Microsoft Teams." You can also search the official Microsoft site at `https://docs.microsoft.com`.

Using Teams for Video Calls

Meetings have evolved over the years. In the old days, everyone would crowd into a room and meet in person. People who weren't in the same location could call into a phone number so that everyone could share a line and hear each other. All that changed when meetings went online with Lync and Skype. Teams is a continuation of these tried-and-true products, and Microsoft has evolved and consolidated its meeting technology with Teams.

TECHNICAL STUFF

Lync was a standard product used for chat and meetings for many years. Then the product name changed to Skype for Business, and now Skype for Business has been gobbled up by Teams. If you have experience with any of these past products, you'll feel right at home in Teams. The interface is different, but the concepts are the same.

A Teams meeting can include many different features. At the most basic level, a Teams meeting provides an online chat group, a voice link, and a shared screen where people can present presentations, share their screens, and see each other through video.

A meeting is often more productive and inclusive when you can see the other participants and watch their reactions and facial expressions. Teams works especially well at making a meeting feel inclusive when the conference room also has video of the entire room. That way people offsite and the people in the room can see each other *and* the presentation at the same time. The people offsite see the presentation and the video of the room on their computer screens. The people in the room see the presentation and the video of those offsite projected on the wall. This functionality makes a meeting with a dispersed team feel very natural and efficient. When you're part of a meeting without video, you can end up feeling like you're on the outside of the meeting and that everyone in the room is on the inside. When there is video, you feel very much connected to the rest of the people because you can see them and they can see you. In order to make this happen, you need to have special hardware designed for Teams.

To conduct a video call in a Teams chat, follow these steps:

1. **Click the Chat icon in the left navigation pane and then click the chat message for the person you want to call.**

   If you don't already have a chat going with the person you want to meet with, you can start one by clicking the New Chat icon (which looks like a pencil writing on a paper).

2. **To start a video call, click the video icon in the upper-right corner of the chat, as shown in Figure 15-10.**

   The video call will start ringing the other person. You can click the video icon or the audio icon to turn off your video camera or mute your audio button, as shown in Figure 15-11.

Click to start a video call

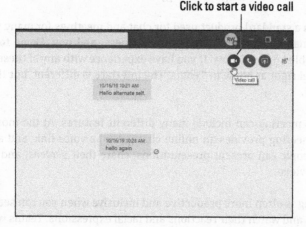

FIGURE 15-10: Starting a video from a chat.

You can turn off your webcam and microphone at any time throughout the call as well. For example, maybe you have a child who runs into the room unexpectedly and you want to turn off your webcam for a moment, or your dog starts barking and you need to mute your microphone. Click the video icon or the audio icon and the webcam will be disabled or the audio will be muted. To enable them again, simply click them again.

TIP

3. **When you're finished with the call, click the red hang-up icon and the call will end.**

You can start a video call from just about anywhere in Teams. Just hover your mouse over the name of the person you want to call and then click the video icon. You can find all your contacts by clicking the Calls icon in the left navigation pane and then clicking Contacts. I generally just hover over a person's name in a channel or start a call from a chat as outlined in the previous steps.

TIP

Click to turn the webcam on or off

During a Teams meeting, most of the Teams window is usually taken up by the presentation someone is discussing. If a presentation is not active, then the screen fills with the video of the person speaking.

You can customize the way these components appear on your computer. To customize these components, all you need to do is hover your mouse over the main display screen to reveal the meeting control icons (see Figure 15-12). In addition to using these icons to turn your webcam and microphone on or off, you can also make adjustments to how your screen appears. For example, clicking the icon of a little monitor with an arrow pointing up into it will pop out the video or the presentation so that you can view different aspects of the meeting on different monitors or on different portions of a large monitor.

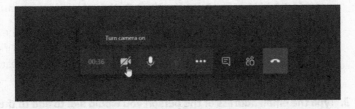

The defaults generally work well, so you may not need to change things most of the time. But just be aware that you can if you want to. The best way to discover this functionality is to hover the mouse over the meeting and test out the icons that appear.

THE GUEST USER EXPERIENCE IN MICROSOFT TEAMS

Anyone you add to Teams who is *not* part of your Microsoft 365 or Office 365 subscription gets added as a guest user. To enable guest access in the Teams Admin Center, follow these steps:

1. **Open your web browser and log in to the Teams Admin Center at** https://admin.teams.microsoft.com.

   Note that you need to be a Teams administrator in order to access the Teams Admin Center. If you signed up for the Microsoft 365 or Office 365 subscription, you're an administrator by default.

2. **In the left navigation pane, click Org-Wide Settings and then click Guest Access.**

   The Guest Access screen appears, where you can toggle this option on or off.

3. **Toggle the setting to allow guest access to Teams.**

   When you toggle on guest access, additional settings appear. There are settings for calls, meetings, and messaging, and you can toggle them on or off based on your preferences.

4. **Click the Save button to save your changes.**

   Guest access is now enabled for Teams.

Guest users can be anyone outside your organization. To add a guest user to your team, follow these steps:

1. **Click the Teams icon in the left navigation pane to see a list of all your teams.**

2. **Next to the team to which you would like to add a guest user, click the ellipsis and select Add Member from the More Options drop-down menu.**

   The Add Members dialog box appears. Make sure the message at the top of the dialog says that you can also add people outside your organization. If you don't see this, refer to the preceding directions to turn on the Guest Access feature in the Teams Admin Center.

3. **Type the email address of the person you would like to add to the team.**

   When the email is verified as valid, you can select it from the drop-down menu that appears.

4. **Enter as many email addresses as you would like to add and then click the Add button.**

5. **Click the Close button to close the dialog box.**

After you've added guest users, you can send them chat messages in the channel and mention them using the @ ("at") symbol.

The guest will receive an email message that invites her to join the team. If her email address is already associated with a user in Teams, then she can immediately start chatting with you. If the guest user is new to Teams, she'll be guided through a setup process and be able to start chatting with you using the web version of Teams.

In addition to adding guests using their email addresses, you can get a URL link to the team and send that link to anyone you want to invite to join the channel. When invitees click the link, they can log in with their Microsoft accounts and they're automatically joined to the team as guests. You can get a link to the team by going to the More Options drop-down menu next to the team and choosing the Get Link to Team option. You find the link on the drop-down menu when you click the ellipsis next to the name of a team.

You can also host online meetings with guest users. Just include your guest's email address when you schedule a meeting in Teams, and your guest will get an email invitation with instructions on how to join your meeting. Your guest can click the link, enter her name, and join the meeting from her browser.

The general experience of collaborating with a guest user is almost identical to working with colleagues on the same Microsoft 365 or Office 365 subscription. However, there are some differences. If you choose to allow it, you can let guest users create channels, participate in channel conversations and private chats, post and edit messages, and share channels. However, guest users cannot create teams, join public teams, view org charts, share files from a private chat, add apps, create meetings, access schedules, access OneDrive files, or invite other guests. There are also many limitations for guests regarding using voice and calling features in Teams.

If you're interested in learning more about this topic, Microsoft has an excellent article titled "What the guest experience is like"; you can find it at https://docs.microsoft.com/en-us/microsoftteams/guest-experience. It goes into all the nitty-gritty detail of working with Teams as a guest, and you can refer to it and the tables it contains whenever you're working with a guest user and you're trying to figure out why something works for you but not for them.

If you've invited someone to a meeting who doesn't have a Teams account, you can also point the guest to the Microsoft article entitled "Join a meeting without a Teams account" for guidance. It's available at https://support.microsoft.com/en-us/office/join-a-meeting-without-a-teams-account-c6efc38f-4e03-4e79-b28f-e65a4c039508.

5

Managing Employees from Home

Chapter **16**

Introducing the Basics of Managing Virtual Employees

The past decade has seen a major shift in the attitudes of companies — and the attitudes of the men and women who run them — toward a more worker-friendly workplace. Today's managers are much more flexible and willing to work with the unique needs of their employees than ever before. Why? Because savvy managers realize that they can get more from employees with a little consideration (and employees increasingly expect this). So, whether employees need to drop off their kids at school in the morning, work only on certain days of the week, or take an extended leave of absence to care for an ill relative, managers are more likely to do whatever they can to accommodate workers' needs.

This shift in attitudes (as well as changes in the nature of work, the improvement of technology, and reduced levels of management in many organizations) has led to its eventual conclusion: virtual employees who spend most of their work hours away from established company offices and worksites, employees managed from a distance, employees who work a variety of shifts or have differing starting and ending times, and employees who telecommute to the office from the comfort of their homes.

Of course, these changes haven't been easy for the managers who are required to implement them. For managers who are used to having employees nearby and ready to instantly respond to the needs of customers and clients, managing off-site employees can be a bit disconcerting. But that doesn't have to be the case. Virtual employees can be just as good as the ones in the office. In fact, they can be more loyal, more effective, and more highly motivated . . . as long as you know how to manage them effectively.

This chapter considers this new kind of work arrangement and how best to work with virtual employees. You explore strategies for effectively managing far-away employees and employees who work differing shifts, and you take a look at the future of telecommuting.

Making Room for a New Kind of Employee

A new kind of employee is out there — the *virtual* employee. Exactly what does *virtual employee* mean? A virtual employee is simply someone who regularly works somewhere outside of the regular bricks-and-mortar offices that house a company's business operations. Virtual employees join employees who have accepted (and often clamored for) a variety of alternative working arrangements, including alternate work schedules and flexible work schedules. Such arrangements can range from something as simple as starting and ending the workday outside the standard (or core) business hours, all the way to working full-time from home.

But don't these kinds of arrangements cost a company more or result in less productive employees? At this time, the evidence says no. At one point, IBM found that it saves an average of 40 percent to 60 percent of its real estate expenses each year by eliminating offices for all employees except those who truly need them. The company recorded productivity gains of 15 percent to 40 percent after instituting a virtual workplace. Hewlett-Packard doubled revenues per salesperson after it created virtual workplace arrangements for its people. And Andersen Consulting discovered that its consultants spent 25 percent more time with clients when their regular physical offices were eliminated.

REMEMBER

Managing people who aren't physically located near you can be particularly challenging, and you have to approach it differently than managing employees who work in the same physical location. Perhaps your employees are located at a different facility or even in a different state (called *remote employees*), or maybe they're telecommuting from their homes, a local library, or even a coffee shop. But regardless of the reason for the separation, these new distance-working relationships make it harder for managers to identify and acknowledge desired behavior and performance. You have to be more systematic and intentional in determining whether employees are fully performing their duties to the same standard as employees housed in a regular office.

Preparing to get virtual

Is your company ready for virtual employees? Are you ready for virtual employees? The following quick-and-easy checklist can help you determine whether your organization is ready and taking steps to make it so:

❑ Your company has established work standards to measure employee performance.

❑ Prospective virtual employees have the equipment they need to properly perform their work offsite.

❑ The work can be performed offsite.

❑ The work can be completed without ongoing interaction with other employees.

❑ Prospective virtual employees have demonstrated that they can work effectively without day-to-day supervision.

❑ Supervisors can manage and monitor employees by their results rather than by direct observation.

❑ Any state or local requirements for virtual workers (including overtime pay requirements) have been discussed with your legal and human resources departments.

❑ The company policy on flexible work arrangements is clear and has been well communicated.

❑ A standard agreement is in place to be used to document the terms of each customized work arrangement.

❑ Employee worksites have been examined to ensure that they're adequately equipped.

If you checked off most of the items on this list, your organization is ready, willing, and able to initiate (or keep) alternative work arrangements with your employees. If you have lots of empty boxes, you have your work cut out for you before you can reasonably expect virtual employees to be a viable option in your organization.

To make your organization more ready for virtual employees, take another look at the checklist. By addressing each box that doesn't have a check mark, you bring your company closer to making virtual employees a reality. For example, if your company doesn't have the equipment virtual employees need to do their work offsite — say, laptop computers and smartphones — then you can budget for and buy them. Or if you don't have a clear company policy on flexible work arrangements, you can create one. As you address each of the unchecked boxes, you're one step closer to your goal.

Understanding changes to the office culture

One of the key concerns for managers when an increasing number of employees become virtual employees is this: What happens to the company's culture (and employee performance) as more workers work outside the office? After all, a company's culture is mostly defined by the day-to-day interactions of employees within a company's four walls. Employees who work outside these interactions probably have no grounding in an organization's culture and have little attachment to other employees or to the organization's values and goals. The result? Employees who are potentially less productive than regular employees, with lowered teamwork and loyalty.

The good news is that you can take a number of steps to help your virtual workers plug into your company's culture, become team players, and gain a stake in the organization's goals in the process.

Consider the following ideas:

>> **Schedule regular meetings that everyone attends — in person or by telephone conference call or Internet videoconferencing system.** Discuss current company events and set aside time for the group to tackle and solve at least one pressing organizational issue — or more, if time permits.

>> **Create communication vehicles that everyone can be a part of.** For example, you can send employees audio or video recordings to listen to when and where convenient. These recordings can cover anything from current company happenings and policies to questions and answers and more.

>> **Hire a facilitator and schedule periodic team-building sessions with all your employees — virtual and nonvirtual — to build working relationships and trust among employees.** Flip to Chapter 19 for more on building trust with employees.

>> **Initiate regular, inexpensive group events that draw out your virtual employees to mingle and get to know regular employees — and each other.** Going out to lunch on the company's tab, volunteering to help a local charity, having a potluck at a local park — the possibilities are endless.

WARNING

As a manager, you need to consider the reality that virtual employees face issues and challenges that conventional in-house employees don't:

>> Virtual employees may find that they're not fairly compensated by their employers for the home resources (office space, computers, electricity, furniture, and so forth) that they contribute to the job. Many employers feel that employees should contribute these items for nothing — as a quid pro quo for being allowed to work outside the office.

>> Virtual employees may feel that their personal privacy is being violated if management efforts are too intrusive. Keep in mind that your employees aren't available 24/7. Respect their work hours and use work phone numbers and email addresses — not home contact information — when you want to communicate.

>> Regular employees may become jealous of virtual employees' "special privileges."

>> Family duties may intrude on work duties much more often for employees who work at home than for employees who work in traditional offices.

These issues don't mean that you should just forget about offering your employees alternative working arrangements. It just means that you need to be aware of them and work to ensure that they don't cause problems for your virtual — or regular — employees.

Weighing the pros and cons of telecommuting

With the proliferation of personal computers — both at work and at home — and the availability of fast and inexpensive Internet hookups and communications software, telecommuting is becoming a common arrangement with many benefits. According to studies, employee productivity can increase by 30 percent, less time is lost as people sit in cars or mass transit to and from work, workers are more satisfied with their jobs, and society (and our lungs) benefits from fewer cars on the road every rush hour.

Although the idea of virtual employees seems to be catching on in the world of business, you, as a manager, need to consider some pros and cons when your thoughts turn to the idea of telecommuting.

Here are some advantages to telecommuting:

>> Depending on the job, employees can set their own schedules.

>> Employees can spend more time with customers.

>> Distracting office politics are often reduced.

>> Employees can conduct more work because everything is there where they need it. (And when they get bored on a Saturday afternoon, they just may do an hour or two of work.)

>> You may be able to save money by downsizing your facilities.

>> Costs of electricity, water, and other overhead are reduced.

>> Employee morale is enhanced because people have the opportunity to experience the freedom of working from their own homes or other locations of their choice.

WARNING

And here are some of the disadvantages to telecommuting:

>> Monitoring employee performance is more difficult.

>> Scheduling meetings can be problematic.

>> You may have to pay to set up your employees with the equipment they need to telecommute.

>> Employees can lose their feelings of being connected to the organization.

>> You must be more organized in making assignments.

For many employees, the prospect of being able to work out of their own homes is much more appealing than merging onto the freeway each morning. For example, Scott still gets out of bed at about the same time he did when he worked at a large corporate publisher, but now his commute is a few steps down the hall instead of an hour and 15 minutes of bumper-to-bumper, smog-filled, Los Angeles stop-and-go traffic. By 9:30 a.m. (15 minutes before his old starting time), he has already made several calls to his East Coast clients, contacted publishing contacts overseas, and created a sales presentation on his computer.

However, telecommuting isn't just a plus for your current employees. It can be a powerful recruiting tool when you're on the hunt for new people to supplement your workforce. As Baby Boomers retire and move on to greener pastures (or golf courses), the younger generations (Generation X and millennials) will have fewer people to replace them. Long story short, a shortage of good workers is going to arise. Anything you can do to attract and retain good employees in the future will become not just a nicety, but a necessity.

Managing from a Distance

With the changing nature of work today, managers have to adapt to new circumstances for managing employees. How can managers keep up with an employee's performance when that employee may not even have physical contact with the manager for weeks or months at a time? The following sections can help.

Increasing your interaction

REMEMBER

Today's managers have to work harder to manage distant employees. If you value strong working relationships and clear communication (and you should), you need to reach out to your virtual employees to be sure adequate communication is taking place. Some of the answers to managing virtual employees effectively lie in a return to the following basics of human interaction:

>> **Make time for people.** Nothing beats face time when it comes to building trusting relationships. Managing is a people job — if you're a manager, you need to take time for people. It's part of the job. And you need to do so not only when taking time is convenient, but also whenever employees are available and need to meet.

>> **Increase communication as you increase distance.** The greater the distance from one's manager, the greater the effort both parties have to make to keep in touch. And although some employees want to be as autonomous as possible and want to minimize their day-to-day contact with you, other employees quickly feel neglected or ignored if you don't make a routine effort to communicate with them. Increase communication by sending regular updates and scheduling meetings and visits more frequently. Also, encourage your employees to contact you (communication is a two-way street, after all), and go out of your way to provide the same types of communication meetings with each work shift or to arrange meetings that overlap work shifts or duplicate awards for each facility.

>> **Use technology.** Don't let technology use you. Use technology as a more effective way to communicate with your employees, not just to distribute data. Promote the exchange of information and encourage questions. You can set up communication channels on your company intranet or within a password-protected area of your company's website. See Parts 2, 3, and 4 for details on three other platforms you can use: Slack, Zoom, and Microsoft Teams.

Providing long-distance recognition

TIP

Every employee needs to be recognized by a manager for a job well done. Just because an employee is out of sight doesn't mean that person should be out of mind. Consider some steps you can take to make sure your virtual employees feel just as appreciated as your regular employees:

>> Ask virtual team members to keep the leader and other team members apprised of their accomplishments, because they can't be as readily seen.

>> Keep a recognition log of remote team members so that they don't fall into the cracks — a particularly important consideration for mixed teams (with both traditional and virtual team members).

>> Make sure that virtual team members are appropriately included in recognition programs by ensuring that remote employees are kept fully in the loop.

>> Provide some "treat" for virtual team members who can't join in face-to-face socials and celebrations.

>> Utilize recognition activities and items that are appropriate for a mobile workforce, such as thank-you cards and gift certificates.

>> Tap into the recognition capabilities of email, such as virtual flowers or greeting cards.

>> Involve executives in recognition activities by way of conference calls, videoconferencing, or periodic in-person awards programs.

>> Make a point of employing a variety of team recognition items (such as coffee mugs, T-shirts, jackets, and so forth) when rewarding members of virtual teams. Such items help remind them of their team membership.

Using the Internet

Managing employees is a challenge when you've got them right there in front of you. However, when your employees are across town — or on the other side of the globe, nine time zones away — this challenge is multiplied many times. The good news is that, just as the Internet has brought the world closer together in many different ways, the Internet can help bring your far-flung employee team closer together while making your job of managing easier. These tools can do just that:

>> **Teleconferencing and videoconferencing:** You can find a number of Internet-enabled teleconferencing websites, including Zoom (www.zoom.us; see Part 3) and FreeConferenceCall.com (www.freeconferencecall.com). Some of these sites provide service for free, but others require you to pay. All

offer a variety of different features, including instant conference calls, scheduled calls, recording, conversation transcription, and more. If you want to conduct videoconferences, many of the teleconferencing companies' sites can also do that. Skype (www.skype.com) allows you to set up videoconferences for free.

>> **Virtual meetings:** If you've got a group larger than just a few people and you want to integrate your computer into the proceedings (to display documents, spreadsheets, graphics, and so forth), consider checking out some of the providers of virtual meeting services. Some of the most popular are Microsoft Teams (see Part 4) and GoToMeeting (www.gotomeeting.com). Prices for these services vary, but most offer a free trial period, so be sure to try before you buy.

>> **Project collaboration sites:** One of the most difficult challenges in managing virtual employees arises when you're working together on a project. Usually team members need to swap a lot of documents and files; plus, occasional get-togethers are necessary to ensure that everyone is working from the same page. Project collaboration sites such as Slack (www.slack.com; see Part 2), Basecamp (www.basecamp.com), and Easy Projects (www.easyprojects.net) make the job much easier and more effective. Most offer a variety of online project collaboration tools such as project milestone charts, project updates and check-ins, shared task lists, virtual brainstorm sessions, and much more. Again, prices and exact services vary, so be sure the system meets your needs before you make a long-term commitment.

Of course, you can still use your telephone, as well as email or text messages, to conduct the majority of your interactions with your virtual employees. And don't forget to schedule an occasional in-person team meeting where everyone has an opportunity to spend some time together and put faces behind the voices. However, when you need to manage a project or pull together a meeting with more than an employee or two, these Internet-based tools give you a distinct advantage.

Managing Different Shifts

The challenge of managing today's employees is made harder by the fact that the nature of work is changing so dramatically and so quickly. Employers have increasingly supplemented traditional work schedules with more flexible scheduling options. Managing employees who work differing shifts is a special challenge for today's managers; this situation can include managing people who work across a number of time zones.

Here are some strategies to consider when making the most of working with shift employees:

>> **Take time to orient shift employees.** All employees need to get their bearings, and shift employees can often be at a disadvantage because they're working outside a company's normal hours. Be sure to let them know what they can expect about the job and the organization, including work policies you expect them to abide by. And create opportunities for them to personally meet all other individuals they need to know or work with.

>> **Give them the resources to be productive.** Giving them the resources can range from the right equipment to do the job, to access to others when they have a question. Other resources include the right instruction and training, especially about company products and services, work processes, internal procedures, and administrative requirements.

>> **Make an ongoing effort to communicate.** The importance of communication is almost a cliché, but you can't underestimate its value. Many employees prefer to silently suffer through poor directions instead of running the risk that they'll seem slow to grasp an assignment — and possibly be labeled as difficult to work with. Constantly check with shift employees to see whether they have questions or need help. Make every personal interaction count to find out how the employees are doing and how you can better help them.

TIP

Some managers schedule meetings at shift change to get two shifts at once. Have key staff contacts from your human resources, finance, and legal departments come in occasionally to answer questions as well.

>> **Appreciate employees for the jobs they do.** Even if an employee is at work only outside the standard work schedule, his need to be recognized for hard work and accomplishments is still as great as any other employee's, although his circumstances make it more inconvenient to thank him. Fortunately, a little appreciation can go a long way. Take the time to find out what may motivate extra performance and then deliver such rewards when you receive the desired performance.

>> **Treat shift employees the way you want them to act.** If you want shift employees to have a long-term perspective, treat them with a long-term perspective. Make them feel a part of the team. Treating shift employees with courtesy and professionalism can help establish your reputation as a desirable employer to work for and, thus, attract additional talent when you need it.

Chapter **17**

Transitioning from Old-School Manager to Virtual Team Leader

W hen leading a virtual team, using an old-school style of management isn't only out, it's outlandish to even think it can work.

If you try to use an old-school style of management with your virtual team, you'll be completely out of your depths in the new world reality of virtual team leadership. The ways of old-school management — which some business schools are still teaching — become a liability on a virtual team where adaptability, emotional intelligence, and a collaborative mindset are required.

More than likely, you know what old-school management looks and feels like. It's top-down, command and control. It's closed-minded and bullying. It always knows best, never asks your opinion, and fears change. It doesn't value diversity of people or ideas. It makes you feel like you just stepped into an episode of *Mad Men*, but no one offered you a scotch. If you use an old-school style of management, you'll likely fail miserably as a virtual team leader.

This chapter examines and compares leadership styles that can work most effectively in a virtual environment. If you've worked in a traditional environment up until now, consider adopting a new mindset and style of management that can serve you and your team in the best way possible. This chapter also offers tips on building a team community and steering clear of common problems that virtual teams face.

Recognizing Which Leadership Style Works Best

What makes a virtual team effective includes building trust and connection, supporting self-directed work, setting clear expectations and goals, providing collaborative opportunities, and engaging in innovative thinking.

These are the skills of an authentic leader. They're also essential skills to adopt when you're the leader of a virtual team. The following sections explain the qualities that make virtual leaders successful, as well as what leadership style and approach work best with a virtual team.

Examining what makes virtual team leaders succeed

REMEMBER

Understanding the mindset of a leader who excels in a virtual environment can help you assess your current leadership style and where you have opportunity to grow. Here are common qualities that have helped virtual team leaders succeed:

>> **Flexibility:** The 9-to-5 model is dead, even for people who work in offices. On virtual teams, work happens at all times of the day (and night) to accommodate team members across the country and around the world. More and more, people are working less traditional business hours. Effective leaders of virtual teams understand that their team has been hired to produce a specific outcome and are willing to adapt to members' various work schedules while keeping an eye on the big picture.

>> **Trust:** Micromanaging from afar is a nuisance to team members and a waste of time for the team leader. Effective virtual team leaders know how to provide employees the resources they need to do the job and then trust them to get it done.

- >> **Communication:** The idea that technology hinders communication is outdated. After all, technology *is* communication. Leaders of virtual teams who communicate most effectively, most often, and most efficiently with technology are the most successful. Effective leaders of virtual teams recognize the need for more communication, feedback, and guidance than onsite teams and step up their game in this area.

- >> **Comfort with technology:** You don't need mad programming skills, but you need a general understanding of the technology that gets your team collaborating and communicating. Effective leaders choose their technology wisely and are quick to put it into practice and lead the way. (See Parts 2, 3, and 4 for details on different platforms that can help you work virtually.)

- >> **Listener:** Effective leaders of virtual teams are empathetic and know when to talk and when to solicit feedback. They know when something is off with a team member and a face-to-face meeting is necessary. They also take time to listen deeply and with a sense of curiosity, so they can discover where to support their team members where they need it most.

- >> **Collaborator:** Leaders must be able to lead people and teams through collaboration. Working with others when you're all under the same roof can be difficult. Adding distance and different time zones to the equation can further complicate things. The best virtual leaders know how to overcome these challenges and foster strong collaboration within their teams.

- >> **Patience:** Some things will take more time when you aren't in close proximity. Effective virtual leaders are used to it and are patient with the process. And they're always looking for ways to streamline and improve.

- >> **Diversity champion:** Leaders who get the best results from their virtual team appreciate diversity in all forms — gender, age, religion, culture, ethnicity, sexual orientation, sexual identity, and, of course, diversity of thought. They adapt to their increasingly diverse employee base and demonstrate sensitivity to a variety of backgrounds, worldviews, and values on their teams.

- >> **Results oriented:** All managers need to be results oriented, but effective virtual team leaders have clear individual accountability in place with agreed methods of monitoring and measuring performance. They worry less about how their team members are spending their time or when they actually do their work and, instead, focus on delivering results.

In addition to having the right mindset, succeeding as a virtual leader requires that you're astute enough to recognize what style of leadership will work with different people and in different situations.

AN OLD-SCHOOL MANAGER'S MINDSET

Most managers aren't complete dinosaurs, but many do have some shades of old-school thinking. Here are a few things that shape their mindset:

- **Seeing is believing.** Old-school managers equate time at your desk or at the office with productive work. If they can't see you doing the work, then obviously you're slacking off. Not only will they micromanage your time, but as an added bonus, they'll constantly ask for updates.

- **Desiring work–life balance is soft.** If you want to attend your kid's school function in the middle of the day or leave work at 5 p.m. every day, then you're not committed to your job. Old-school managers see these types of requests as outrageous and don't place any value on providing flexibility to their employees so that they can manage the increased demands of everyday life.

- **I'm in charge. Now let me beat my chest.** Old-school managers don't want to be challenged, and they rarely use collaboration skills. Their body language will almost always communicate superiority, whether they cut you off in a meeting, don't listen to your ideas, or take your good ideas and make them their own. They'll look for every opportunity to demonstrate they're in charge. These managers expect that you'll never challenge authority by asking questions, offering feedback, or voicing disagreement; they prefer to be surrounded by yes people who do as they're told.

- **I deserve reverence and respect.** Generational bias is a real thing, and old-school managers simply don't get it. They rarely tap into the breadth of new skills and new insights of their team. Because of experience or education, they believe they obviously know more than anyone at the table.

- **Stay the course. You'll hear from me when you mess up.** Old-school managers can go weeks or even months before they provide you with feedback. When they do, it's because you messed up. The once-a-year performance appraisal is their preferred method of letting you know what they think of your performance, which usually leads to a lot of unwelcomed surprises. Your only recognition for your good work is your paycheck.

You can quickly realize that none of these behaviors will make the cut in a virtual team environment. Your proverbial ship will sink fast. Successful remote workers are most likely more educated than you and want their ideas to be heard and considered. They value transparency, feedback, flexibility, and innovation. In addition, what's more important to them than a paycheck is contributing to a team goal that's meaningful.

Determining whether you're a micromanager, coach, or hands-off manager

Managing and leadership are different, and both are necessary when leading a virtual team. Management requires you to plan, organize, monitor, and execute the work to be done, including

>> Clarifying roles and goals

>> Communicating priorities

>> Organizing resources to get the work done

>> Putting in place measures to analyze success

>> Setting deadlines and holding others accountable

Meanwhile, leadership is establishing direction and influencing team members' behavior through recognition, coaching, support, and communication. As a virtual team leader, doing all these things at one point or another is necessary. However, many virtual team leaders sometimes spend more time in one area or even neglect an area all together. Where a virtual team leader spends the majority of her time usually has to do with her style and what comes most naturally to her. The following sections review three common styles of leadership and when they're appropriate.

REMEMBER

Each of these styles works in different situations, with different team members, at different times. Skilled virtual team leaders know what's going on with each of their team members and adapt their approach and style accordingly.

Directive style

A *directive style* comes naturally to you if you're most comfortable with having control over what gets done and how it gets done. This style is most appropriate when a team member is new, asks for help, needs to gain specific skills or knowledge to reach her goals, or is stuck in some way and needs you to walk her through a process step by step. A directive manager

>> Provides very specific direction

>> Keeps close tabs on the work and how it's being done

>> Gives immediate feedback when something doesn't meet her expectations

>> Sets goals and expectations for the team member

>> Defines processes and procedures for getting the work done

>> Closely monitors results

WARNING

This style of leadership — which is more controlling and can come across as micromanaging — doesn't work well long term and can quickly demotivate your remote team members. In emergency or high-risk situations, this style can be extremely effective because it's fast and clear. But, if this happens to be your natural style, consider opportunities where you can use a more facilitative or hands-off approach with your virtual team.

Facilitative style

A *facilitative style* helps employees use their own internal resources to solve problems and develop skills and knowledge. This style of leader takes time to coach team members and is passionate about their growth. If this is your natural style, you most likely connect with your team directly on a regular basis and are always looking for ways to collaborate. You also do a good job at providing regular feedback and coaching.

By asking open-ended questions, listening closely, and guiding your team members where to look for answers, the facilitative approach relies on your team members' innate abilities and empowers their self-development. A facilitative manager uses questioning techniques to

>> Encourage team members to identify what motivates them

>> Involve team members in problem solving and goal setting

>> Ask team members to develop a plan of action to address any performance issues

>> Provide coaching and support as needed

>> Work together with team members to agree on performance measures and deadlines

REMEMBER

A facilitative style of leadership can work well in a virtual environment but can also cramp the productivity and creativity of high performers on your team who prefer a hands-off approach.

Leaders who excel at using this style are experts at asking great questions. Here are some facilitative questions that you can use:

>> What do you want to have happen?

>> What's already working? What's not working?

>> What has worked for you in the past?

- >> What have you already tried or done?
- >> What are the reasons this didn't work as well as you had hoped?
- >> What is the situation from your point of view?
- >> What is the situation from other perspectives?
- >> What's another way of looking at it?
- >> What needs to happen in order for you to . . .?
- >> What's getting in your way?
- >> What will you take away from this?
- >> If you had to do it over again, what would you do differently?
- >> What resources are available to you?
- >> What would be a courageous action?
- >> What support can I provide you?

Hands-off style

If the *hands-off style* is your natural approach, then you probably agree with the concept of hiring the best and then getting out of their way. You have a great deal of trust in your team members to complete the work. If they're experienced, they have a sense of fulfillment and foster higher levels of creativity.

This style can also work well in leading a virtual team when team members clearly know their role and can deliver results quickly. Collaborative technology and project management software can help you to stay abreast of progress and obstacles while still allowing team members to self-direct their work.

WARNING

Be careful of being too hands-off and becoming disconnected from your team or missing out on details that may indicate a team member is struggling or unhappy. Being hands-off has its benefits, but problems can also more easily hide until it's too late to correct them.

Comparing control-based and trust-based leadership

In a virtual team environment, leaders should focus not on making the team more stable but on making it more *flexible*. The essential difference between the traditional control-oriented team approach and a collaborative, trust-based team approach can be broken down like this:

>> **Control-based, traditional approach:** Maintaining control is a leader's most important job.

>> **Trust-based, collaborative approach:** Anticipating and preparing others for change is a leader's most important job.

When you approach leadership as a collaborative effort — as the person who helps your team foresee and prepare for continuous change — you strengthen your team, build high levels of trust, and demonstrate your value as a leader. Table 17-1 outlines the differences between the two approaches.

TABLE 17-1   **Control-Based versus Trust-Based Leadership**

Control-Based Leadership	Trust-Based Leadership
Control-based leaders believe their power comes from their position.	Collaborative leaders believe that power comes from building trust and cohesion on a team.
Control-based leaders determine and plan the work.	Trust-based leaders determine and plan the work jointly with their team members.
Roles and responsibilities are narrowly defined.	Roles and responsibilities are broad and evolve and shift, depending on need.
Control-based leaders view cross-training as inefficient and unnecessary.	Collaborative leaders consider cross-training the norm and an important part of team effectiveness.
Control-based leaders rarely solicit feedback and input from the team.	Collaborative leaders view feedback and input from the team as a pillar of team culture.
Important information is kept confidential and only between managers.	As much information as possible is freely shared at all levels.
Training focuses on technical skills and solving issues.	Training focuses on building emotional intelligence, leadership, communication, and technical skills.
Control-based leaders discourage and even punish risk taking.	Collaborative leaders encourage and support thoughtful risk taking in the spirit of innovation.
People work alone.	People work together.
Rewards are based on individual performance.	Rewards are based on individual performance contributions to team performance.
The leader determines the best methods.	The team collaborates to analyze and improve methods and processes.
Performance reviews happen once a year.	Performance feedback and coaching happens regularly and consistently.

REMEMBER

On a virtual team, effective teamwork is your greatest strength and most valuable competitive advantage. Trust-based leadership is what to focus on to build and sustain a team environment that brings out the best in your people and garners the best results.

Taking the Opportunity to Grow

Companies that have been around for a while are struggling with making the shift to virtual teams and flexible working arrangements. Why? Because they have a traditional corporate culture with clear lines of authority, established communication methods, old-style performance management systems, a professional work environment, teams that work independently from one another, a keen focus on the bottom line, and a tendency toward being risk averse.

If you've been managing in this type of culture, you most likely are used to the consistency of rules and roles, the way that decisions are made, and the methods by which information is disseminated. It may even bring you a sense of calm and control that feels comfortable.

Due to technology, new forms of communication, and talent spread across the world, traditional cultures have seen a major shift in how they operate, which can be quite a struggle. However, this reality also presents a major opportunity for growth if managers embrace the innovations of technology and a new leadership philosophy.

So, the question is: How do you manage in this new team culture when you work for a traditional company? It's about experimenting, being willing to take risks, trusting your team to make decisions, and pushing authority to the individuals who know the work the best. The following sections help you organize your approach for making the change to a virtual leader.

Pushing the boundaries of culture and C-level expectations

You may not know it yet, but you have the chance to be a trailblazer. You have the opportunity to shift how work gets done, goals are accomplished, and technology is used to communicate. And in some cases, ignoring corporate cultural norms that don't serve your virtual team is unquestionably an important part of the growth process. But taking the leap to establish a new foundation won't be easy.

In fact, a research study on virtual team effectiveness in 2016 glaringly showed an obvious disconnect between how executives perceived the productivity of virtual teams and how the team perceived their results. More than half of all virtual team members reported that increased productivity was a benefit of virtual teams, compared to only 13 percent of executives who agreed. Why the disconnect? Here are some assumptions:

>> Many executives haven't worked in a virtual team environment and come from a more traditional approach managing people and teams. If they can't see you doing the work, they don't believe that actual work is taking place. They may be holding onto a biased way of thinking about how work gets accomplished and what productivity looks like.

>> Executives continue to measure results through traditional methods, such as sales revenue, earnings per share, and quality or service levels when other important ways can measure value that include innovation and collaboration.

>> Virtual teams and remote work are new to the company culture and executives don't understand how to shift their mindset to embrace and support this new world of work.

REMEMBER

If you're leading a virtual team in a traditional culture, you may find that the cards are stacked against you. Success requires you to have a plan of action that includes the following:

>> **Pushing consistent communication to the company, highlighting team projects, progress, and impact to the bottom line:** Your job is to raise awareness about how awesome your team is doing and how it's having a positive impact on others.

>> **Sharing recognition frequently for innovative ideas that are moving forward and for projected financial results if they're implemented:** This proves that your team is creating value.

>> **Introducing remote new hires to the company in a fun, engaging way and sharing what other teams they'll be supporting or working with:** Generate excitement for the level of experience and knowledge that your new team members bring to the company.

Knowing when to manage up

No other relationship can impact your team as much as the relationship you have with your direct manager. Having a solid foundation of trust and openness creates an environment that supports your virtual team members in getting the resources they need to solve problems and address opportunities. If your manager doesn't understand the value your team brings to the table, she won't go to bat for you when issues come up or won't support the work your team is doing if ever questioned.

TIP

Getting your direct manager in your corner is something to take seriously. Here are a few ideas to help you get started:

>> **Be clear and aligned on your team's purpose.** What value does your virtual team bring to the company?

>> **Understand your manager's goals and what drives her.** When you present progress updates or ask for additional resources, describe how your team can help your manager reach her goals.

>> **Nurture the relationship.** Get to know your manager as a person and build trust. Doing so helps you discover more about her style and what's important to her.

>> **Be strategic and anticipate what she needs from you.** Examples include progress reports, stats on what's in the pipeline, error rates, and so on.

>> **Keep your manager in the loop.** Never let your manager get blindsided by a hiring or firing decision. Be sure she's up to date on team dynamics, changes, or resource requirements.

>> **Ask your manager for what you need and provide feedback.** If you need more direction, clarity around goals, recognition for a job well done, ask. She can't read your mind.

>> **Go above and beyond whenever possible.** If your team frequently overdelivers, that creates real value that your manager can easily tout to others in the company.

Recognizing Common Virtual Team Issues

Virtual team issues are similar to in-person team issues, but they may look a bit different and require a different set of skills if you're a traditional manager. If you're used to managing employees you can see every day, you may be surprised by some issues that virtual teams face — and the skills you need to overcome them. This section reviews the most common virtual team issues to help your transition to managing virtual teams be less rocky.

Poor communication

Communication quality and quantity are vital to virtual team success. Unfortunately, research has proven that poor communication is one of the top fail points for virtual teams. Old-school one-way communication won't work.

Good communication leads to good outcomes in new and old virtual teams. Experienced teams that communicate effectively were 19 times more likely to report that their members were highly engaged. Likewise, newly formed teams that communicate effectively are 12 times more likely to accomplish their goals and 55 times more likely to be responsive to customers.

When virtual team leaders and executives viewed communication within the team as strong, they were 31 times more likely to indicate the team accomplishes its goals and 21 times more likely to view the team as effective in responding to customers.

TIP

Be sure to spend the time setting up communication agreements with your virtual team members. Check out Chapter 18 to find out more about best practices in virtual team communication.

Lack of clarity, direction, and priorities

This issue is largely related to poor communication (see the preceding section). Old-school managers may limit discussion of roles and responsibilities to an annual review or face-to-face meeting, which doesn't happen often. Virtual team leaders know that all team members need crystal-clear expectations to ensure productivity and reduce the incorrect assumptions that can fester when there is no regular dialog. And it's ongoing dialog, not just an annual event. Research shows that establishing clear rules of engagement early — and sticking to them — is the key to virtual team success. You're largely responsible for having this conversation and working collaboratively with your team members to establish how and when work will happen, holding them accountable to the agreements, and taking corrective measures, if necessary. When virtual team leaders and executives indicated the team had high levels of accountability, they were

>> Thirty-two times more likely to indicate that the team accomplishes its goals

>> Forty-one times more likely to indicate that the team meets deliverables on time and within budget

>> Twenty-four times more likely to view the team as effective in responding to customers

Loss of team spirit and morale

As a virtual team leader, you're responsible for creating a clear and compelling direction for the team and making sure each individual is connected to the team vision. Old-school managers may assume that team members already understand how they contribute and why they matter, but that mindset and lack of communication can undermine team spirit.

REMEMBER

Creating and nurturing strong morale on your virtual team won't happen overnight — it's created through hundreds of everyday interactions. That's why you need to encourage cohesiveness every time you communicate with team members. That can look like always asking for their opinion, making time for recognition on every team call, or explaining the impact of their work accomplishments on the business.

Lack of trust

You've never met them in person. You can't see what other people are doing. There is a delay in getting responses immediately, and you're rarely working (or in some cases awake) at the same time. It's easy to see why trust can be an issue for an old-school manager.

TIP

To get up to speed with virtual teams, set the example and trust your team members to do the job that they're hired to do. Establishing a culture of strong accountability, setting clear goals and expectations, and creating awareness of each other's contributions also helps to build trust.

Lack of social interaction

For all its perks, working remotely can be isolating. Old-school managers are used to relying on chatting and quick check-ins with team members around the office. Virtual team members miss out on the office banter and in-person friendships that enrich their work lives. In study after study on virtual teams, the research reveals that getting together in real life is important.

TIP

Teams that meet in person frequently have higher effectiveness ratings (defined as meeting goals, team productivity, and engagement) than those that meet two to three times a year. Make it a priority as a virtual team leader to budget for your team to get together and check in on each team member regularly for some non-work conversations.

Tech issues

Not everyone is a technology expert, but people on virtual teams need to be competent at using technology in order to connect with their team. Tech fails — or simply nonuse or underusage of technology — is one of the biggest issues facing virtual teams and leaders. Old-school managers must quickly become fluent in using the team's technology, or the entire team may suffer the consequences.

In fact, in a study conducted with more than 150 remote workers at various Fortune 500 companies, one of the biggest challenges for newly formed virtual teams was figuring out how to effectively use technology. Mastering collaborative technology is imperative for the leader so that she can create efficiency, workflow tracking, and connection within her team. The research showed that teams that rate themselves as effective at using collaborative technology are

>> Ninety-eight times more likely to come up with innovative solutions

>> Seventy-four times more likely to deliver on time and within budget

>> Thirty-seven times more likely to accomplish goals

Flip to Parts 2, 3, and 4 for details on navigating three popular platforms for working at home: Slack, Zoom, and Microsoft Teams.

Cultural clashes

Good communication on virtual teams is vital — even more so when teams cross cultures. Old-fashioned, narrow thinking about people and their backgrounds is dangerous on a virtual team. Virtual team leaders must practice openness and acceptance and encourage others on the team to do the same. Miscommunication on a virtual team can happen in so many different ways than what can happen on an in-house team. Examples include nonverbal cues, voice inflection, or cultural and language nuances that are misunderstood. Virtual teams have a greater responsibility — and challenge — to be inclusive.

IN THIS CHAPTER

» Grasping why good communication is essential

» Recognizing the limitations of text-only communication

» Giving consistent and frequent feedback

» Creating best practices with communication agreements

» Discovering and using different communication styles

Chapter **18**

Adopting Best Practices in Communication

Communication is everything for your virtual team.

If done effectively, it can influence, build trust, empower, and energize your team members. And, of course, if done haphazardly and without thoughtful consideration and collaborative agreement, it can create frustration, confusion, detachment, rework, and even conflict for everyone involved.

Simple, positive approaches to how you and your team communicate can initiate personal shifts in attitude, behavior, style, and focus that have a positive ripple effect throughout your team. The result is establishing powerful communication habits that create happier and more productive, engaged employees, higher levels of respect and trust, as well as improved customer service.

In this chapter, you consider important communication practices to implement with your virtual team. You discover how to recognize and adjust when communication isn't working and what communication method is appropriate when. You find practical strategies for providing consistent feedback, working with different communication styles, and establishing communication agreements. After reading this chapter, you can walk away with ideas that you can implement immediately with your virtual team.

Identifying Four Components to Transform Your Communications

Good communication doesn't just happen all by itself. It requires a commitment to engaging in practices that make it successful. Everyone on your team should ponder four key components before engaging with others. Getting in the habit of using these mindful and thoughtful communication techniques can positively transform your virtual team relationships:

>> **Consider purpose and intent.** You communicate in everything you do. You don't even need to think about it — but you should. Before you speak, write an email, or turn on your laptop camera, consider the purpose and intent of your communication. These questions can help you:

- Why am I sending this message? What do I want recipients to do with it?

- What is their communication style, pace, and knowledge level? How should I adjust?

- What content do they need?

- How much information do they need?

- What is the chance of a misunderstanding?

- What is our relationship like?

Based on the answers to these questions, you can determine how to frame your communication, how much information to share, and what communication method to use.

>> **Consider assumptions.** You know the old adage about making assumptions — everyone makes them and sometimes they're wrong. That's why you need to consider the expectations and beliefs of both the sender and the receiver of any communication before you assume anything. If you're the sender, ask yourself these questions:

- What do I know and believe about this person?

- What assumptions might he make that can impact how he interprets my communication?

- How can I provide more clarity?

As the receiver, ask yourself these questions:

- What do I know and believe about this person?

- What assumptions can impact how I alter this communication?

- How can I get more clarity?

Based on how you answer these questions, you'll have a greater understanding about the questions you should ask, the level of detail you should provide, and the communication method that will work best.

>> **Make use of body language.** By choosing to communicate using a method where your body language is visible such as video, you have a higher chance of ensuring that your intention behind the message is understood correctly. Body language is the natural way people broadcast their true thoughts and feelings, even if the words they use don't match. For example, someone may say, "Yes, I understand," but if his body language says something different, you may stop and ask more questions to make sure he gets it. When you solely rely on words alone, getting your feelings and attitude across is difficult, if not impossible, which is a valuable and intricate part of communicating. Make sure you talk about the importance of body language and how you'll use video technology with your virtual team to limit misunderstandings, confusion, and conflict.

TIP

>> **Incorporate a feedback loop.** A *feedback loop* (see Figure 18-1) ensures that the message sent is the message received. Having the receiver of the communication repeat back to the sender of the communication what she heard and understood in her own words ensures clarity and understanding.

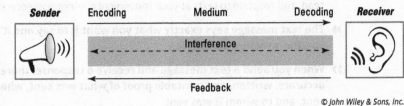

FIGURE 18-1: The feedback loop.

© *John Wiley & Sons, Inc.*

Looking Closer at Text-Only Communication

Not that long ago cell phones just made phone calls. No text, no apps, no calendars, no games, no emoji. Just a phone that was a complete marvel because it wasn't tethered by a cord to a wall. But enough of the nostalgia. Studies show that texting has replaced voice calls and even emails as the primary form of communication. In fact, in a recent poll by *Time*, 32 percent of respondents said they'd rather communicate by text than phone, even with people they know very well. This shift to text isn't just for personal communication. It's even truer in the business world, where people prefer to email or text with colleagues.

Even though more and more people are using text-only communication (instant message [IM], phone text, and chat functions) in the workplace, it does have its pros and cons, which the following sections discuss. The following sections also point out how you can effectively use text-only discussions in your virtual teams.

Examining the pros and cons

The following are the pros to using text-only communication, which includes texts, IMs, and chats:

>> **When you text, you can expect an immediate answer.** Of the 6 billion daily text messages in the United States, the average response time is three minutes. Email response times are getting slower in the wonderful world of spam, and voice calls often aren't answered due to inconvenience or intentional avoidance.

>> **Sending and receiving texts is a breeze.** You don't even need to open an app.

>> **You don't need to worry about time zones.** Similar to email, you can send, read, and respond to texts at your convenience — not someone else's.

>> **The text message says exactly what you want it to say and it's sent to specific, targeted audiences.**

>> **When you send a text message and receive a response, there is an accurate, written, and printable proof of what was sent, when it was sent, and to whom it was sent.**

WARNING

And here are the cons of using text-only communication:

>> **They're an interruption.** Although texts are immediate, people can become overwhelmed when they pop up and interrupt their work, so they may not respond right away or even ignore the communication all together.

>> **They can hinder interpersonal skills.** Developmental psychologists have been studying the impact of texting, and they're especially concerned about younger adults because their interpersonal skills haven't yet fully formed. Most older adults already had fixed social skills before the era of smartphones, although these skills have eroded recently with high text usage.

>> **Without body language, facial expressions, or vocal tone, text messages can be misinterpreted or misunderstood.** It's far too easy for a sarcastic comment to be misconstrued as genuinely hurtful. The real meaning of your message gets lost through the medium.

Your message can be miscommunicated in the following ways:

- **Unspoken feelings:** With text-only communication, you can miss out on the opportunity to discover feelings behind a message or a person's general attitude and understanding about the message that you're conveying. Your intent can easily get lost in translation when you only use words to communicate.

- **Tone of voice:** Tone of voice is an important aspect of communication when working virtually. By using text-only communication, you lose the opportunity to build your personal brand, trust, and influence with team members. Using your voice, you can come across technical, verbose, factual, direct, enthusiastic, friendly, funny, or informal. If you're concerned with building team culture, consider choosing another communication method other than text-only communication.

>> **Diminished language:** Texting creates poor grammar habits. An entire vocabulary of shortened (misspelled) words, acronyms, and emoji not only can lead to confusion and misunderstanding, but it also makes communication much less formal and even can make genuine statements seem insincere. Most important, using poor grammar is highly unprofessional.

>> **Impersonal communication:** When people communicate primarily via text, they're much less likely to have meaningful conversations. For highly sensitive or emotional conversations, such as an apology or a contentious issue, people are avoiding having real conversations and instead taking the easy way out and using text.

Using text-only communication effectively

REMEMBER

The big question is how to use texts, chats, and IMs effectively while still encouraging meaningful communication on your virtual team. It boils down to choosing the right medium for the right message. Ponder two important questions when considering your communication purpose and intent:

>> **What's the chance that the message can be misunderstood?** Consider whether the message is highly technical or contains a lot of details. Ask yourself whether the receiver of the message has the knowledge and skills to understand or comprehend it.

>> **What is the risk to the relationship?** Think about your current relationship with this person or group. Have you had a recent conflict or issue that may have damaged trust? If so, then you need to consider the risk to the relationship if the receiver misreads your message and makes any assumptions about its intent. Do you know the receiver well? Does he trust you and believe that you have his best interest in mind?

Depending on your answer to these questions, you can choose the right method of communication. Figure 18-2 shows a virtual team communication method matrix that can help you determine what method of communication is best to use, ranging from impersonal to more personal methods of communication.

Virtual team communication method matrix

	Low	Medium	High
High	Voice mail or Phone conversation	Videoconference	In person
Medium	Email Chat rooms Voice mail	Phone conversation or Videoconference	Videoconference or In person
Low	IM Text Email	Phone conversation Videoconference	Videoconference In person

Chance of misunderstanding (vertical axis) / *Relationship risk* (horizontal axis)

FIGURE 18-2:
The virtual team communication method matrix.

© John Wiley & Sons, Inc.

TIP

If you want your team to become better communicators, build communication agreements that incorporate different methods of communicating for different situations and reasons. A *communication agreement* basically defines how your team will communicate, by what method, and for what purpose. The later section "Establishing Best Practices with Communication Agreements" discusses how to set up agreements and what to include in them. Be sure to discuss the communication method matrix and agree on when texting is and is not appropriate.

Providing Consistent and Frequent Feedback

Feedback is a gift — and on a virtual team, it's the gift that keeps on giving. Feedback is an opportunity to help others grow and develop on your team, including you. Creating a team culture where constructive feedback is given freely and accepted with care and thoughtfulness is a vital part of building trust. Also, if you've done a good job providing regular feedback to your employees, there should never be any surprises during performance discussions. Employees should have a clear understanding of how they performed toward achieving goals and meeting expectations, as well as what areas they need to work on improving.

One aspect of giving feedback is taking the initiative to have a clear dialogue with each team member. Providing regular feedback keeps the lines of communication open between you and your virtual team members and creates an environment where everyone can succeed. Taking the time to discuss, clarify, and agree on role expectations will enable you to provide feedback that's meaningful down the road. It also helps set up an environment that encourages all your virtual team members to do their very best.

The following sections examine the importance of setting clear expectations and providing frequent, effective feedback to create a strong virtual team relationship with each team member.

Establishing clear expectations

In order to provide valuable feedback, you need to be sure of what you expect from your team members and discuss it with them. This is the best way to make feedback meaningful and in the spirit of helping your team members improve or supporting them in continuing to perform at a high level. To establish expectations, keep the following in mind:

>> **Designate an expected standard level of performance for each team member.**

>> **Discuss agreements or expectations with your virtual team members when they're hired, as well as throughout their tenure.** You can discuss expectations by expressing the what, when, how often, or how much. Here are two examples:

- "Complete your weekly progress update by Friday at 3 p.m. using the team progress update form on Google Drive. Provide information on your wins/accomplishments and obstacles/solutions, as well as your plan for the following week."

- "Respond to all customer complaints via the website within one hour and be sure that their issue was handled to their satisfaction at the end of each interaction. Provide a follow-up call within 24 hours to thank them for their business and for bringing the problem to our attention."

WARNING

When your feedback blindsides your team members, it usually means that you didn't establish clear expectations from the beginning.

Recognizing the importance of two-way feedback and performance discussions

TIP

When providing feedback to the team, keeping the following key elements in mind is important so that the feedback is clear and understandable and achieves the desired results:

>> **Choose the right communication method.** Depending on what the feedback is for, be sure to choose the right communication method using the matrix provided in the earlier section, "Using text-only communication effectively."

>> **Make it specific.** Craft your communication using clear, objective examples of the behavior or performance that you observed (positive or negative).

>> **Know that timing is everything.** Feedback needs to take place as close as possible to the performance event or behavior that you observed or heard.

>> **Keep it positive and corrective.** Regularly give feedback for performance that needs to be adjusted or for performance that you want to see continue.

>> **Share the impact.** Effective feedback lets the team members know how their behavior or performance affects the team, department, or company. Taking time to explain the impact of the behavior or action removes the feeling of it being a personal opinion.

>> **Allow for team member input.** Your team members should always have an opportunity to share their perceptions. There may be additional information that you need to know.

>> **Turn it into an opportunity.** Feedback is an excellent opportunity to work together to establish an action plan for improvement to redefine expectations or goals or to put developmental plans in place if necessary.

By using these feedback strategies consistently, you can create a culture of transparency and openness that can help your virtual team experience the greatest levels of success.

Giving feedback: The how-to

Most team leaders aren't experts at giving feedback. Most virtual leaders usually don't have a good template for providing feedback that is simple, to the point, and clear, and offers an opportunity for collaboration.

The following five-step feedback model walks both leaders and team members through the feedback delivery process to ensure the feedback is clear, effective, and respectful:

1. **Describe the facts.**

   Express and explain the specific concrete behaviors or actions that you noticed, heard about, or witnessed firsthand. Discuss facts only, no judgment, which means no adjectives or general traits.

2. **Focus on the impact of the behavior or action.**

   State how the behavior or action impacted the result and/or the individual, team, organization, or customers in a positive or negative way. By focusing on the impact and not the person, you help to keep your team member from getting defensive.

3. **Offer some time for reflection.**

   Provide an opportunity for your team member to reflect on the feedback and provide insight about the situation. Involve her in considering the impacts and what may happen if it continues.

4. **Work together to come up with a solution or reinforcement.**

Collaborate to gain commitment to specific future actions or changes in behaviors, or reinforce the positive behavior that you want to see continue.

5. **Follow up to chat about progress or questions.**

Plan a time to follow up in the near future to discuss any progress or questions the team member may have. Follow-up also provides the opportunity to offer recognition if she was able to turn around a particular behavior quickly.

In a virtual environment, all types of communication are vital to success. However, giving feedback to your virtual team members is one of the most critical (and most often overlooked) components of effective communication.

Shifting focus from individual accountability to team accountability

If your virtual team is truly a team and not a bunch of individuals working as lone rangers in remote places around the globe, then creating team accountability for results is the way to go. Although your virtual team consists of unique individuals with distinctive skills, the team as a whole needs to understand what it's responsible for accomplishing collectively.

TIP

Here are tips for creating team accountability:

>> **Define a common purpose and goal.** Be sure to provide feedback on the team's purpose and what the team is meant to accomplish. Discuss how important each role is to the team's success, and have all team members provide feedback on how they impact the goal.

>> **Discuss role expectations and what success looks like.** Clarify what each team member is responsible for and where people need to collaborate and why. Gather feedback from the team to create a story of what success for the team looks like.

>> **Measure and track.** Use technology to measure and track team progress. This tip should be visible to all and improves accountability when it's obvious that one team member isn't pulling his weight.

>> **Collaborate and coach.** Look for opportunities in team meetings to ask questions, encourage insight and participation with problem solving, and offer coaching and support when necessary.

>> **Hold each other accountable.** Agree up front how team members will hold each other accountable. Practice how to provide feedback to each other.

>> **Communicate and recognize.** Constantly communicate progress and provide feedback on successes. Explain how certain behaviors or skills have helped the team move forward. Generously share recognition and feedback when things are working to keep the team moving in the same direction.

>> **Continually discuss improvement opportunities.** Create space for reflection as an approach to continuous improvement where the team provides feedback on what's working well and where improvements need to be made. Work together on formulating new solutions.

Establishing Best Practices with Communication Agreements

Every virtual team needs to agree on guidelines about how you'll communicate, the technology and methods you'll use, and what's acceptable and unacceptable concerning response times, participation levels, and more. Taking a mindful approach to communication is the best strategy to steer clear of accidental communication that can quickly wreak havoc on your virtual team.

REMEMBER

Mindful communication involves planning and coordination between team members to agree on communication expectations for a variety of situations. It supports transparency, helps to address difficult situations such as conflict or problem solving, and increases team and personal engagement.

On the other hand, accidental communication is when your team has no plan in place for communication, which creates a reactive culture. There is a lack of coordination and alignment of goals and usually an avoidance and fear of dealing with conflict and difficulty solving common team issues. The following sections discuss a few mindful communication agreements to discuss with your team.

Choosing appropriate communication methods

Agreeing when to pick up the phone, scheduling a video call, or even getting the team together in person is important. Talking through what communication methods are appropriate and when to use them is important for building team trust. Furthermore, understanding the level of comfort different team members may have for using different methods is also helpful. Some team members may prefer to text, whereas others may prefer to email. Individual team members or the team as a whole can make agreements and may choose a preferred method of communication as a group.

Here's when to use each mode of communication and the best practices when you do use them:

>> **IMs:** Use IMs when

- The issue is fast and easy to resolve.

- You can keep it simple and to the point and complete the conversation in a few minutes.

- Then information isn't confidential, sensitive, or highly technical.

- You don't have to share personal information or company information.

When you use IMs, follow these best practices:

- Use them to clarify information, inquire about information or resources, or check availability.

- Consider your audience.

- Be brief and to the point.

- Check for spelling errors and use proper grammar.

- End the IM conversation appropriately. Don't leave people hanging.

- Limit the use of acronyms and emoticons.

- Give people time to respond.

- Ask yes-or-no questions.

- Set your IM status appropriately.

- Turn on IM when working remotely.

>> **Email:** Use email when

- The information needs to be delivered to more than one person.

- You want to be sure it was received and/or you want a record.

- You want to be able to easily retrieve it at a later date.

- You're providing an outline or list to help organize your information.

- You want time to compose your thoughts and information and revise your message if needed.

- It's not personal or emotional.

When you use email, follow these best practices:

- Use your subject line as your headline. State the level of importance or action required in the subject line and use the words *URGENT* or *IMPORTANT* sparingly.

- Only carbon copy (cc) people who need a record of the email. Limit the use of reply all. Don't spray messages.

- Know when to bail on email and pick up the phone or have a face-to-face meeting.

- If you need a particular response, decision, or action taken, clearly state it in the email and be specific. Set clear expectations so the receiver can meet them.

- Don't use email for sensitive or emotional topics or if you believe your intentions have a high probability of being misunderstood. Never send an inflammatory email; instead, take a break.

- Avoid reading between the lines about the sender's intent. Assume good intent. If you have questions about the meaning, pick up the phone and ask.

- Handle important topics/decisions or bad news regarding a customer over the phone or in person.

- Check for spelling, punctuation, and grammar errors. Use spell check every time.

- Don't use all caps; it reads like you're yelling.

- Limit emails to a single topic.

- Don't use acronyms or company jargon that the receiver may not understand.

- Get back to people in a timely manner, or let them know when to expect a response.

- Always have a proper signature line in your emails that includes your contact information.

- Track and easily search ongoing communication on an important topic by limiting your email to a single topic.

- Remember that your email communication represents you. Is it making the right impression?

- Appropriately use blind carbon copy (bcc).

>> **Phone or voice mail:** Use phone or voice mail when

- It's personal.
- You want to make sure your message is understood.
- You want an immediate response.
- You want to build the relationship.
- You want to be able to interpret the other person's reaction.
- The message is complicated and would be too difficult to communicate via email.
- You have several questions or topics to discuss.

When you use phone or voice mail, follow these best practices:

- Be clear and outline your ideas.
- Let people know how much time you think the phone call will take and agree on an ending time.
- Set expectations for the call and what you want to accomplish.
- Engage in active listening techniques during the call.
- Ask questions to clarify understanding and eliminate any confusion.
- Plan for a follow-up call if appropriate.
- Review your voice mail before hitting send.

Agreeing on expected response times

Every virtual team should discuss and agree on a time frame for answering an email or text. You also want to agree on whether an acknowledgement is necessary every time and when others should be copied. Make this more of a guideline for people to follow rather than a hard-and-fast rule.

TIP

Recognize that different time zones may impact response times. If you're working on a global team, having every team member agree to using status notifications to help set expectations for response times is helpful.

Setting the rules for handling conflicts

Conflict on your virtual team is inevitable, so you need to have a formal process or agreement for managing it. For conflicts that escalate beyond the team's ability to resolve them, you'll need an escalation path for assistance within the larger organization and HR. Team members should discuss the following questions:

>> Who do you involve when they need to resolve a conflict?

>> When is it appropriate to bring in a third party to help mediate or coach?

>> Who makes a final decision in the case of a deadlock where the conflict can't be resolved?

>> What method of communication is appropriate when conflicts arise?

REMEMBER

Don't let conflicts fester. Agree on expectations that help the team deal with the conflict productively.

Choosing a problem-solving model

Understanding some basic techniques for idea generation and decision-making is vital when bringing your virtual team together to problem-solve. Having these tools in your back pocket can help to ensure that your communication stays on track and moves forward.

Here are a few problem-solving models to consider:

>> **Brainstorming:** This method is common for a group of people to creatively generate a high volume of ideas on any topic. It encourages open thinking when a team or group is stuck.

>> **Fishbone diagram:** Also referred to as an *Ishikawa diagram* or the *cause-and-effect diagram*, this model allows a team to identify, explore, and display all the possible causes related to a problem and discover its root cause.

>> **Five whys:** With this model, you ask why again and again until the root cause of an issue becomes obvious.

>> **Pareto chart:** Use this model to focus your efforts on the problems that offer the greatest potential for improvement by showing their relative frequency or size in a descending bar graph. It's based on the proven Pareto principle that 20 percent of the sources cause 80 percent of the problems.

>> **Flowchart:** This model identifies the various steps in a process or components within a workflow to understand the steps, duration, and costs.

Agreeing on a process for communicating outside the team

Effective communication on any team has three distinct directions:

>> **Downward:** Downward communication represents the flow of information from leadership through the team. Examples include

- Purpose and vision

- Goals, strategy, and objectives

- New organizational rules, regulations, and guidelines

- Organization-wide practices and procedures

- Role definitions and job instructions

- Performance feedback and recognition

- Talking points from executive leadership meetings

>> **Upward:** Upward communication represents the flow of information from your virtual teammates to leadership. Examples include

- Problems (working conditions and working relationships)

- Suggestions for improvement

- Customer feedback or trends

- Complaints

- Information gathered from meetings with other team members

>> **Horizontal:** Horizontal communication is the flow of information across the team or to other teams laterally or diagonally, which supports collaboration and coordination. Examples include

- Problem solving

- Joint projects

- Innovation

- Recognition

- Support and education

- Information gathered from team meetings

Figure 18-3 represents this cascade of information.

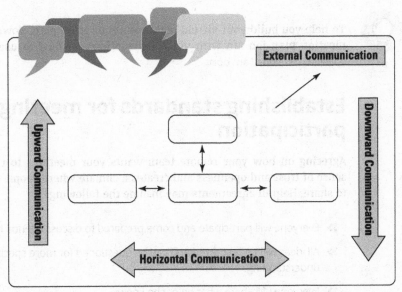

FIGURE 18-3:
Communication
channels.

© John Wiley & Sons, Inc.

Putting together your plan

On a virtual team, discuss and agree on a communication plan so that information is shared with the right people at the right time. Here are eight areas to focus on with your team members and questions to answer when building an effective communication plan:

>> **Sources:** Where or who are you receiving information from that needs to be cascaded through your internal network? If you aren't receiving information, where do you go to get it?

>> **Stakeholders/audience:** Who needs to know this information that you're receiving?

>> **Objectives:** Why do they need to know it? What should they be able to do with it?

>> **Methods:** What are the ways that you can communicate to them?

>> **Role:** Who is responsible for communication?

>> **Frequency:** How often does communication happen (daily, monthly, quarterly)?

>> **Alignment:** What are the ways you can align your message to important goals or strategies to create value?

>> **Feedback:** How will you incorporate a feedback loop?

TIP

To help you build your virtual team communication plan, download a communication plan job aid with video instructions on how to use it at www.team communicationplan.com.

Establishing standards for meeting participation

Agreeing on how your remote team wants your meetings to run establishes a sense of trust and openness and creates a climate where people are more willing to share. Helpful agreements may include the following:

>> Everyone will participate and come prepared to discuss agenda items.

>> All ideas will be respected and can be questioned for more specifics or deeper understanding.

>> Everyone will share what he or she knows.

>> The focus of the meeting will be on the set objective and creating a strategy or solution to accomplish the objective.

>> If you don't speak up, we'll assume you agree.

>> We will start and end on time. If you arrive late, leave early, or miss the meeting all together, you'll be responsible for getting the information you need.

>> Team members will agree on next steps and action plans together and hold each other accountable for follow-through.

>> Confidentiality will be maintained.

Utilizing the DISC Assessment Tool

Influential and successful communicators understand themselves and how their communication affects others. They also understand their reactions to other people and know how to adapt their communication approach based on the situation.

One of the most effective ways to help your team members understand their communication style and the style of others is through an assessment tool called DISC. DISC is a simple and practical assessment that helps team members leverage the various communication styles on their team. Table 18-1 describes each communication style and strategies for effective communication.

TABLE 18-1   **The DISC Assessment Tool**

DISC Styles	Style Descriptions
Dominance style (D)	Tends to take an active, assertive, direct approach to obtaining results. Likes communication to be direct, to the point, and focused on the bottom line.
Influence style (I)	Tends to approach others in an outgoing, gregarious, socially assertive manner and can be impulsive, emotional, and reactive. Likes communication to be positive and inspiring and appreciates the opportunity to brainstorm and persuade others.
Steadiness style (S)	Tends to prefer a more controlled, predictable environment and is steady, stable, sincere, deliberate, patient, and group oriented. Prefers communication to be two-way and is a great listener and provides empathetic feedback when prompted.
Conscientious style ©	Tends to have high standards and prefers that things be done the right way. Tends to be conscientious, controlled, complex, cautious, precise, courteous, and tactful. Wants communication to be professional and include details. Makes a decision after gathering all the facts.

6

Adding Balance and Peace to Your Work-at-Home Life

Create a culture of connection — even virtually — and focus on team wellness and boundaries.

Adopt mindfulness practices for working at home and thriving in the digital age.

Take breaks for stretching, both away from your desk and in your chair.

Chapter **19**

Building Trust and Wellness in the Virtual Workplace

You may be leading remotely, but your employees pay attention to what you do and how you lead every single day. You're the role model who sets the tone for how the team will handle conflict, build relationships, and support one another. As a leader, if you don't walk the walk, you can be sure that you won't have a high-performing, cohesive team. Why would your team trust you if you say one thing, but you do something different?

This chapter focuses on how you can lead by example and set the stage for a connected team culture that is healthy and productive. Even if you're not a manager, you can find plenty of tips for building trust with colleagues and staying healthy as part of working from home.

Building a Connection Culture

Building meaningful relationships starts with you. When remote employees join your team, what you do in the first 48 hours to welcome them to the group sets the standard for how the rest of the team will connect. Valuing the unique skills, abilities, and backgrounds of all your team members helps them feel appreciated and cared for. Openly encouraging dialogue, debate, and feedback provides the opportunity for contribution. All these examples can help you to build a culture of connection and create a team of high-performing, happy remote workers.

The following sections help you understand what you need to do to step up as a virtual leader and how you can be an inspiration to your team.

Being a leader your team wants to follow

REMEMBER

Chances are, you've had both good bosses and bad bosses, and you can probably easily explain the differences in approach, credibility, and style. Why not make the decision to be a leader that people choose to follow?

TIP

Here are a few tips to help you:

>> **Don't ask anyone to do anything that you wouldn't do yourself.** Don't reinforce common hierarchy standards. If you want your team members to believe that you have their backs and aren't above any type of work, prove it by stepping in when needed.

>> **Lead in alignment with a strong sense of purpose and values.** Make sure your team knows what you stand for.

>> **Be vulnerable and courageous.** It's okay to acknowledge failure. Show your team that learning from mistakes is an opportunity to grow.

>> **Share information with your virtual team early and often.** When you have new information, share it. Be as transparent as possible.

>> **Create space for innovative solutions to be considered.** Be open to trying something that hasn't been done before. Give people license to present new ways of doing things. Encourage creative thinking by using brainstorming in meetings.

>> **Be a skillful listener.** Practice effective listening. Acknowledge what is being said by repeating back in your own words what you believe was the meaning behind the message.

>> **Practice self-care.** Model healthy behaviors working from home. Exercise, don't text or email after 6 p.m., and check out when you take vacation. (You can find out more about setting healthy boundaries later in this chapter.)

Getting to know your team members

The challenge for the virtual leader is to transcend the boundaries of space and develop a supportive, collaborative connection with your team. Many of the best ways to establish a personal connection are also fun and sometimes even a little silly.

TIP

Humor and laughter put people at ease and help you open up, so don't brush aside these ideas immediately. Instead, figure out which ones you can try with your own team over the next few weeks:

>> **My Window:** Ask team members to take a picture of what's outside their window and upload it ahead of your virtual meeting. Team members share a story about what's outside their window.

>> **Highs and Lows:** Have each team member share a high and a low from the past week.

>> **TableTopics:** Invest in a card deck of TableTopics (www.tabletopics.com) and ask questions that allow people to share their insights and opinions on different topics.

>> **Two Truths and a Lie:** Use this activity to get people to share three things that the team wouldn't know about them. Two of the facts are true and one is a lie. Your team members have to guess the lie. This activity always leads to some amazing discoveries about your team members.

>> **Our Global Team Map:** Have a map of the world and a virtual pin in each location you have an employee. Ask your team members to share something unique about their country, city, or hometown.

>> **A Day in the Life:** If your team is coming together for the first time, have your team members put together a collage about their lives that includes their families or friends, hobbies, pets, favorite movies, favorite books, and so on.

>> **Dine Together:** This is another great idea to get to know more about someone's heritage or ethnicity. Have each team member share a favorite family dinner recipe. Once a quarter, send a grocery list and gift card to each team member to buy the ingredients and cook the recipe. Have a virtual dinner together while your team member shares information and interesting facts about her family recipe.

Reaching out and building rapport

A key reason to take the time to connect with your virtual team members is to build rapport. Building a sense of camaraderie on your virtual team or increasing accountability and engagement is impossible if you don't have a plan for reaching out and staying connected.

Effective virtual team leaders create time in their schedules for building relationships and rapport. They make a conscious effort every day to build more effective relationships. If you want to know how you're doing, rate yourself on how well you can answer the following questions:

>> How effectively are your team members meeting expected results and performance measures?

>> What performance will be needed from them in three to six months given their role and where the business is headed? Are they prepared?

>> What are their aspirations at work this year and in the future?

>> What makes their work (and their objectives) meaningful and satisfying to them?

>> Why are they here? What motivates them? What stresses them?

>> How do they like to be recognized, acknowledged, and rewarded for a job well done?

>> What limits them from delivering their best? What are their derailers?

>> What support, tools, resources, skills, or empowerment do they need from you as their manager to be more effective?

TIP

Adopt a reach-out strategy with your team to keep your finger on the pulse of what's happening with each team member and make sure they're getting the support and feedback they need to achieve their very best. Don't try to adhere to a rigid schedule; instead, reach out as needed in 10-, 20-, or 30-minute sessions. Table 19-1 shows reach-out recommendations.

TABLE 19-1   **Reach-Out Recommendations**

Reach-Out Timing	Purpose	How Often	Questions
30 minutes	Talent development/ career advancement discussion. This reach-out needs an analysis conversation with a *future focus*.	Quarterly	Where are you? Where would you like to be?
			What do you love to do? When are you in the zone? How does this fit with our strategy?
			What is needed in the department and from your role to move the needle forward? What's needed now? What's needed in the next 18 months?
			What skills or experiences would you like to develop to help you grow in this role or in the future?
			What's your plan for development and how can I support you in getting there?
			Based on our conversation, what will you start/stop/continue doing as a result?
20 minutes	Tactical conversation with a *current focus* used to assess and support what tasks and projects they're involved in that are making progress toward their goals and development plans.	Monthly	What opportunities exist right now on this project or task to move the needle?
			What one or two things are you focusing on to grow?
			What opportunities are available to develop the skills we discussed?
			How can I best support you?
			Based on our conversation, what will you start/stop/continue as a result?
10 minutes or less	Feedback conversation with a *just-in-time focus* used to provide immediate feedback, coaching, and support.	Weekly	Can I sit in on this call with you?
			How about we brainstorm your approach with this customer/vendor/team member?
			Would you like to role-play how you'll handle this conversation?
			Tell me how it went. What was challenging? How did you handle it?
			What feedback do you need from me?
			Based on our conversation, what will you start/stop/continue as a result?

Focusing On Workplace Wellness

Health and wellness are an integral part of your workday whether you work in an office or your home. In fact, engaging remote teams in wellness is even more important because of the isolation of working from home and the sedentary nature of working on a computer for most of your day.

Many remote workers report that one of the top advantages of remote work is the flexibility to find time to run to the gym or take a yoga class. Running and yoga aren't for everyone, though, and *wellness* refers to a holistic approach to health that includes the full spectrum of physical health (exercise and nutrition), as well as mental health, financial health, emotional wellness, social wellness, intellectual wellness, and environmental wellness. Having a menu of options and support systems in place goes a long way toward creating inclusion among your team and encouraging holistic health and wellness at work.

Workplace health and wellness is a broad category, so this section provides some helpful information and several options for keeping your virtual team healthy in mind, body, and spirit.

Considering wellness best practices

Due to the digital revolution, virtual teams have some great wellness options. And because virtual teams connect every day via various collaboration tools, intranets, or work-based social media (check out some platforms in Parts 2, 3, and 4), the stage is already set to connect your virtual team to a comprehensive menu of wellness options.

TIP

Here are a few best practices to consider:

>> **Look at what's already in place.** You may not need to reinvent the wheel. If your organization is larger, wellness options may already be available to you and your team. Explore the resources available.

>> **Lead by example.** In addition to introducing your wellness program and encouraging full participation, be an active user of the program. Your participation will be a motivator for you to stay healthy as well.

>> **Be inclusive.** Unlike teams who are located in the same building, virtual teams connect people from across the country and around the world. When compiling your wellness program, be aware of time differences, ability levels, and cultural nuances of your team so that everyone feels welcome and can participate in their own time.

>> **Share and celebrate successes.** Nothing encourages success like recognition. Your wellness program should include opportunities for team members to post their progress — or frustration, for that matter — and receive the encouragement and support they need.

>> **Keep it fun.** Don't make it heavy handed; design the program so people *want* to participate, but don't feel pressured to do so. Have a low barrier for trial. Make it easy — and fun — to get involved.

Starting your team wellness program

TIP

Looking for some ideas for your health and wellness program? Here are a few ideas to kick-start your brainstorming:

>> **Host a virtual team retreat.** If you're fortunate enough to have the opportunity to get together face to face, include an active activity on the agenda. Bring in a yoga instructor, go for a team hike, bring in a stress reduction expert. . . . You get the idea.

>> **Create a healthy workspace.** Put together a series of guidelines and helpful tips for creating a safe and productive workspace at home. Include guidance on choosing an ergonomic desk and chair; finding good lighting; maintaining an organized, clutter-free space; reducing eye strain from too much screen time; and so on. (See Chapter 1 for even more ideas.)

>> **Set up a one-stop wellness shop.** Create a wellness web page on your intranet or social media that includes a series of helpful links and resources. Include videos for meditation, yoga, stretching, and stress reduction, and a wellness message board where team members can post their own content.

>> **Start a virtual team fitness challenge.** Team goals can be a great motivator. Get the team together to run or bike (virtually, of course) and have team members log miles on their own. Or create a training plan for an actual team event, like a 5K, a triathlon relay race, or an adventure race. Create roles for every team member (for example, athletes, fundraisers, and those offering logistics support), and then meet up in the designated city for the event. Accomplishing a team goal that uses different muscles other than your brain is an extraordinary motivator.

>> **Get cookin'.** Compile a healthy recipe cookbook full of team members' favorites, cook, and then share a meal together for a virtual lunch or dinner once a month.

- » **Create healthy reminders.** Use an app or create calendar reminders throughout the day prompting the team to do healthy things like stretching at their desks, doing ten push-ups, practicing a gratitude break, doing a few jumping jacks, drinking a glass of water, and so on.

- » **Manage money wisely.** Research and post TED Talks on financial planning, preparing for retirement, saving for college, and prepping taxes, which is especially valuable for independent contractors.

Maintaining Healthy Boundaries

For many people, the idea of working from home sounds heavenly. No commute, no cubicle, no annoying coworkers, no more expensive dry cleaning, no more office politics — the list goes on.

To others, banishment from the office doesn't sound ideal. They may be concerned about social isolation, boredom, and career limitations, as well as fear that they won't be productive working on their own.

TIP

When you work from home, it's your responsibility to set up your space, your schedule, and your boundaries to create a healthy work–life balance. Here's a great list of best practices to help you and your team have healthy boundaries:

- » **Set up a dedicated workspace.** Create your space and make it work for you. Don't try to reproduce a corporate office. Make it your own by filling it with things that make you happy (family pictures, diplomas, awards), safe (ergonomic desk and chair), and productive (good lighting, efficient filing system, stable Internet connection). Don't bring your work into the rest of the house, and try to never bring it into the bedroom. (Chapter 1 has more information on setting up your workspace at home.)

- » **Set working hours.** Working on a virtual team is all about flexibility, but to maintain boundaries and to be transparent with your colleagues, you must establish working hours. You can (and should) still block time for picking up kids from school or taking your favorite spin class at the gym, but the consistency of working hours can ground you.

- » **Schedule lunch and breaks.** Just as you do in an office, you need to eat and take breaks. Make sure you book them throughout your day.

>> **Get dressed.** Yes, working in your PJs and sweats is tempting, but you need to maintain some professionalism. That doesn't mean you have to put on a power suit and a full face of makeup, but no one needs to see your bedhead on video calls, so take a shower and make yourself presentable. More than likely, you'll also feel productive.

>> **Go walking, preferably outside.** Get some real-world time every day, even if it's just to stand out on your porch for 15 minutes. Walk, get some sun, smell the fresh air. There's no better way to quickly get some perspective and clear your head.

>> **Set clear boundaries with nonwork friends.** Just because you don't work in an office doesn't mean you're available for unannounced visits from friends. A quick reminder usually does the trick.

>> **Don't do chores.** Setting parameters is key. If you've scheduled an hour in your day to run personal errands, that's fine. Just don't get in the habit of haphazardly jumping back and forth between work projects and home projects. You won't do either one well.

>> **Drink plenty of water.** In the absence of an office watering hole, keep a large water bottle on your desk and sip it throughout the day.

>> **Stop working when the workday is done.** Although being connected to your virtual team is important, it's equally important to shut off when the workday ends. If you're available all hours of the day, people will expect you at all hours and your work–life balance will be nonexistent.

Chapter 2 has additional pointers on establishing habits for work-at-home success.

Chapter 20

Using Mindfulness in Your Daily Life

M indfulness is portable: You can be mindful anywhere and everywhere, not only on the meditation cushion or yoga mat. You can engage in a mindful state of mind while giving a presentation, feeding the cat, or hugging a friend. By cultivating a mindful awareness, you deepen your day-to-day experiences and break free from habitual mental and emotional patterns. You notice that beautiful flower on the side of the road, you become aware and release your tense shoulders when thinking about work, and you give space for your creative solutions to life's challenges. All the small changes you make add up. Your stress levels go down, your depression or anxiety becomes a bit more manageable, and you begin to be more focused. You need to put in some effort to achieve this, but a totally different effort from the kind you're probably used to; you're then bound to change in a positive way.

This chapter offers some of the infinite ways of engaging this ancient art and modern science of mindfulness in your daily life, even when you're working at home.

Using Mindfulness at Work

Work. A four-letter word with lots of negative connotations. Many people dislike work because of the high levels of stress they need to tolerate. A high level of stress isn't a pleasant or healthy experience, so welcome any way of managing that stress with open arms.

WARNING

If you think that you're suffering from work-related stress, you need to consider talking to your manager or other appropriate person about the situation. Poor management standards are linked to unacceptably high levels of stress, and changes need to be made to ensure that stress is kept at reasonable levels.

So, how can mindfulness help with work?

>> Most important, mindfulness gives you the space to relate to your stress in a more healthy way.

>> Mindfulness has been found to lower levels of stress, anxiety, and depression.

>> Mindfulness leads to a greater ability to focus, even when under pressure, which then results in higher productivity and efficiency and more creativity.

>> Mindfulness improves the quality of relationships, including those at work.

REMEMBER

Mindfulness isn't simply a tool or technique to lower stress levels. Mindfulness is a way of being. Stress reduction is the tip of the iceberg. One business organization trained in mindfulness aptly said: "Mindfulness goes to the heart of what good business is about — deepening relationships, communicating responsibly, and making mindful decisions based on the present facts, not the limits of the past." When employees understand that giving mindful attention to their work actually improves the power of their brain to focus, their work becomes more meaningful and inspiring.

Beginning the day mindfully

Watching the 100-meter race in the Olympics, you see the athletes jump up and down for a few minutes before the start, but when they prepare themselves in the blocks, they become totally still. They focus their whole beings completely, listening for the gunfire to signify the start. They begin in stillness. Be inspired by the athletes: Begin your day with an inner stillness, so you can perform at your very best.

TIP

Start the day with a mindfulness exercise. You can do a full formal meditation, such as a body scan or a sitting meditation, or perhaps some yoga or stretching in a slow and mindful way. Alternatively, simply sit up and feel the gentle ebb and flow of your own breath, or listen to the sounds of the birds as they wake up and chirp in the morning. Other alternatives include waking up early and eating your breakfast mindfully, or perhaps tuning in to your sense of smell, sight, and touch fully as you have your morning bath or shower; see what effect that has. That's better than just worrying about your day.

Dropping in with mini meditations

When you arrive at work (even if the commute is from your bedroom to your home office), you can easily be swept away by it all and forget to be mindful of what you're doing. The telephone rings, you get email after email, and you're called into endless meetings. Whatever your work involves, your attention is sure to be sucked up.

This habitual loss of attention and going from activity to activity without really thinking about what you're doing is called *automatic pilot mode.* You simply need to change to mindful awareness mode. The most effective way of doing this is with one- to three-minute mini meditations, feeling the sensation of your own breath as it enters and leaves your body.

The breathing space meditation (a type of mini meditation) consists of three stages. In the first stage, you become aware of your thoughts, emotions, and bodily sensations. In the second stage, you become aware of your own breathing. And in the third and final stage, you expand your awareness to the breath and the body as a whole. Follow these steps:

1. **Sit comfortably with a sense of dignity, but don't strain your back and neck.**

    You can sit upright or stand; even lying down on your back or curling up is acceptable. Sitting upright is helpful, because it sends a positive message to the brain — you're doing something different.

2. **Practice step A — awareness — for a minute or so.**

    Reflect on the following questions, pausing for a few seconds between each one:

    -   **What bodily sensations am I aware of at the moment?** Feel your posture, become aware of any aches or pains, or any pleasant sensations. Just accept them as they are, as far as you can.

    -   **What emotions am I aware of at the moment?** Notice the feelings in your heart or belly area or wherever you can feel emotion.

- **What thoughts am I aware of, passing through my mind at the moment?** Become aware of your thoughts, and the space between yourself and your thoughts. If you can, simply observe your thoughts instead of becoming caught up in them.

3. Practice step B — breathing — for a minute or so.

Focus your attention in your belly area — the lower abdomen. As best you can, feel the whole of your in-breath and the whole of each out-breath. You don't need to change the rate of your breathing — just become mindful of it in a warm, curious, and friendly way. Notice how each breath is slightly different. If your mind wanders away, gently and kindly guide your attention back to your breath. Appreciate how precious each breath is.

4. Practice step C — consciously expanding — for a minute or so.

Consciously expand your awareness from your belly to your whole body. Get a sense of your entire body breathing (which it is, through the skin). As your awareness heightens within your body, notice its effect. Accept yourself as perfect and complete just as you are, just in this moment, as much as you can.

When you're working, give a mini meditation a go:

>> **When?** You can do a mini meditation at set times or between activities. So, when you've finished a certain task or job, take time to practice a mini meditation before heading to the next task. In this way, you increase the likelihood of your being calm and centered, rather than flustered, by the time you get to the end of the day or workweek. If you don't like the rigidity of planning your mini meditations ahead of time, just practice them whenever the thought crosses your mind and you feel you need to go into mindfulness mode.

You can also use meditation to cope with a difficult situation, such as your boss irritating you. One way of coping with the wash of emotion that arises in such situations is to do a three-minute breathing space meditation like the one earlier in this section.

>> **How?** Use any posture you like, but sit up if you want to energize yourself through the practice. The simplest form of mini meditation is to feel your breathing. If you find your mind wanders a lot when feeling your breath, you can say to yourself "in" as you breathe in, and "out" as you breathe out. Alternatively, count each out-breath to yourself, going from one to ten. As always, when your mind drifts off, simply guide the attention gently and kindly back, even congratulating yourself for noticing that your mind has wandered off the breath. Be sure to accept and embrace mind wandering as part of the mindfulness process.

>> **Where?** You can do a mini meditation anywhere you feel comfortable. Usually, meditating is easier with your eyes closed, but that's not so easy at work! You can keep your eyes open and softly gaze at something while you focus your attention inward. Try going for a slow walk for a few minutes, feeling your breathing and noticing the sensations of your feet as they gently make contact with the earth. Or if the weather is nice, perhaps you can lie down in the sunshine while lying on some grass as you practice some mindfulness.

TIP

You may dearly want to try out the mini meditation at work, but you simply keep forgetting. Well, why not make an appointment with yourself? Perhaps set a reminder to pop up on your computer or a screen saver with a subtle reminder for yourself. One worker put a card on her desk with a picture of a beautiful flower. Each time she saw the picture, she took three conscious breaths. This helped to calm her and had a transformative effect on the day. Or try a sticky note or a gentle alarm on your cell phone — be creative in thinking of ways to remind yourself to be mindful.

Going from reacting to responding

A *reaction* is your almost automatic thought, reply, and behavior following some sort of stimulus, such as your boss criticizing you. A *response* to a situation is a more considered, balanced choice, often creative in reply to the criticism, and leads to solving your problems rather than compounding them.

You don't have to react when someone interrupts you in a meeting, takes away your project, or sends a rude email. Instead, having a balanced, considered response is most helpful for both you and your relationship with colleagues.

For example, say you hand in a piece of work to your manager, and she doesn't even say thank you. Later on, you ask what she thinks of your work, and she says it's okay, but you can tell she doesn't seem impressed. You spent lots of time and effort in order to write a superb report, and you feel hurt and annoyed. You *react* by either automatically thinking negative thoughts about your manager and avoiding eye contact with her for the rest of the week, or you lash out with an outburst of accusations and feel extremely tense and frustrated for hours afterward. Here's how you can have a mindful *response* to this situation instead.

TIP

Begin to feel the sensations of your breath. Notice whether you're breathing in a shallow or rapid way because of your frustration, but try not to judge yourself. Say to yourself, "in . . . out" as you breathe in and out. Expand your awareness to a sense of your body as a whole. Become mindful of the processes taking place inside you. Feel the burning anger rising from the pit of your stomach up through your chest and throat, or your racing heart and dry mouth when you're nervous. Honor the feeling instead of criticizing or blocking the emotion. Notice what happens if you don't react as you normally do or feel like doing. Imagine your breath soothing the feeling. Bring kindness and curiosity to your emotions. This isn't an easy time for you — acknowledging that is an act of self-compassion.

You may discover that the very act of being aware of your reaction changes the flavor of the sensation altogether. Your relationship to the reaction changes an outburst, for example, to a more considered response. Your tone of voice may subtly change from aggressive and demanding to being slightly calmer and more inquisitive. The point is not to try to change anything, but just to sit back and watch what's going on for a few moments.

TIP

To help you to bring a sense of curiosity when you're about to react to a situation at work, try asking yourself the following questions slowly, one at a time, and giving yourself time for reflection:

>> What feeling am I experiencing at the moment, here at work? How familiar is this feeling? Where do I feel the feeling in my body?

>> What thoughts are passing through my mind at the moment? How judgmental are my thoughts? How understanding are my thoughts? How are my thoughts affecting my actions at work?

>> How does my body feel at the moment? How tired do I feel at work? What effect has the recent level of work had on my body? How much discomfort can I feel at the moment in my body, and where is the source of it?

>> Can I acknowledge my experiences here at work, just as they are? Am I able to respect my own rights, as well as responsibilities in the actions I choose? What would be a wise way of responding right now, instead of my usual reaction? If I do react, can I acknowledge that I'm not perfect and make my next decision a more mindful response?

Perhaps you'll go back to your manager and calmly explain why you feel frustrated. You may become angry, too, if you feel this is necessary, but without feeling out of control. Perhaps you'll choose not to say anything today, but wait for things to settle before discussing the next step. The idea is for you to be more creative in your *response* to this frustration instead of *reacting* in your usual way, if your usual way is unhelpful and leads to further problems.

The benefits of a considered, balanced response as opposed to an automatic reaction include

>> Lower blood pressure, reducing the strain on your heart

>> Lower levels of stress hormones in your blood stream, leading to a healthier immune system

>> Improved relationships, because you're less likely to break down communication between colleagues if you're in a calmer state of mind

>> A greater feeling of being in control, because you're able to choose how you respond to others instead of automatically reacting involuntarily

REMEMBER

Don't sweep your frustration or anger under the carpet. Mindfulness isn't about blocking emotions. Instead, mindfulness enables you to do the opposite: You allow yourself to mindfully feel and soothe the emotions with as much friendliness and kindness as you can muster. Even forcing a smile can help. Mindfulness effectively overcomes destructive emotions. Expressing out-of-control anger leads to more anger — you just get better at it. And suppressing anger leads to outbursts at some other time. Mindfulness is the path to easing your frustration through being genuinely curious and respectful of your own emotional experiences.

Solving problems creatively

Your ideas need room. You need space for new perceptions and novel ways of meeting challenges, in the same way that plants need space to grow or they begin to wither. For your ideas, the space can be in the form of a walk outside, a three-minute mini meditation, or a cup of tea. Working harder is often not the best solution; working smarter is.

If your job involves dealing with issues and problems, whether that involves people or not, you can train yourself to see the problems differently. By seeing the problems as challenges, you're already changing how you meet this issue. A *challenge* is something you rise to — something energizing and fulfilling. A *problem* is something that has to be dealt with — something draining, an irritation. Studies have found that people who learn to see problems as positive challenges have a more enjoyable experience of navigating a solution.

TIP

To meet your challenges in a creative way, find some space and time for yourself. Write down *exactly* what the challenge is; when you're sure what your challenge is, you find it much easier to solve. Try to see the challenge from a different person's perspective. Talk to other people and ask how they'd deal with the issue. Become mindful of your immediate reactive way of dealing with this challenge, and question the validity of it.

Practicing mindful working

Mindful working is simply being mindful of whatever you do when you work. Here are some examples of ways of being mindful at work:

» **Start the day with a clear intention.** What do you need to get done today? What attitude do you want to bring to your day? Perhaps it's kindness or focus, for example. How will you ensure you're best able to achieve what you intend to do? What barriers can prevent you from achieving your intention and how can you best remove or manage them? For example, if your intention is to be focused and you're likely to get distracted in your home office, can you work somewhere else?

» **Be mindful of your everyday activities.** For example, when typing, notice the sense of touch between your fingers and the keyboard. Notice how quickly your mind converts a thought into an action on keys. Are you striking the keys too hard? Are your shoulders tense; is your face screwing up unnecessarily? How's your posture? Are you taking breaks regularly to walk and stretch?

» **Before writing or checking an email, take a breath.** Is this really important to do right now? Reflect for a few moments on the key message you need to get across, and remember, it's a human being receiving this message — not just a computer. After sending the message, take time to feel your breath and, if you can, enjoy it. Notice how easy it is to be swept away for hours by the screen.

» **When the telephone rings, let the sound of the ring be a reminder for you to be mindful.** Let the telephone ring a few times before answering. Use this time to notice your breath and posture. When you pick it up, speak and listen with mindfulness. Notice both the tone of your own voice and the other person's. If you want to, experiment by gently smiling as you speak and listen, and become aware of the effect that has.

» **When you get a text message or other ping sound from your smartphone, just pause for a moment.** Do you need to check your phone right now or are you in the middle of something? If it's not an ideal time to check, is now a good time to switch off your phone so that you can focus and finish the work you're doing? These small moments of choice can make a difference to your whole day.

» **No matter what your work involves, do it with awareness.** Awareness helps your actions become clear and efficient. Connect your senses with whatever you're doing. Whenever you notice your mind drifting out of the present moment, just gently bring it back.

» **Make use of the mini meditations (discussed earlier in this chapter) to keep you aware and awake at work.** The meditations are like lampposts, lighting wherever you go and making things clear.

Debunking the multitasking myth

Everyone does it nowadays: texting as we walk, or checking emails as we talk on the phone. People multitask to be efficient, but most of the time it actually makes you *less* efficient. And from a mindfulness perspective, your attention becomes hazy rather than centered.

Many studies by top universities show that multitasking leads to inefficiency and unnecessary stress. Some reasons to avoid multitasking and to mindfully focus on just one task at a time instead are that doing so will help you to

>> **Live in the moment.** In one hilarious study, researchers asked people who walked across a park whether they noticed a clown on a unicycle. People who were glued to their phones didn't notice it! Others did.

>> **Be efficient.** By switching between two tasks, you take longer. It's quicker to finish one task and then the other. Switching attention takes up time and energy and reduces your capacity to focus. Some experts found a 40 percent reduction in productivity due to multitasking.

>> **Improve relationships.** A study at the University of Essex found that just by having a phone nearby while having a person-to-person conversation had a negative impact. Give your partner your full attention as much as possible. Most people don't realize how much of a positive effect simply giving your partner your mindful awareness has.

>> **Destress.** A study by the University of California found that when office workers were constantly checking email as they were working, their heart rates were elevated compared with those of people focusing on just one task.

>> **Get creative.** By multitasking, you over-challenge your memory resources. There's no space for creativity. A study in Chicago found that multitaskers struggled to find creative solutions to problems they were given.

Finishing by letting go

You may find letting go of your work at the end of the day very difficult. Perhaps you finish your to-do list, but all you can think about is work. You may spend the evening talking angrily about colleagues and bosses, or actually doing more work to try to catch up with what you should've finished during the day. Not letting go impacts the quality and quantity of your sleep, lowering your energy levels for the next day. This unfortunate negative cycle can spin out of control.

REMEMBER

Draw a line between your work life and home life, especially if your stress levels feel unmanageable. Meditating as soon as you finish working provides an empowering way of achieving this. You're saying "enough." You're taking a stand against the tidal wave of demands on your limited time and energy. You're doing something uplifting for your health and well-being, and ultimately for all those around you, too. And you're letting go.

To let go at the end of the day most powerfully, choose a mindful practice that you feel works best for you. Or take up a sport or hobby in which you're absorbed by gentle, focused attention — an activity that enables the energy of your body and mind to settle, and the mindfulness to indirectly calm you.

Living Mindfully in the Digital Age

The digital age has brought huge benefits — from saving lives in emergencies to sharing information with the world, the advantages are countless. But without mindfulness, living in the digital age can drive you crazy! If you don't turn your phone or computer off from time to time, your attention can be completely hijacked by websites, incoming messages, social media, games, and more. Gadgets are so compelling.

If you think that the digital age is getting to be too much, check out the suggestions in this section to get yourself back in control.

Assessing your level of addiction to technology

Nowadays, people seem to use their phones a lot. A recent survey of more than 4,000 users found that

>> Average smartphone users check their phones 47 times a day.

>> Eight-five percent of smartphone users check their phones when speaking with friends and family.

>> Eighty percent of smartphone users check their phones within an hour of waking up or going to sleep.

>> Almost half of all smartphone users have tried to limit their usage in the past.

When you find you're spending more time on your phone than interacting with real people, it may be time to reassess your phone usage. Smartphone addiction is often fueled by Internet overuse, because it's often the games, apps, and online worlds that are most compelling.

Here's a quiz to get an idea of just how addicted you are to your phone:

1. **You're doing some work and a phone rings in another room. Do you**

(a) Take no notice. It must be someone else's. Your phone is normally off.

(b) Ignore it and check it later.

(c) Walk casually to pick it up.

(d) Run to pick up the phone, sometimes tripping over or stubbing your toe in the process, and getting annoyed by anyone in the way.

2. **You're planning a vacation, but the hotel has no Wi-Fi and no phone signal. Will you go?**

(a) Yes, why not?

(b) Oh, I'd love the chance to get a break from my devices. Heaven!

(c) Probably wouldn't go there.

(d) No way! How can I have a vacation without my phone and/or laptop — that doesn't make sense. I need a good phone signal and superfast Internet 24/7.

3. **Where's your phone right now?**

(a) My what? Oh, phone. . .. Uh, no idea. I'm not sure if I have a phone actually.

(b) Somewhere around here.

(c) In this room.

(d) It's right here — my beautiful, precious phone.

4. **What do you use your phone for?**

(a) Phone calls, of course. What else is it for?

(b) Calls and texts from time to time. Mainly emergencies.

(c) Call and texts and picking up emails sometimes, too. A few pictures.

(d) Everything. It's my life! Facebook, Twitter, WhatsApp, Instagram, Snapchat, email, texting, photos, video, playing games, fitness, Skype. Oh, yes, and occasionally phone calls, too.

5. **Do you keep your phone nearby as you sleep?**

(a) No way!

(b) Sometimes. Or just for my alarm clock. Don't really check last thing at night or first thing in the morning.

(c) Quite often. I send the odd text and maybe have a peek at my messages first thing in the morning, too.

(d) Every night. I sleep with my phone. It's the last thing I look at before falling asleep and the first thing I see when I wake up. It's a compulsion.

Add up your score: Letter a is 1 point, b is 2 points, c is 3 points, and d is four points.

5–10 points: You're not really addicted to your phone at all — you're probably too busy meditating.

11–15 points: You like your phone, but not that much. You're still in control, and you can live comfortably without it.

16–18 points: You're pretty dependent on your phone for many things. You may like to take a little break from your phone from time to time.

19–20 points: You love your phone. What if you lose your phone? Or it gets stolen? Make sure you have some moments in the day where you take a break from your device and do some mindful walking or stretching, or sit and meditate away from your phone. If you feel that your phone usage is out of control, try some of the tips in the next section to help, or consider getting professional help if you feel overwhelmed.

Using mindfulness to get back in control

If you've discovered that you're using digital devices to the point that they're having a negative impact on your work or social life, it's time to get back in control.

You can manage overuse of digital devices in many ways. It's not as hard as you may think. In fact, when you start using some of these strategies, you may find that you don't even want to look at your devices.

TIP

Here are some techniques that you can try:

>> **Engage in other activities.** You can participate in a new hobby regularly, such as knitting, gardening, or playing an instrument. By paying mindful attention to your hobby and keeping your phone and computer out of the way, you'll develop greater mindfulness. And you can also get on with a few

household chores — you'll feel good when they're done. Again, keep your devices switched off and try focusing on the chore — it can be soothing and enjoyable to polish the dining room table or clear your desk with full attention and a little smile.

>> **Make good use of airplane mode, or switch your phone off.** This prevents calls and alerts from coming through.

>> **Set boundaries.** Just before you go to bed, it's important not to look at screens too much. TVs, computers, and phones emit a light that signals to your body that it's still daytime. If you look at your phone in bed, you may have trouble falling asleep and may wake up tired.

Also, you may not want to be disturbed at other specific times in the day. For example, when walking through the park, keep your phone off and enjoy the nature and people around you. And obviously, when you're with friends or family or eating a meal, switch your phone off or leave it out of the way. If distancing yourself from your phone sounds like a challenge, just try it once and see how it goes. Eventually, leaving your gadgets behind can feel freeing.

>> **Switch off notifications.** Does your computer beep each time an email comes through? Does your phone make a noise each time someone contacts you on social media or sends you a message? If so, you can end up with perpetual distraction. Every time you're doing one task, you're distracted by another. The more you keep switching your attention, the less your mindful awareness develops. Turn off as many notifications as you can. This way, you can focus on doing whatever you need to do with awareness.

>> **Be kind to yourself when you slip up.** Ever had that feeling of frustration when you've spent the last hour or so just surfing the web rather than finishing your work? Everyone has. But when you do eventually catch yourself doing this, don't beat yourself up too much. It's okay. Everyone has downtime and gets distracted. Say to yourself, "It's okay. Let me take a break from my computer and phone and have a little mindful walk. Then I'll come back with a smile and get on with my tasks. Everyone gets too caught up with the barrage of technology sometimes."

REMEMBER

If you feel you need more help to reduce your Internet usage, consider an evidence-based therapy like cognitive behavioral therapy or acceptance and commitment therapy to ease your compulsive behavior and change your perception about Internet usage. Professional help can offer alternative ways of dealing with the underlying emotions and thoughts that may be fueling your smartphone use.

Using technology to enhance mindful awareness

If you're looking for a way to enhance your mindfulness, you may want to avoid technology altogether — and that's understandable. Use of technology can distract your mind. But for you, using digital devices may be part of your everyday life. Switching them off for an extended period may seem impossible to achieve. In such a case, you can make good use of mindfulness apps, websites, and more.

TIP

You can download and use apps for mobile devices like phones and tablets. Simply search for "mindfulness" or "meditation" in the app stores and you'll find lots of resources — take your pick. New apps come out every week! Popular ones at the moment are Calm, Headspace, and Insight Timer, but there are many more.

TIP

If you use social media a lot, following people or organizations that offer mindful images, tweets, and resources may help you. You can also use software to help you focus mindfully on your work. For example, software called SelfControl is available free for Mac computers, and equivalent software products are available for Windows PCs.

Chapter **21**

Stretching during the Workday

Your body wasn't designed to sit for hours at a time. Do you think the cavemen would've survived if they had sat still all day? No, they would've been a buffet lunch for some hungry *T. rex*. But nowadays, no one has to run from giant carnivores every day. As a matter of fact, in the last 50 years, our lifestyles have changed so dramatically that we've developed an entirely new set of problems because of it: stress headaches, low-back pain, muscular tightness and imbalance, repetitive stress injuries such as carpal tunnel syndrome, and the special selection of aches and pains brought on by the ordeal of modern travel.

This chapter is composed of two sections — one that shows you exercises to do away from your desk (or confined space) to combat the constricting effects of sitting for long periods of time and another for when you must stay sitting. Either way, these exercises go a long way toward helping your work-at-home life evolve into a healthier, more comfortable form of existence.

Step Away from the Desk: Standing Stretches

Whether you're a student, a traveler, a computer jockey, or a couch potato, there comes a time when you tend to sit for way too long. Sitting too long on a regular basis can, over time, shorten your hip flexors and the muscles in your hamstrings, chest, and back, resulting in uncomfortable muscle tension.

REMEMBER

Experts recommend getting up out of your chair a couple of times an hour or, more specifically, taking 3- to 5-minute breaks every 20 to 40 minutes. Whenever you get up from your desk in your home workspace, choose from the following selections of stretching exercises to help lengthen your muscles, reduce stress and tension, and get your blood pumping again — and, in turn, sitting still will feel a lot less like hard work.

Standing chest stretch

Do this simple chest stretch several times a day, especially if you find yourself sitting a lot. You can actually do the stretch anywhere. It helps keep your chest muscles from tightening and shortening, which prevents that hunched-over look.

To do this stretch, follow these steps:

1. **Stand up tall and clasp your hands together behind your back just above your tailbone (see Figure 21-1a).**

    TIP

    If you have difficulty getting your hands together behind your back, try holding the end of a small towel in each hand.

2. **Take a deep breath and, as you exhale, keep your arms straight and gently lift your hands toward the ceiling away from your back (see Figure 21-1b).**

    Lift your arms as high as you can while standing straight and avoid bending forward.

3. **Hold this stretch for 30 seconds.**

REMEMBER

A few do's and don'ts for this stretch:

>> Do stand up tall with good posture.

>> Do keep your knees slightly bent.

>> Don't tense or lift your shoulders.

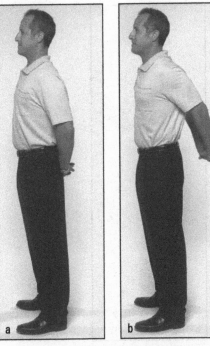

FIGURE 21-1:
Standing chest
stretch.

© Tilden Patterson (www.tildenphoto.com)

Standing abdominal stretch

After sitting for an extended period of time, the muscles in your abdomen and chest can become shortened and your back rounded. To counterbalance these effects, stretch your chest and abdomen in the exact opposite direction. It feels great!

To do this stretch, follow these steps:

1. Stand with your feet shoulder-width apart and knees slightly bent.

2. Place your hands on the lowest part of your back, right where your buttocks meet your lower back, with your fingers pointed downward (see Figure 21-2a).

3. Inhale and, as you exhale, squeeze your buttocks (to prevent compression in your lower back), lean back, and slightly push your hips forward (see Figure 21-2b).

4. Hold this stretch for 30 seconds and then come back to upright position.

5. Perform this exercise twice.

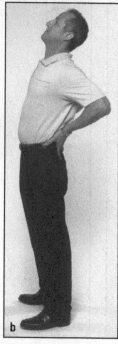

FIGURE 21-2:
Standing
abdominal
stretch.

REMEMBER

A few do's and don'ts for this stretch:

>> Do squeeze your shoulder blades together as you lean back.

>> Do lift your chin so your neck stays in line with the rest of your spine.

>> Don't bounce or force the stretch, which puts stress on your lower back.

Standing side reach with legs crossed

After sitting for a long time, your sides get all scrunched together, so nothing can feel better than a good side reach. Feel this stretch along your rib cage and shoulders as you bring oxygen to your entire body.

To do this stretch, follow these steps:

1. **Stand tall with your arms at your sides.**

2. **Cross your left leg over your right leg, keeping both feet flat on the floor (see Figure 21-3a).**

TIP

If you find it uncomfortable or awkward to cross your legs, try moving your front leg forward an inch or two. If it's still awkward, or you have trouble balancing, simply perform this stretch with your legs uncrossed and your feet together.

3. **Inhale and, as you exhale, lean to the left and reach your left arm toward the floor (see Figure 21-3b).**

4. **Hold the stretch for 30 seconds, and then come back to starting position.**

5. **Cross your right leg over your left leg, keeping both feet on the floor, and repeat the stretch leaning to the right.**

FIGURE 21-3:
Standing side reach.

© Tilden Patterson (www.tildenphoto.com)

REMEMBER

A few do's and don'ts for this stretch:

>> Do keep your hips facing forward.

>> Do keep your arms to your sides.

>> Don't bounce or twist.

>> Don't hold your breath, but instead breathe regularly.

Standing hamstring and calf stretch

Two areas that can get tight after sitting for a long time are the backs of your thighs and your calves. This one stretch can get both areas at the same time.

To perform this exercise, follow these steps:

1. **Stand tall with both feet together and your arms at your sides.**

2. **Step out with your left leg, keeping your back heel on the floor and your front toes pointing toward the ceiling.**

3. **Bend your right knee slightly and inhale.**

4. **As you exhale, hinge at your hips and tilt your pelvis back, placing both your hands just above your bent knee (see Figure 21-4).**

TIP

   If you're not feeling the stretch in your calf, try to flex your foot more (lift your toes more toward the ceiling). If you're not feeling the stretch in your hamstrings, try tilting your pelvis back farther and lengthening your back more if you can.

FIGURE 21-4: Standing hamstring and calf stretch.

© Tilden Patterson (www.tildenphoto.com)

5. Hold the stretch for 30 seconds, and make sure to keep your spine lengthened, your chest lifted, and your tailbone reaching toward the wall behind you.

6. Repeat the stretch on the other side.

A few do's and don'ts for this exercise:

» Do breathe slowly and rhythmically.

» Do keep most of your weight on your bent leg.

» Don't round your back or drop your chest too far toward your bent leg.

Standing hip flexor stretch

This stretch targets your hip flexors with pinpoint accuracy and, as an added bonus, can even tone your thighs and buttocks!

To do this stretch, follow these steps:

1. Start in a forward lunge position, with both knees bent and your arms at your sides.

   Make sure your feet are far enough apart so when you bend your knees your front knee doesn't jut forward past your toes.

2. Inhale and, as you exhale, squeeze your buttocks and tilt your pelvis under so your hipbones point upward and your tailbone points downward (see Figure 21-5).

3. Hold the stretch for 30 seconds and then sink your hips down toward the floor to lower your body another inch or two.

   If you have trouble keeping your balance, move your back leg out to the side an inch or two. This adjustment gives you a wider base of support. Make sure your abdominals are tight and pulled in.

4. Hold this lowered position for another 30 seconds, breathing comfortably and normally.

5. Release the stretch and bring your feet together.

6. Repeat the stretch on your other leg.

FIGURE 21-5:
Standing hip flexor stretch — lunging forward with your pelvis tucked under.

© Tilden Patterson (www.tildenphoto.com)

REMEMBER

A few do's and don'ts for this exercise:

>> Do keep your buttocks squeezed and your pelvis tucked under.

>> Do keep your toes pointed forward.

>> Do stabilize your spine by keeping your back straight and your abdominals lifted.

>> Don't bend your knees more than 90 degrees or let your front knee jut forward. These positions place stress on your knees.

Have a Seat: Stretches for the Professional Desk Jockey

This section gives you a few stretches to do when you can't get away from your desk. Doing these stretches several times during the day can help energize you and keep those aches and pains away.

Shoulders and neck stretch with circles

This stretch is designed to release the tension that can build up in your neck and shoulders after sitting with poor posture for too long. The shoulder circles relax your shoulders and get you sitting up tall again, while the neck stretch lengthens and relaxes the muscles in your neck. This stretch is great if you're prone to rounded shoulders.

To do this exercise, follow these steps:

1. **Sit tall in your chair with your feet flat on the floor, your abdominals lifted, and your hands at your sides.**

2. **Slowly rotate your shoulders forward, up, back, and down as if you were drawing a circle with your shoulders (see Figure 21-6a).**

   Breathe deeply as you repeat this motion four to six times.

3. **At the end of the last repetition, hold your shoulders down and back.**

4. **Tilt your head to the left, moving your left ear toward your left shoulder.**

   Make sure to keep your right shoulder down (see Figure 21-6b).

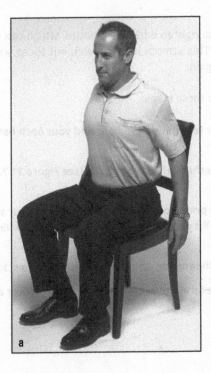 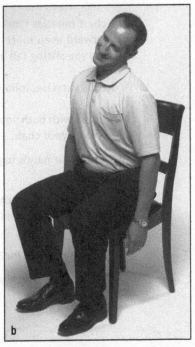

FIGURE 21-6:
Shoulder circles
and neck stretch.

© Tilden Patterson (www.tildenphoto.com)

5. **Slowly roll your head toward your chest, drawing a half-circle with your chin.**

   Continue the motion until you tilt your head all the way across toward the right shoulder. Bring your head back to the upright position and relax.

6. **Repeat on the other side.**

A few do's and don'ts for this exercise:

>> Do keep your posture tall and abdominals lifted.

>> Do keep your shoulder blades down as you perform the shoulder circles.

>> Don't raise one shoulder while you're performing the neck stretch. Make sure to keep both of your shoulders level at all times.

Chest stretch

If you sit for a long time, this stretch is one of the most effective ones to counteract the rounded shoulders and rounded back that can form over time when you hover over that keyboard.

Your chest muscles tend to tighten with bad posture, which can pull your shoulders forward even more. This stretch helps stretch out those worn-out muscles and gets you sitting tall again.

To do this exercise, follow these steps:

1. **Sit tall with both your feet flat on the floor and your back flat against the back of your chair.**

2. **Clasp your hands together behind your head (see Figure 21-7a) and inhale.**

3. **As you exhale, gently press your elbows back, squeeze your shoulder blades together, and lift your chin and chest toward the ceiling (see Figure 21-7b).**

4. **Hold the stretch for 30 seconds, and then release back to starting position.**

5. **Repeat this stretch several times each hour of sitting still or at least a few times a day.**

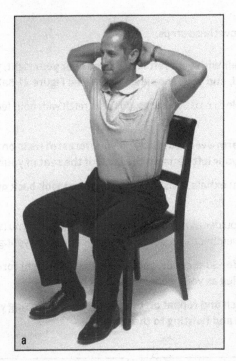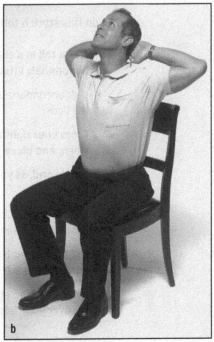

FIGURE 21-7:
Chest stretch
with hands
behind head.

© Tilden Patterson (www.tildenphoto.com)

A few do's and don'ts for this exercise:

REMEMBER

>> Do breathe slowly and rhythmically.

>> Do keep your chest lifted and your abdominals tight.

>> Don't compress or arch your lower back.

Seated spinal rotation

Have you ever been so focused on what you're working on at your desk that you forget there's a world going on around you? Well, this stretch not only relieves tension in your hips and back, but also is a good excuse to look up and see what's going on in the outside world.

To do this stretch follow these steps:

TIP

1. **Sit up tall in a chair with your left leg crossed over your right, your abdominals lifted, and your shoulders down (see Figure 21-8a).**

   If it's uncomfortable to cross your legs, do this stretch with both feet flat on the floor.

2. **Cross your right arm over your body so your forearm rests on your left thigh, and place your left hand on the back of the seat of your chair.**

3. **Inhale and, as you exhale, twist at your waist and look back over your left shoulder.**

   Look over your shoulder as if you were trying to look behind you (see Figure 21-8b). Remember to keep your shoulders down and your gaze level.

4. **Hold the stretch for 30 seconds, gently pressing your right forearm against your left leg as you deepen the stretch.**

5. **Release the stretch and repeat on the other side by crossing your right leg over your left and twisting to the right.**

FIGURE 21-8:
The spinal rotation that stretches your back, hips, and neck.

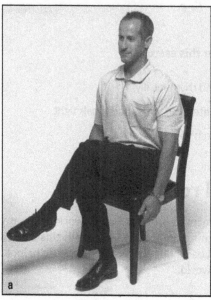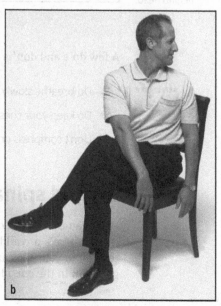

© Tilden Patterson (www.tildenphoto.com)

REMEMBER

A few do's and don'ts for this exercise:

> » Do sit up tall — no slouching.

> » Do keep your hips facing forward.

> » Don't tense up your shoulders and neck.

Seated forward bend

You should feel this stretch along the back of your legs or hamstrings. By hinging at your hips and using the weight of your upper body, you also get a good stretch in your lower back.

To do this stretch, follow these steps:

1. **Sit on a chair with your feet flat on the floor and your abdominals tight (see Figure 21-9a).**

2. **Inhale and, as you exhale, bend forward at the hips as far as you can comfortably stretch, letting your arms and head hang down toward the ground (see Figure 21-9b).**

3. **Hold this stretch for 30 seconds or four to five slow, deep breaths.**

4. **Slowly roll back up, stacking one vertebra on top of the other until you're sitting up tall.**

REMEMBER

A few do's and don'ts for this stretch:

> » Do feel this stretch in the back of your legs.

> » Do gradually deepen the stretch with each breath.

> » Don't force the stretch.

Wrist and forearm stretch

This stretch can help combat the discomfort caused by repetitive stress injuries like carpal tunnel syndrome. You should feel this stretch throughout your forearms and wrists.

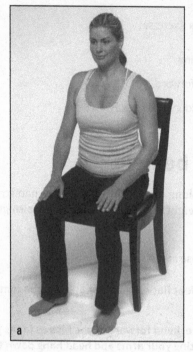

FIGURE 21-9:
The seated
forward bend.

a

b

© Tilden Patterson (www.tildenphoto.com)

To do this stretch, follow these steps:

1. **Sit up straight in your chair with the palm of one hand touching the fingers of the other hand.**

   Point your fingers upward and keep your elbows lifted toward the ceiling (see Figure 21-10).

2. **Inhale and, as you exhale, gently press the heel of your hand against your fingers.**

3. **Hold this stretch for 30 seconds, and repeat on the other side.**

REMEMBER

A few do's and don'ts for this stretch:

» Do sit up tall with good posture.

» Don't tense or lift your shoulders.

» Don't hold your breath.

» Don't let your elbows drop.

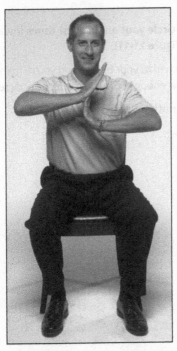

FIGURE 21-10:
The sitting wrist
and forearm
stretch.

Seated ankle circles

As you get older, you naturally lose range of motion in your joints, but particularly in the ankle joint. Ankle circles help increase range of motion in the joint, and they also make walking feel much more comfortable. So, go ahead take your shoes off.

To do this exercise, follow these steps:

1. Sit up tall with your feet flat on the floor.

2. Place your hands under your right knee and clasp them together.

3. Use your hands to lift your knee, lifting your foot a few inches off the floor.

TIP

4. **Inhale and, as you exhale, circle your ankle eight times inward and then eight times outward (see Figure 21-11).**

    Imagine there's a pencil attached to your big toe and you're trying to draw the largest circle you can. Go slow enough so you draw a perfectly round circle.

5. **Repeat this stretch on your other ankle.**

FIGURE 21-11:
Performing the seated ankle circles in a chair.

© Tilden Patterson (www.
tildenphoto.com)

REMEMBER

A few do's and don'ts for this exercise:

>> Do sit up tall with your back straight.

>> Do support the weight of your leg with your hands.

>> Don't rush the movement.

STRESS! HOW IT AFFECTS YOU AND YOUR BODY

Excess stress can lower your immune system, make you depressed, and make you sick, but according to Pamela Peeke, MD, MPH, too much stress can also make you fat! How? Stress activates the flight-or-fight response, a physiological reaction designed to help your body react decisively in an emergency. When confronted with a perceived threat, your brain commands your adrenal glands to dump a large amount of the stress hormone cortisol into your bloodstream. One of the functions of cortisol is to quickly release energy stored in fat cells. Your muscles use the energy to help avert the emergency. The problem is that, even after the emergency is over, the level of cortisol in your bloodstream remains elevated to help encourage you to restock your stores of fat.

In addition, stressed-out women who carry weight in their abdominal area secrete significantly more cortisol than women who don't have excess fat around their waistline, according to a study from the University of California at San Francisco. And because abdominal fat tissue has up to four times the number of receptors for cortisol as does fat elsewhere in the body, the cells in this area are the most likely to store fat as a result of cortisol. Unfortunately, this excess tummy doesn't just spill over your belt; it's an indicator of increased risk for stroke and heart disease, two major killers of people over 50 years old.

What's the solution? When it comes to reducing stress, experts consistently point to regular exercise, which can also help combat cardiovascular disease. And there's nothing more effective to help you reduce the muscle tension brought on by excess stress than a good, invigorating stretch.

7

The Part of Tens

IN THIS PART . . .

Increase your chances of virtual team success with the right technology, a clear vision, effective communication strategies, and more.

Make the most of Slack with ten useful tips on responding promptly, viewing analytics, watching out for new apps, and beyond.

Chapter **22**

Ten Predictors of Virtual Team Success

Virtual teams have different needs than teams that are located in the same office. If you're not careful, the literal distance between team members can create figurative distances. From there you can expect communication breakdown, reduced productivity, disengagement, confusion, mistrust, and ultimately, failure. And when virtual teams fail, usually the virtual part gets the blame — not the lack of planning for their specific needs.

This chapter can safeguard you from virtual team failure. Here are the top predictors of success for your virtual team. Think of this chapter as a checklist to guarantee your virtual team success.

Having the Right Technology

Virtual teams rely heavily on technology to connect team members. Technology is essential for virtual teams, but even though technology exists to enable team communication and collaboration, it can't replace good management.

REMEMBER

Make sure your technology choices support exactly what your team needs. Think about functionality when making your technology decisions. Consider using platforms that integrate all types of communication and include the following key components:

>> Collaboration

>> Project management

>> Document sharing and creation

>> Video and audio conferencing

>> Instant messaging

>> Scheduling/shared calendar

>> Social networking

Most highly effective virtual teams have tools that support these functions. Check out Parts 2, 3, and 4 for more discussion on technology.

Hiring the Right Team Leader

If you're the person responsible for finding the virtual team leader for your organization, make sure you do your research and hire the leader who best meets your team's needs. When conducting your search, keep in mind that a virtual team leader must

>> Have mad skills. What kind of skills? Think management skills, interpersonal skills, communication skills, collaboration skills, and team-building skills.

>> Have the ability to establish clear roles and expectations — and then get out of the way.

>> Trust her team and instill that culture of trust throughout the team (see Chapter 19).

>> Be intuitive, flexible, comfortable with hands-off management, and experienced with the technology that connects the team.

WARNING

Not all managers are cut out for leading a team they don't see face to face every day. Leaders who excel at managing co-located teams may not necessarily be great leaders of virtual teams. A management style that favors a top-down, hierarchical structure, a heavy supervisory role, and a strong clock-watching philosophy isn't going to be successful in a virtual team environment (see Chapter 17).

Hiring the Right Team Members

Virtual team members also need a special skill set. In fact, a virtual team's success is based in large part on the strength of its members. Virtual team members need to have a few common characteristics, including

>> Independence

>> Resilience

>> Communication skills

>> Organization skills

>> Self-motivation

>> The ability to focus

>> Experience using a variety of technology tools

REMEMBER

Job skills are great, but even more important are soft skills, such as problem solving, empathy, conscientiousness, and emotional intelligence. Courtesy and respect become more important when workers are remote and nonverbal communication is limited.

Establishing Clear Team Vision and Values

Your team's vision statement drives behaviors, creativity, commitment, engagement, and determination.

The best vision statements are aligned with company values, are visible and achievable, are inspirational, and define a future state. Make sure that they're clear, memorable, and ambitious, as well as developed by consensus. One of the important things in the vision and values in inclusion. Everyone needs to have a say and a sense of ownership.

REMEMBER

The vision of virtual teams is no different, but the values of virtual teams should include accountability, trust, respect, and emotional intelligence. These values are critical to virtual team success.

Aligning Team Goals with Company Goals

One of the most important responsibilities of a leader is to show his team how to align behaviors, activities, and priorities with the company's strategic goals. These responsibilities are no different for virtual team leaders. In fact, they may be even *more* important because the team is dispersed.

WARNING

Don't create team goals in a vacuum. Make sure they're in line with the company's overall goals, which ensures that a team's work — big or small — is impacting the business. Aligning team goals with company goals also makes the work more meaningful and dramatically increases employee engagement. If your team members know how their work impacts the business, they'll care more about achieving the team's goals and improving the company's performance.

Having a Solid Team Agreement in Place

Every team needs a written working agreement, which is the first step to good team building. In addition to minimizing friction between teammates, an agreement is great for introducing new team members to the group culture. Most of all, the agreement gives all team members a template for what's expected during their day-to-day work.

REMEMBER

Creating team agreements must be an inclusive process, not dictated by upper management. Only your team truly knows what it needs. The team working agreement is a contract between all members. Treat it as a living document by revisiting it periodically and making updates as needed.

Using a Communication Strategy

Virtual teams need solid communication strategies to survive. When team members are spread across multiple cities and countries, creating and then using policies and practices to ensure connectivity across multiple communication channels is critical. (Chapter 18 discusses how to develop and use a communication strategy.)

REMEMBER

The first general rule is to give each communication method you use a designated purpose. Every team member needs to have a game plan for how to best get in touch with teammates for different situations. This clarity will help avoid wasted time, frustration, and missed connections.

Your virtual team communication strategy needs to include a variety of scheduled and unscheduled communication methods in order to make sure that it's managing workflow, hitting targets and goals, and getting the support it needs to be successful. Be sure to schedule events like regular team video calls, one-on-one meetings between each team member and the leader, and regular milestone and project update meetings. With unscheduled or less structured communication methods such as live chats, instant messaging, and social networking, team members can use less formal written communication styles and can (and should!) connect to discuss nonwork topics like getting a quick answer to a question or to recap Sunday's football game. These informal communication tools keep teams connected and engaged but aren't the most effective way to track progress or manage tasks.

Agreeing on a Process for Team Workflow

Having a team workflow process is another success factor for virtual teams. It's basically the road map for how things get done on your team. You want to create an environment for people to do their best work. Great workflows keep everyone on the same page, reduce confusion, eliminate bottlenecks, and create efficiency.

TIP

Although many tools and systems are available to help, keep it simple. Project management tools can get detailed, which is often required, but fight the urge to overcomplicate things. Evaluate processes regularly and eliminate steps that are unnecessary.

Using an Onboarding Strategy for New Team Members

Gone are the days when new hires were welcomed in person and introduced around the office. Virtual employee onboarding occurs through phone call or video chat, and new hires rarely meet their team members face to face. That's where having your team vision, goals, agreements, communication strategy, and workflow already in place really pays off.

TIP

Those policies and practices guide your onboarding process. Don't make successful onboarding for a new virtual team building all business; include introductions, discussions about team culture, and time to get to know coworkers and their after-hours interests.

Actively Managing Executive Perceptions

Is a virtual team like the proverbial tree falling in a forest? If you can't see the team at work, is work happening? Research confirms that a productivity perception gap does exist. Even when team members and team leaders report that virtual team productivity is strong, executives overseeing them often don't share that same opinion.

TIP

The answer to solving the perception gap is detailed planning and communication with results and data. Virtual teams are measured in large part by metrics, so you already have the milestones and progress to report. Formalize the communication process with executives to make sure they're receiving regular communications on your team's contribution.

Chapter **23**

Ten Great Slack Tips

This chapter offers ten quick tips on getting started with Slack, getting it to
stick in your organization, and maximizing its benefits.

Respond Promptly to New Users' Requests, Questions, and Feedback

Fundamentally, Slack isn't an individual tool; it's a group one. Many employees
will have legitimate questions about using Slack at your organization. Others will
make suggestions about how to use Slack differently or better.

REMEMBER

Don't ignore or, even worse, reflexively dismiss those ideas. Respond promptly to
feedback. You'll get more mileage out of Slack when more people in your organization use it.

Regularly View Slack Analytics

You can use Slack to view the most and least active workspace members and channels. With respect to users, you can easily see the number of messages that each user has sent, as well as their days active. (Doing this does not violate members' privacy; you can't read their messages.)

For example, maybe you rolled out Slack a year ago. During that time, one of your employees has posted a mere four messages in it. What's more, Slack calculates that he's been active for only one day. Equipped with this information and depending on his particular job, you shouldn't show him the door. Instead, tap him on the shoulder and talk to him about why he's invisible on Slack. Maybe something deeper is going on at work or at home.

Tread Lightly with New Hires

New employees may become overwhelmed trying to consume a year's worth of material in a bunch of channels. You can't expect them to digest thousands of messages, documents, decisions, and content in public channels within a week of starting their jobs.

TIP

New employees should go to each channel's highlights to see the most important discussions.

Establish Slack as the Default Medium for Internal Communication

To get the most bang for your buck, the default communication method for an organization, group, or department should be Slack. Sure, Slack may not make sense when sending messages to employees at different companies. But in the Slack universe, the idea that, within the walls of any given company, Fernando from finance routinely emails Maxine in marketing is absurd.

Emphasize Slack's Carrots More than Its Sticks

"Want to" almost always beats "have to." If employees give you static about using Slack, emphasize the former first and the latter only if necessary.

Keep an Eye Out for New Slack Apps

New productivity apps arrive all the time. Every month or so, poke around the Slack App Directory to see what new tchotchkes developers have released. You can bet that some new ones will be worth exploring.

Tell Overly Exuberant Slack Members to Tone It Down

No one likes a loud mouth or a troll. Many people have worked with knuckleheads who always had to have the last word on an email chain. You've probably met a few people who can't leave well enough alone.

A negative or aggressive employee may act as a bully on Slack and discourage others from using it. This behavior can be particularly troublesome when new employees join and organizations begin using Slack.

If someone goes over the line, it's imperative to nip the trend in the bud. Respectful disagreement with someone in a public manner is fine, but outright hostility and inappropriate comments are unacceptable in any environment — and that includes a Slack workspace.

Publicize Your Status and Availability

Just as with an email out-of-office (OOO) message, you don't want people expecting to hear from you in Slack when you're snorkeling in Belize or just off the grid. Let other users know your status availability (see Chapter 7).

Try Before You Buy

TIP

Sadly, some of your colleagues may not share your enthusiasm for Slack. After all, no technology sports a 100-percent adoption rate, and Slack is no exception. Before waiting for management to sign up for a company-wide premium plan, consider taking Slack's free version for a spin with your group, team, or department. Chapter 4 has details on Slack's different versions.

Know When to Turn Slack Off

You may find it peculiar to end this list of Slack tips by telling you to stop using it. You read right, though. You don't want to be a slave to any tool — and that certainly includes Slack. Take the lead from Slack's succinct and refreshing company mantra: Work hard and go home.

Index

A

Aa icon, 107
acceptance, building resilience with, 36
accessing
  message drafts, 104
  Slack workspaces with web browsers, 61–62
  Zoom files, 237–238
  Zoom meeting registration forms, 203
accountability, individual *vs.* team, 338–339
accounts (Zoom)
  adding users, 176–177
  creating, 164–167
  deactivating, 178
  deleting users, 178–179
  managing, 176–183
  unlinking users from, 179–180
Achievable and Agreed On, in SMART goals, 23
Active Speaker layout (Zoom), 196
Activity area (Microsoft Teams), 248–249
ad hoc meetings (Microsoft Teams), 288
adding
  animated GIFs in Zoom, 235–236
  channel prefixes, 90–91
  code, 115–117
  contacts to Zoom directory, 216–218
  emojis
    in Microsoft Team chats, 283–284
    in Zoom, 235–236
  external contacts to Zoom directory, 217–218
  files in Microsoft Teams chats, 284–285
  formatting to messages in Zoom, 234–236
  GIFs in Microsoft Teams chats, 283–284
  internal contacts to Zoom directory, 217
  members to existing channels, 93–95
  people to chats in Microsoft Teams, 281
  personal notes to profiles in Zoom, 224–225
  personal touches, 19–20

stickers in Microsoft Teams chats, 283–284
text snippets, 115–117
users
  to private channels, 83
  to Zoom accounts, 176–177
add-ons (Zoom Meetings & Chat), 155
Admin role (Zoom), 183
administrative roles
  Primary Owner, 66–67
  Workspace Admins, 67
  Workspace Owner, 67
agendas, for virtual meetings, 47
agreements, for teams, 398
airplane mode, 373
alignment
  communication and, 345
  leadership and, 352
  of team goals with company goals, 398
@all, using in Zoom, 233
allowing access to Zoom meetings, 203–204
alternative hosts (Zoom), 189
AMA (Ask Me Anything) feature, 90
Amazon Web Services (AWS), 159
analytics (Slack), 402
animated GIFs, adding in Zoom, 235–236
annotating, Zoom Rooms and, 158
Any.do (website), 27
Apple Watch app, 62
applying text formatting in Zoom, 234–235
apps (Slack), 403
Apps screen (Microsoft Teams), 263
Asana (website), 27
Ask Me Anything (AMA) feature, 90
Ask to Start Video action (Zoom), 211
#ask_the_ceo channel, 90
assessing addiction level to technology, 370–372
assumptions, in communication, 330–331

About the Authors

Tara Powers: As a team builder, leadership champion, strategic advisor, and speaker, Tara is on a mission to help fast-growing companies and socially responsible organizations to lead innovatively and authentically and in alignment with their values.

As a 20-year talent development professional, Tara has worked with more than 200 companies and 15,000 leaders around the globe, building custom programs and launching coaching and training initiatives that deliver high touch and high impact. She is the founder of Powers Resource Center (www.powersresourcecenter.com) and is a sought-after speaker at leadership conferences, executive strategy meetings, and corporate team-building events.

For the past four years in a row, Tara's leadership programs have earned the prestigious recognition as a Top 10 Leadership 500 Award winner by HR.com, with more than 4,500 companies applying and 600,000 people voting on the programs. Tara has consistently served as a judge for the well-known Brandon Hall Group Excellence Awards that focuses on talent development programs and attracts entrants from leading corporations around the world.

In addition to *Virtual Teams For Dummies*, Tara is the coauthor of *Success University for Women in Business*, an international best seller. She's also a Five Behaviors of a Cohesive Team Authorized facilitator and Everything DISC Solutions provider.

Tara's commitment to her clients is to serve as a catalyst for change, to be a business partner that takes your team collaboration, employee engagement, and leadership credibility to the next level, and to deliver results that make you want to do that happy dance. Tara resides in Colorado with her husband, two beautiful daughters, and a Catahoula rescue puppy named Houston.

Shamash Alidina: Shamash has been teaching mindfulness since 1998 and has been working in the field of mindfulness on a full-time basis since 2010. He formally trained for three years at Bangor University's Centre for Mindfulness in Wales. He also holds a master's degree in chemical engineering and a master's degree in education. He runs his own successful training organization (www.shamashalidina.com) to introduce mindfulness to the general public, give talks, workshops, and coaching, as well as offer fully online mindfulness teacher training. He has taught mindfulness all over the world, including in the United States, Australia, New Zealand, the Middle East, and Europe. Shamash is also cofounder of the world's first Museum of Happiness in London. He is the author of *Mindfulness For Dummies*.

LaReine Chabut: LaReine is a lifestyle and fitness expert, certified fitness instructor, and personal trainer. She has appeared on CNN, Fox News, *EXTRA*, *Access Hollywood*, and other TV programs. She is the author of *Stretching For Dummies*.

Peter Economy: Peter is the Associate Editor for *Leader to Leader* and the best-selling author of more than 50 books. He is the coauthor of *Managing For Dummies*.

Bob Nelson, PhD: Bob is the founder and president of Nelson Motivation, Inc., a management training and consulting firm based in San Diego, California. He is the author of the bestselling book *1001 Ways to Reward Employees* and (with Peter Economy) *The Management Bible*. He is the coauthor of *Managing For Dummies*.

Phil Simon: Phil is the award-winning author of several books, including *Message Not Received: Why Business Communication Is Broken and How to Fix It*. He is a recognized technology authority, Slack trainer, dynamic public speaker, college professor, and longtime Slack power user. He is the author of *Slack For Dummies* and *Zoom For Dummies*.

Rosemarie Withee: Rosemarie is president of Portal Integrators (www.portalintegrators.com) and founder of Scrum Now (www.scrumnow.com) in Seattle, Washington. Portal Integrators is a Scrum-based software and services firm. Rosemarie earned a master of science degree in economics at San Francisco State University and an executive master of business administration degree at Quantic School of Business and Technology. In addition, Rosemarie studied marketing at UC Berkeley Extension and holds a bachelor of arts degree in economics and a bachelor of science degree in marketing from De La Salle University, Philippines. She is the author of *Microsoft Teams For Dummies*, among other titles.

Publisher's Acknowledgments

Senior Acquisitions Editor: Tracy Boggier
Compilation Editor: Georgette Beatty
Project Editor: Elizabeth Kuball
Copy Editor: Elizabeth Kuball

Production Editor: Tamilmani Varadharaj
Cover Photos: © Moyo Studio/Getty Images

Take dummies with you everywhere you go!

Whether you are excited about e-books, want more from the web, must have your mobile apps, or are swept up in social media, dummies makes everything easier.

Find us online!

Leverage the power

Dummies is the global leader in the reference category and one of the most trusted and highly regarded brands in the world. No longer just focused on books, customers now have access to the dummies content they need in the format they want. Together we'll craft a solution that engages your customers, stands out from the competition, and helps you meet your goals.

Advertising & Sponsorships

Connect with an engaged audience on a powerful multimedia site, and position your message alongside expert how-to content. Dummies.com is a one-stop shop for free, online information and know-how curated by a team of experts.

- Targeted ads
- Video
- Email Marketing

- Microsites
- Sweepstakes sponsorship

20 MILLION PAGE VIEWS EVERY SINGLE MONTH

15 MILLION UNIQUE VISITORS PER MONTH

43% OF ALL VISITORS ACCESS THE SITE VIA THEIR MOBILE DEVICES

700,000 NEWSLETTER SUBSCRIPTIONS TO THE INBOXES OF

300,000 UNIQUE INDIVIDUALS EVERY WEEK

# of dummies

Custom Publishing

Reach a global audience in any language by creating a solution that will differentiate you from competitors, amplify your message, and encourage customers to make a buying decision.

- Apps
- Books
- eBooks
- Video
- Audio
- Webinars

Brand Licensing & Content

Leverage the strength of the world's most popular reference brand to reach new audiences and channels of distribution.

For more information, visit **dummies.com/biz**

PERSONAL ENRICHMENT

Staying Sharp
9781119187790
USA $26.00
CAN $31.99
UK £19.99

Facebook
9781119179030
USA $21.99
CAN $25.99
UK £16.99

Guitar
9781119293354
USA $24.99
CAN $29.99
UK £17.99

Investing
9781119293347
USA $22.99
CAN $27.99
UK £16.99

Beekeeping
9781119310068
USA $22.99
CAN $27.99
UK £16.99

Digital Photography
9781119235606
USA $24.99
CAN $29.99
UK £17.99

Meditation
9781119251163
USA $24.99
CAN $29.99
UK £17.99

Pregnancy
9781119235491
USA $26.99
CAN $31.99
UK £19.99

Samsung Galaxy S7
9781119279952
USA $24.99
CAN $29.99
UK £17.99

iPhone
9781119283133
USA $24.99
CAN $29.99
UK £17.99

Crocheting
9781119287117
USA $24.99
CAN $29.99
UK £16.99

Nutrition
9781119130246
USA $22.99
CAN $27.99
UK £16.99

PROFESSIONAL DEVELOPMENT

Windows 10
9781119311041
USA $24.99
CAN $29.99
UK £17.99

AutoCAD
9781119255796
USA $39.99
CAN $47.99
UK £27.99

Excel 2016
9781119293439
USA $26.99
CAN $31.99
UK £19.99

QuickBooks 2017
9781119281467
USA $26.99
CAN $31.99
UK £19.99

macOS Sierra
9781119280651
USA $29.99
CAN $35.99
UK £21.99

LinkedIn
9781119251132
USA $24.99
CAN $29.99
UK £17.99

Windows 10
9781119310563
USA $34.00
CAN $41.99
UK £24.99

SharePoint 2016
9781119181705
USA $29.99
CAN $35.99
UK £21.99

Fundamental Analysis
9781119263593
USA $26.99
CAN $31.99
UK £19.99

Networking
9781119257769
USA $29.99
CAN $35.99
UK £21.99

Office 2016
9781119293477
USA $26.99
CAN $31.99
UK £19.99

Office 365
9781119265313
USA $24.99
CAN $29.99
UK £17.99

Salesforce.com
9781119239314
USA $29.99
CAN $35.99
UK £21.99

Coding
9781119293323
USA $29.99
CAN $35.99
UK £21.99

dummies.com

dummies
A Wiley Brand

Learning Made Easy

ACADEMIC

9781119293576
USA $19.99
CAN $23.99
UK £15.99

9781119293637
USA $19.99
CAN $23.99
UK £15.99

9781119293491
USA $19.99
CAN $23.99
UK £15.99

9781119293460
USA $19.99
CAN $23.99
UK £15.99

9781119293590
USA $19.99
CAN $23.99
UK £15.99

9781119215844
USA $26.99
CAN $31.99
UK £19.99

9781119293378
USA $22.99
CAN $27.99
UK £16.99

9781119293521
USA $19.99
CAN $23.99
UK £15.99

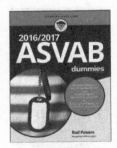

9781119239178
USA $18.99
CAN $22.99
UK £14.99

9781119263883
USA $26.99
CAN $31.99
UK £19.99

Available Everywhere Books Are Sold

Small books for big imaginations

9781119177173
USA $9.99
CAN $9.99
UK £8.99

9781119177272
USA $9.99
CAN $9.99
UK £8.99

9781119177241
USA $9.99
CAN $9.99
UK £8.99

9781119917721
USA $9.99
CAN $9.99
UK £8.99

9781119262657
USA $9.99
CAN $9.99
UK £6.99

9781119291336
USA $9.99
CAN $9.99
UK £6.99

9781119233527
USA $9.99
CAN $9.99
UK £6.99

9781119291220
USA $9.99
CAN $9.99
UK £6.99

978111917702
USA $9.9
CAN $9.9
UK £8.99

Unleash Their Creativity